Making Democracy Matter

Making Democracy Matter

IDENTITY AND ACTIVISM IN LOS ANGELES

KAREN BRODKIN

RUTGERS UNIVERSITY PRESS
New Brunswick, New Jersey, and London

Library of Congress Cataloging-in-Publication Data

Brodkin, Karen.
    Making democracy matter : identity and activism in Los Angeles/
Karen Brodkin.
        p. cm.
    Includes bibliographical references and index.
    ISBN-13: 978-0-8135-3979-9 (hardcover: alk. paper)
    ISBN-13: 978-0-8135-3980-5 (pbk. : alk. paper)
        1. Political participation—California—Los Angeles—Case studies.   2. Political
activists—California—Los Angeles —Interviews.   3. Community development—
California—Los Angeles—Case studies.   I. Title.
JS1007.A15B76 2007
322.409794'94—dc22   2006015184

A British Cataloging-in-Publication record for this book is available from the
British Library.

Manufactured in the United States of America

Contents

PREFACE

THIS BOOK IS ABOUT A cohort of activists who came of age in Los Angeles in the 1990s, but it has personal roots in an event that took place in 1986 while I was teaching women's studies at Oberlin College, a small, mainly white liberal arts college in Ohio known for its liberal politics. The previous year, as part of a nationwide campus antiapartheid movement, Oberlin students had held a large demonstration at the annual Board of Trustees' meeting, demanding that the school divest itself of investments in apartheid South African corporations. The administration responded by threatening fifty-nine student protesters with suspension; hearings were to be held in the spring of 1986. Each student was allowed to have two faculty advocates. Given that the faculty hardly exceeded two hundred, and that a large portion were in sympathy with the students, virtually all the supportive faculty were present at the hearing. And since the proceedings were to be open, most of the student body filled the auditorium and overflowed onto the quad outside, where loudspeakers were set up.

The administration and the trustees were unprepared for the crowd and asked if there were a smaller group who would meet privately with them. Students discussed the proposal among themselves, and sent ten or twelve elected spokespeople off with the trustees. I sat with a group of faculty who had been active in some combination of civil rights, SDS, and antiwar activism in the sixties and seventies. We muttered to each other knowingly that the trustees were going to co-opt the students, and we darkly predicted they would sell out by accepting some form of punishment.

Students left in the room yelled to the departing spokespeople, "What are we supposed to do?" One said that there was a boom box; another said that there were a bunch of mikes around the auditorium.

Confusion reigned for a short time, but no one left. Soon students started to take up the mikes and say whatever was on their minds. Not all of it had much to do with the matter at hand; some suggested dancing; others brought up various campus and lifestyle issues. We faculty rolled our eyeballs.

But within an hour, the discussion turned political and focused on whether or not there should have been a subcommittee negotiating. There was a lot of discussion about process—about whether students not threatened with suspension should have the right to decide what action to take. Someone noted that white men seemed to be doing all the speaking; another that few students of color were speaking; still another that few women were speaking. So they decided that every third speaker needed to be a student of color or a woman. Students listened to each other quietly and spoke respectfully no matter how off the wall comments were. Various speakers tried to get fellow students to stay on topic, but no one cut anyone off or sought to impose any order with regard to content.

It was a slow, messy process, but it was effective. A very large, heterogeneous group moved from confusion to consensus. The consensus that emerged—among those facing charges and the rest of the audience—was that there was really nothing to discuss with the administration, that they should drop all charges, or, that failing, students facing charges wanted a full hearing on everything they were charged with, and they were willing to risk expulsion.

When the spokespeople, administrators, and trustees returned after about two hours, one of the spokespeople announced that they had reached a compromise. Many in the audience yelled out words to the effect of "no compromises!" The students on the negotiating team looked at each other, shrugged, turned to the administrators and said, "We're not the leaders anymore," and handed the mike to a student who had been in the auditorium. That student then announced the consensus to a very surprised bunch of administrators and trustees. They huddled briefly and asked for twenty-four hours to think and get back to the students. When they did, they decided to drop all charges.

I was stunned by the process as well as by the outcome, having predicted neither. As an anthropologist, I had read, taught, and written admiringly about this sort of democratic process in small-scale societies. But I had never seen it in action until that evening. I say this despite the fact that democracy, as ideal and practice, were vital parts of early civil rights, student, and women's movements of the sixties. But consensus worked best in very small groups. Also, by the late sixties and seventies I think my generation of activists had become neither so patient nor respectful.

I subsequently encountered some of the same openness, patience, and willingness to listen that Oberlin students exhibited among a more colorful spectrum of California student activists when I came to UCLA the following year. If the emerging cohort of activists was reinventing democracy and democratic political selves, I wanted to learn how they were doing it.

I also became curious about comparing the paths to activism of today's activists with those of my generation. I underwent a sharp political transformation as a college student in the early sixties, first watching, later participating in part of the civil rights movement, and then traveling to newly revolutionary Cuba in 1964. As a white, suburban kid I was amazed by the impacts these social movements had not only on the activists but on the non-activists, who seemed also to be transformed by the wider social environment that these movements created. In Cuba especially, people on the street spoke of themselves as owners of the revolution, and as knowledgeable and ready to remake the world better than it was. A whole populace seemed politicized and empowered. By the late sixties, I experienced a similar personal transformation in the consciousness-raising groups of the women's liberation movement. The extraordinary energy and clarity of vision unleashed by this movement felt not all that different from what I had seen in the early days of the Cuban Revolution and in the civil rights movement.

Those two experiences—of making democracy and of giving birth to oneself as a social actor—are at the heart of this book. All social movements engage in these projects, but in their own ways. They generate their own ideas about what democracy looks like and how to practice it, and the nature of those who can act democratically. And they generate personal rebirthings, in the ways people come to see themselves, each other, and the world. Rebirth is also about becoming a particular kind of social person, of creating a politicized social self, or identity. Those identities are also collective, the constituencies the movement seeks to represent.

MY FIRST AND DEEPEST APPRECIATION goes to the sixteen activists who spent many hours in interviews and conversations about their political lives, practices, and ideals. Because they are experts, political intellectuals as well as narrators of their own lives, I have used their names throughout the book so readers will be able to get to know them and their ideas. I know that I've presented only a small slice of their ideas about politics and identity, theory, and practice. My hope is that I got it right.

Thanks also to Vivian Rothstein, organizer and mentor to many activists, for pushing me to focus on the emerging political generation and for introducing me to such an exciting group of people. Staff and officers of HERE Local 11, SEIU Locals 399 and 1877, and LAANE/SMART offered me time in their staff meetings to conduct surveys and to talk with the organizers. I thank deeply all the organizers of these groups for their interest, thoughtful contributions, and the time they gave from very heavy schedules.

I am also deeply grateful to Tritia Toyota, who took time out from her dissertation on new Chinese-American activists and volunteered to conduct interviews with three of the narrators.

Wally Marks made it possible to transcribe the interviews, for which I remain deeply grateful. And I thank Chrys Ritchie for her excellent transcription.

I have benefited greatly from the funds of knowledge about activism in Los Angeles, past and present, from ongoing conversations with Vivian Rothstein, Juan Gomez Quiñones, Devra Weber, Carol Wells, Kent Wong, Ruben Lizardo, Margarita Ramirez and the staff of the Liberty Hill Foundation, Lyn Goldfarb, David Kamper, Monica Russel y Rodriguez, Marqueece Harris-Dawson, Mandla Kayise, Kimi Lee, and Kim McGillicuddy.

For guidance to sources, dates, and archives at UCLA, I thank Marjorie Lee and Judy Soo Hoo of the Asian American Studies Library, and Yolanda Ritter of the Chicana/o Studies Library, as well as the staff of the University Archives, and Kathleen Parent of the UCLA Registrar's Office. And for sources on the history of Los Angeles activism, I am happily indebted to Sarah Cooper and Michelle Welsing of the superb Southern California Library for Social Studies. Early on in the project Sabrina Motley and Becca Howes-Mischel offered critical research assistance, for which I offer deep thanks.

For the photos, I thank Roxane Auer, Joann Lo, Suyapa Portillo, Eileen Ma, Stephanie Monroe, Javier Gonzalez, Michelle Mascarenhas, Liz Sunwoo, Aquilina Soriano-Verzosa, and John Delloro for use of their personal photos. I thank Danny Feingold and Jim Robbins for opening LAANE's photo archives, and LAANE for permission to use them. I'm also grateful to Kent Wong and to UFCW Local 770 for permission to use their photos. And hardly least, I'm delighted that Roxane Auer has offered one of her photos for the book's cover.

I have been blessed throughout this project with supportive friends, interlocutors, and critical readers of many drafts. Longtime collaborator Dorothy Remy was there at the beginning to talk through my fuzzy ideas. Tritia Toyota helped persuade me that this project deserved a book. As the book took shape, Devra Weber, Sarah Cooper, Juan Gomez Quiñones, Vivian Rothstein, Cynthia Strathmann, Suyapa Portillo, John Delloro, Michelle Mascarenhas, Roxane Auer, and Dorothy Holland read various chapters and offered valuable feedback. And as a full manuscript developed, it gained a great deal from thoughtful readings and incisive critiques from KarenMary Davalos, Valerie Matsumoto, Joann Lo, Eileen Ma, Tritia Toyota, and Lynn Stephen.

I've also benefited from feedback at presentations of parts of this work at the Culture, Boundaries, Power seminar at Columbia University, organized by Hannah Lessinger; at a colloquium at the Jefferson School in conjunction with the journal Science and Society in New York; at the meetings of the American Anthropological Association, the Society for the Anthropology of North America, the Center for the Study of Women in Society at the University of Oregon, and the Lavender Languages Conference at American University. I especially thank Margaret Hallock and Nicholas Shigeru Sakurai for their thoughtful conversations at the latter two talks.

Far from least, I am especially grateful to Sandra Morgen for wrestling her way through several versions of the whole book when her own workload was enormous. Her incisive thoughts put a finger on what was needed to pull it all together.

Carollee Howes, my life partner, has lived with this project from start to finish. She's vetted more drafts than anyone ought to read, and pushed me to get to the analytic heart of the matter, all the while being consistently supportive and encouraging.

And finally, my thanks to my editor Leslie Mitchner, copy editor Lyman Lyons, and the staff at Rutgers for being pure pleasure to work with.

LIST OF ORGANIZATIONS

AFL-CIO	American Federation of Labor-Congress of Industrial Organizations, the national federation of labor unions, www.aflcio.org.
AGENDA	A multiracial community-based group in several neighborhoods in Los Angeles, www.scopela.org/components.html.
APALA	Asian Pacific American Labor Alliance, www.labor.ucla.edu/apalabor, www.apalanet.org.
CFJ	Californians for Justice, www.caljustice.org.
CARECEN	Central American Resource Center/Centro de Recursos Centroamericanos, www.carecen-la.org.
CBE	Communities for a Better Environment, www.cbecal.org.
CHIRLA	Coalition for Humane Immigrant Rights of Los Angeles, www.chirla.org.
CIWA	Coalition of Immigrant Worker Advocates.
FACTS	Families to Amend California's Three Strikes. "Three strikes" refers to California's law requiring a life sentence for persons convicted of three felonies. www.facts1.com.
GWC	Garment Worker Center, an independent worker center affiliated with and sharing offices with Sweatshop Watch, an organization that monitors working conditions in the garment industry and publicizes abuses of workers. www.garmentworkercenter.org.
HERE	Hotel Employees and Restaurant Employees International Union, www.unitehere.org.
IDEPSCA	Instituto de Education Popular del Sur de California (Institute for Popular Education of Southern California)

JfJ   Justice for Janitors, the SEIU drive to organize and
                    represent   cleaners   of   commercial   buildings,
                    www. seiu1877.Org/ourlocal/#janitors.
KIWA   Korean Immigrant Workers Alliance, www.kiwa.org.
LAANE   Los   Angeles   Alliance   for   a   New   Economy,
                    www.laane.org.
MEChA   Mesa Estudiantil de Chicanos de Aztlan. A national fed-
                    eration of Chicana/o and high school and college
                    student   organizations,   www.azteca.net/aztec/mecha/
                    index.shtml.
MIWON   Multi-ethnic Immigrant Workers Organizing Network,
                    www.chirla.org/programs.htm.
OI   Organizing Institute of the AFL-CIO, a program for
                    recruiting and training new labor organizers.
PWC   Pilipino Workers' Center, www.pwcsc.org.
SEIU   Service Employees International Union.
SMART   Santa Monicans Allied for Responsible Tourism (sister
                    organization to LAANE), www.laane.org/smart/index.
                    html.
UNITE   Union of Needletrades, Industrial and Textile Employ-
                    ees, formed from the merger of the International Ladies
                    Garment Workers Union and the Amalgamated Clothing
                    and Textile Workers Union in 1995.
UNITE   Union created by merger of UNITE and HERE,
HERE   www.unitehere.org.

About the Narrators

Roxane Auer spent the last thirty years in the Los Angeles area. She grew up in Topanga Canyon and Malibu, graduated from UCLA, and moved to Silver Lake and then Echo Park, where she still lives with her partner Scott, two cats, and three dogs. Her first job was with Communities for a Better Environment, but in 1996 she went to work for the labor movement and has been doing that work ever since. For this she credits UNITE HERE Local 11 and Los Angeles Alliance for a New Economy for developing a cooperative work environment and giving her the opportunity early on to run her own campaigns. She also credits her family and community for the endless support they provide. She currently works as a lead research analyst at UNITE HERE Local 11. She notes, "I can't wait to see what the entire labor movement does in the next ten years. The beauty of sticking with it through difficult times is seeing tangible change; it gives me hope for the future. I think anyone who feels depressed or saddened by the front pages, as I do, should dedicate time to changing something locally that they care about. It makes it easier to be patient and never lose hope. I believe eventually the pendulum will swing towards justice once again."

John Delloro was largely influenced by his hard-working immigrant parents and has committed himself to the movement for socioeconomic justice. Throughout his childhood, his parents worked long hours to support him and his brother. Their struggle taught him the centrality of work in structuring people's lives and how power in the workplace is essential to controlling one's life. He currently works as the southwest area manager for SEIU Local 1000, the union for California state workers. Previously, he was a staff director for SEIU Local 399, a health-care workers union, and helped establish and coordinate its

member-organizer program and worked on the campaign that led to a
union at his mother's hospital. He has also worked as an organizer for
AFCSME and the Culinary Union (HERE Local 226) in Las Vegas. He
was one of the founding executive board members of the Pilipino Workers' Center of Southern California, and recently served as the president
of the Los Angeles chapter of the Asian Pacific American Labor Alliance.
He deeply loves his partner Susan Suh and two children Mina and
Malcolm Jae Delloro-Suh.

JAVIER GONZALEZ began working for SEIU Local 1877 in 2000. Before
that he was a wage-and-hour investigator with a labor-management,
industry-funded janitorial watchdog organization. In this position
he initiated and led the initial investigation and filing of what eventually became a $21 million lawsuit on behalf of janitors against major
chain supermarkets. Before this, Javier was a day-labor and community
organizer.

At Local 1877 Javier worked on successful campaigns to organize
workers in Los Angeles, Orange County, and at Los Angeles International Airport (LAX). As the political director, he has worked on several
election, initiative, and other campaigns for worker gains, and also to
build power. Building political power from the local union has allowed
for greater support from elected leaders to fights the union engages in.
Part of the role the local union has focused on includes being active with
members on a variety of community issues as they relate to housing,
education, reform, immigrant rights, civil and human rights, and quality of life issues.

TORI TAEHUI KIM immigrated to the United States from Korea in 1978
when she was six years old. She grew up in Colorado, and attended college and law school at Harvard University. After graduating from college
in 1993, Tori lived in Korea for a year and a half, seeking to reconnect
with her Korean roots and learn about the social and political movements that had dominated the country after her emigration. Upon
returning to the United States, Tori began work with Korean Immigrant
Workers Alliance in Los Angeles, where she served as a staff attorney
for two years after receiving her law degree in 1998. Tori is now an
attorney at the law firm of Wilmer Cutler Pickering Hale and Dorr LLP

in New York, where she combines a general litigation practice with pro bono work on behalf of immigrants.

AISHA LIVINGSTONE worked as an organizer for the Los Angeles Alliance for a New Economy until 2002. She has since left the activist community.

JOANN LO gained much of her experience in social activism as a student at Yale University, where she earned a degree in environmental biology in 1997. After graduation, Joann worked as an organizer for SEIU Locals 399 and 1877. She then worked at the Garment Worker Center as lead organizer when garment workers in Los Angeles led a boycott campaign against the young women's retailer Forever 21. The campaign resulted in a settlement of their lawsuit against the company and in Forever 21's commitment to work with GWC and workers to try to improve conditions in the garment industry. Joann is now field coordinator for Enlace, a strategic alliance of low-wage worker unions and workers centers in the United States and Mexico. Her parents are immigrants from Taiwan who live in Ohio, where Joann grew up. Joann lives with her husband Matt and their cat Django in Los Angeles.

EILEEN MA identifies herself as a queer Chinese-American woman. The second of two daughters of Chinese immigrants, she grew up in New York and has been working as an organizer since her graduation from Columbia University in 1993. She became immersed in the labor movement, becoming a field trainer for the AFL-CIO Organizing Institute and an active member and young leader within the Asian Pacific American Labor Alliance. By the year 2000, Eileen's "love affair" with union organizing virtually ended, though she continues to believe in organizing and the good work of so many grassroots union activists. She found inspiration at Health Access, working on statewide health-care reform, spearheading their Los Angeles efforts until 2002 when she relocated with her partner to New York City. As of 2006, Eileen is working for Power U Center for Social Change, an organization working to address environmental racism and gentrification, and to fight for social and economic justice in low-income communities of color in Miami. She is inspired by and proud to have helped organize a small movement of residents fighting for justice in Overtown, the historic but disenfranchised black community of Miami. Eileen continues to challenge herself to find the right place and the right ways to use her strength, work, and privilege in a lifelong struggle to advance a vision of the world and of social change that she believes in, a struggle that is especially challenging for queer women of color. She travels through life armed with the love of a cherished life partner, indulged by a loving family and forgiving friends, emboldened by the legacy of Audre Lorde, and accompanied by two lazy cats.

DOUGLAS MARMOL works at LAX for HMS Inc. and has been a worker organizer with HERE Local 11 for almost a decade. He has been active in and been a lead organizer on the living wage campaign at LAX, on campaigns to unionize airport concession workers, and on the Hotel Workers Rising campaign. He is currently an organizer with HERE's Coalition for a New Century, a community revitalization and union-organizing drive in the community near LAX. In 2002 Douglas participated in the first-ever California Lesbian, Gay, Bisexual, Transgender Leadership School, cosponsored by the UCLA Labor Center and Pride at Work. He is among the organizers of the Labor Center's second California LGBT Leadership School in 2006.

NORMA MARTINEZ-HOSANG has been a community and labor organizer and trainer in the Los Angeles region for the last ten years. She served as a field organizer and lead organizer with Californians for Justice, overseeing several large-scale precinct and voter-education efforts across Southern California. She then went on to serve as lead organizer for the California Nurses Association, leading several successful union election campaigns. She is a former board member of the National Organizer's Alliance. She is currently the Southern California Regional Organizer for Health-Access, a California statewide organization that organizes for single-payer health insurance and other reforms that will make health care affordable and accessible for all Californians.

MICHELLE MASCARENHAS is the co-director of SOUL (School of Unity and Liberation), an Oakland-based training center that is working to lay the groundwork for a powerful liberation movement by supporting the development of a new generation of young organizers—especially young women, young people of color, queer youth, and working-class young people. She became politically active through the labor movement in Los Angeles before devoting a decade of her life to working with students and parents to bring healthy fool to schools in low-income neighborhoods in Los Angeles and nationally.

STEPHANIE MONROE began working with LAANE while at UCLA and continued after she graduated in 1995. While still at LAANE she founded and directed SMART and organized a volunteer-driven campaign to defeat an anti-living-wage ballot measure in Santa Monica. She moved to the Bay Area in 2001 and served as research director for the new California Works Foundation, then helped found and establish the California Partnership for Working Families (CPWF), a statewide alliance between LAANE, Working Partnerships, U.S.A., East Bay Alliance for a Sustainable Economy, and the Center on Policy Initiatives in San Diego. She continued as field director for CPWF until June 2005. At the same time Stephanie was beginning to study and take courses for a career in naturopathic medicine. Solving her own health problems made her aware of the ways that health could be a vehicle to spiritual empowerment. She sees natural medicine and organizing as two streams of her life goal of helping to empower others, materially and spiritually.

QUYNH NGUYEN returned to Los Angeles to work with the United Food and Commercial Workers Local 770, where she organized packinghouse and community campaigns. She then went on to become the national organizing director of APALA. She is currently taking some time off to raise her two young children.

MILTON PASCUAL is currently a lead organizer for AFSCME. He moved from HERE Local 11 to AFSCME in 2001 and spent most of the next three years organizing workers at the University of Maryland, where the union won a landslide victory. He is proudest of the workers' success at building strong cooperation between African-American and Hispanic workers. Milton also met his wife, Maria Claudia Pascual, during that campaign. He is now out west, working on an organizing drive at New Mexico State University. He hasn't forgotten HERE for giving him his start, and says, "I'll never forget where I came from, and I'll never forget the people who were there for me. My family has been my inspiration."

SUYAPA PORTILLO crossed the Mexico-U.S. border wet, cold, and empty-handed on a November night in the early 1980s. That story (see chapter 3) has become part of her family history and informs her organizing, researching, and teaching work. Although she was born in Copán, Honduras, her home has been in Highland Park, Los Angeles for most of her life. She attended Pitzer College in Claremont, California, where she double majored in psychology and Latin American literature. She has a masters degree in history and is completing her doctoral dissertation research in Honduras in the history of modern Latin America at Cornell University. Since graduating from college in 1996, she has organized in a variety of campaigns: KIWA, SEIU Local 399, Los Angeles Coalition for Quality Health Care, Screen Actors Guild, AFSCME Local 1108, CHIRLA, briefly for a HERE Local 11 campaign, as well as volunteer work and coalition work on issues dealing with immigrant border crossing, sex trafficking, immigrant health and social services, solidarity work in support of maquila workers and indigenous communities in Chiapas, Mexico, and now in solidarity with banana workers in Honduras and Central America. Growing pains within several of these organizations around Los Angeles challenged her to see the problems and discrimination women and queer organizers face in Los Angeles.

Her work in solidarity with indigenous communities inspires and informs the most difficult of decisions in her professional and political life. She sees that we are witnessing a revolutionizing of union movements throughout the Americas to democratize and to recognize women. Women are the vanguard for new models of organizing. Los Angeles persists in her memory and heart and she hopes to return to teach, research, and continue organizing on the streets of her adopted city. She now shares her life with Eileen Ma and their two cats.

AQUILINA SORIANO-VERZOSA is a founder and current executive director of the Pilipino Workers' Center of Southern California, a nonprofit organization serving and organizing the low-wage Pilipino immigrant community in Los Angeles. She has been working in the Pilipino community for ten years, both in Los Angeles and in the Philippines. She studied for her BA in Asian American Studies at the University of California, Los Angeles. She is also an appointed member on the Justice and Peace Commission of the Los Angeles Archdiocese. A mother of two, she sees her work for social justice as a lifelong endeavor that she hopes to pass on to her daughters.

ELIZABETH SUNGMIN SUNWOO is currently coordinating the Multi-ethnic Immigrant Worker Organizing Network (MIWON), a multiethnic, multi-industry network of immigrant-worker-based organizations that seeks to build the political consciousness and participation of immigrant workers in their fight for better living and working conditions. Key strategies are to fight for legalization and worker rights and to act as a collective voice for low-wage immigrant workers in Los Angeles. Elizabeth was also an organizer with the Korean Immigrant Workers Alliance (KIWA) and has a masters degree in Labor Studies.

Making Democracy Matter

Introduction

DURING THE 1990S, new forms of social-justice activism crystallized into a vibrant social movement whose key constituents were working-class people of color, both U.S.-born and new immigrants. These trends were especially visible in the nationwide resurrection of a grassroots labor movement spearheaded by immigrant workers and workers of color, with women prominent among them. In her important new work, Vanessa Tait (2005) shows this movement to be a complex mix of independent worker centers in largely immigrant and African-American communities that incubated in the 1980s and exploded in the 1990s. These organizations took on a mix of workplace issues and broader issues like racism, immigration policy, and environmental justice. Their success encouraged progressive forces in labor unions and the AFL-CIO's turn to organizing in the 1990s. Unions and independent worker centers have been building ongoing synergistic relationships marked by a mix of mutual support and conflict, largely around issues of democracy. Emphasizing democratic, decentralized organizing and coalition building, this movement joins independent workers centers and progressive union locals with a range of community-based groups (Bronfenbrenner et al. 1998; Clawson 2003; Lichtenstein 2002; M. Louie 2001; Mantsios 1998; Tait 2005; Tillman and Cummings 1999).

In its emphasis on developing political consciousness, knowledge, and agency among those with whom they work, this new movement is part of a larger tradition of making democracy that has run through many social movements. The Student Nonviolent Coordinating Committee's (SNCC) organizing in Mississippi in the early 1960s is perhaps the most famous exemplar. It emphasized one-on-one organizing that created political knowledge from personal experience that gave people the courage to challenge the Jim Crow social order in Mississippi (Payne 1995; see also Polletta 2002). SNCC's Bob Moses called it the organizing tradition, and clarified by contrasting it with the mobilizing tradition, best exemplified in the civil rights movement by Martin Luther King's Southern Christian Leadership Conference. King relied on huge, periodic mass mobilizations and civil disobedience more than grassroots education and leadership building.

Other movements created their own versions of an organizing tradition. Black and white women SNCC veterans created consciousness-raising, the hallmark practice of second-wave feminism (Cade 1970; Evans and Boyte 1986; Giddings 1984). Building a movement from experiences was also critical to forming the more recent black women's health movement, and subsequent health movements among other women of color as well. The black women who created the National Black Women's Health Project in 1984 found that the agendas and priorities of white women's groups—especially the narrowness of support for abortion—simply did not speak to the range of health assaults they faced that stemmed from the deeply institutionalized racism of U.S. society. They had to invent their own movement by reinventing themselves through self-help groups. The self-help groups "addressed their physical, spiritual, emotional, and psychological health needs" in a "safe, validating environment for us to learn how to come together to share our stories, to be appreciated for the struggles we have participated in, to review our circumstances, and to make decisions designed to change our lives and our health circumstances" (Silliman et al. 2004, 71). The workers' movements of the 1990s is connected to this tradition in its emphasis on building widespread political agency and individual and collective leadership among those they organize.

New movements also share with their antecedents a set of democratic political visions that emphasize creating among participants the democracy the movement wishes to see in society. The white New Left practices of the 1960s referred to this aspect of participatory democracy as "prefigurative": "By 'prefiguring' within the current practices of the movement the values of freedom, equality, and community that they wanted on a grand scale, activists were helping bring them about" (Polletta 2002, 6; see also Darnovsky, Epstein, and Flacks 1995; Flacks 1971). Democratic practice was simultaneously means and end, current practice and future vision.

Los Angeles was an early center of this new labor movement. Immigrant workers in building cleaning, hospitals, home health care, hotel work, and auto parts and other manufacturing plants undertook enormously visible and successful organizing drives. New, progressive leadership of key unions and of the county Federation of Labor welcomed immigrant workers and their organizing efforts. They were an early and strong force behind the AFL-CIO's organizing emphasis in the mid-nineties and for changing its national policy on immigration.

Much of the city's labor dynamism came from unions working collaboratively, working alongside immigrant worker advocates, and working with a variety of community groups. Office cleaners, hotel and hospital workers, and day laborers all involved community organizations in their contract and unionization drives. Grassroots organizing and creative mobilizations that dramatized social injustice generated popular and political support beyond working-class communities, from college campuses and from many sectors of the middle class. Together with campaigns to adopt municipal living-wage ordinances, the new labor movement mobilized a wide spectrum of public support for low-wage workers (Gottlieb et al. 2005; Milkman 2000; Milkman and Wong 2000; Waldinger et al. 1997).

The 1990s in Los Angeles were a time of intense and broadly framed social justice activism. Part of labor's revitalization came from its active involvement with campus and community organizations in which new immigrants and their children played prominent roles. Many young people of color and children of immigrants became politically involved in supporting workers' efforts to unionize and in campaigns against the anti-immigrant and racist voter initiatives that dominated California electoral politics for much of the 1990s. Immigrant worker initiatives and anti-racist efforts on college campuses, in high schools, and in communities of color shaped the political practice of a large cohort of young activists who came of age in this decade (Brown 1999; Hamilton 1994; E. Kaplan 2003, 2005; Seif 2004; Gottlieb et al. 2005).

This cohort of labor, immigrant worker, and antiracist activists in Los Angeles were also part of a wider, but more inchoate, national and global movement. For some (Sklair 1998; Stiglitz 2002; Tabb 2001), the Battle of Seattle—the huge demonstrations against the 1999 meetings of the World Trade Organization in that city—marked the birth of a global coalition across multiple differences led by this new generation of young activists and united against neoliberal capitalism. The images of "teamsters and turtles" linked together working-class and environmental issues, and joined them to the issues of economic imperialism and racism. Since then, the movement against global neoliberalism, its economic and political practice, and its ideology, has become worldwide, demonstrating and holding alternative forums wherever the world's capitalist elite hold their meetings. Los Angeles was the site of the 2000 Democratic National Convention. Los Angeles activists who had a few years earlier first become involved in antiracist and labor activism were actively engaged in planning for the massive protests (and equally massive police repression) that challenged the neoliberal policies of the Democratic Party.

In short, a social justice movement flowered in Los Angeles during the 1990s. The innovative message of this upsurge was to redefine what working-class America looked like, and what a socially just public policy for that working class should be. In other words, it showed to a broad public that America's working people were black and brown, women as well as men, and that they were entitled to much better than they got. It put antiracism, working-class women, living wages, health care, education, and housing on the map as both working-class issues and human-rights issues. It also helped to reshape the organization of social activism to emphasize horizontal and democratic organization and coalition building.

The creative strategies, the networks among organizations, the coalitions, the mix of sites—schools, workplaces, city council—and the messages that linked issues as well as people to one another all contributed to weaving many discrete struggles into a feeling of movement that was broadly owned. For the generation of activists who came of age during these years, the nineties cohort, it was the formative movement.

The sense of optimism this movement generated was dashed in the aftermath of 9/11. Despite an extraordinary anti-Iraq war movement— Los Angeles and many other U.S. cities saw their biggest anti-war demonstrations since the sixties—the Bush administration went to war, and has since transformed late twentieth-century neoliberalism into a twenty-first-century permanent war economy and society. Its support for privatization of public services, deep cuts in domestic programs, and tax rebates to the rich have made the lives of most Americans more difficult. So, too, have large corporations' accelerated efforts to cut back on benefits, wages, and full-time jobs.

George Bush's reelection in 2004 exacerbated a widely perceived crisis of the left. There has been much talk from liberal pundits and public intellectuals about how to revive the Democratic Party by moving rightward to appeal to conservative voters. There is a relative silence in these venues about building a wider participatory democracy or more robust visions of social justice.

While liberals and labor attached to the Democratic Party hoped to save some shreds of New Deal liberalism through party politics, many progressives worked outside these circles to continue the social movements they had begun in the nineties (Gottlieb et al. 2005). Los Angeles unions and immigrant worker-rights organizations continue to pursue a progressive social justice agenda through organizing. Health care and hotel worker unions with whom many activists in this book worked continue to win important victories despite the hostile political climate. For example, the Hotel Employees and Restaurant Employees International Union (HERE) faced a serious crisis with the post-9/11 crash of tourism in Los Angeles. As workers were laid off and union membership shrank, the financially stressed union struggled, successfully, to keep all staff employed. HERE merged with the Union of Needletrades, Industrial and Textile Employees (UNITE), itself battered by massive outsourcing of garment manufacturing, and began a campaign to negotiate hotel contracts across the nation at the same time in order to maximize their power in the face of centralized opposition by national chains of luxury hotels. In San Francisco in the fall of 2004, the employers' group locked out workers and refused to negotiate. Unable to win by picketing alone, the union built support around the idea of fairness and justice for workers. Both San Francisco popular opinion and that of its mayor swung toward union support. Local support combined with support from several large professional associations that cancelled meetings at San Francisco hotels, ultimately allowing the mayor to negotiate an end to the lockout.

In health care, since 2000 the Service Employees International Union (SEIU Local 399) has organized Los Angeles's largest hospital chain, Catholic Healthcare West, and since 9/11 has gone on to a statewide campaign to unionize workers at Tenet, the state's largest hospital chain. Unions like them are part of a wider effort to incorporate the younger generation in their efforts to revive the labor movement from within. These unions initiated the Change to Win Coalition, which argued that labor needed to pursue a more active and innovative organizing mission to survive, and in 2005, with several other large unions, left the AFL-CIO to pursue that path.

Politics may well be the art of the possible, but social movements are the force that expands the range of what is possible. As this book went to press, a million or so people in Los Angeles alone, largely immigrants and their families, took to the streets on March 25 and May 1, 2006, against xenophobic and punitive anti-immigrant legislation. Their actions, demanding full amnesty and legalization, are challenging the limits within which immigration policy is being debated. Now more than ever, it is important to examine the kind of movement that immigrant workers in Los Angeles helped bring into being.

SOCIAL MOVEMENT ENERGY

Much of the movement's impact came from the sense that this was a *movement*. Like many other armchair progressives and sometime activists in Los Angeles, I was drawn into it. Like the much briefer, but intense outpouring of massive opposition to the Iraq war, it had a particularly contagious energy that drew people to participate, even if they had not been active recently, or ever. We know a fair amount about the organizational foundations of social movements from resource mobilization theorists, as well as the effectiveness of rank-and-file involvement and community-based organizing in the labor movement.[1] But these literatures do not speak to the wider passions and involvement that are invoked when there is a social movement happening. Where does this sense of movement come from? What is it made of?

In her history of the women's health movement, Sandra Morgen (2002) tries to get at the experience and the personal meaning of belonging to a movement (as well as the structures and organization that scaffold the experiences). At its core, she argues, are foundational stories that "create shared history and sustain collective identity, the core lived experience of belonging to a social movement" (Morgen 2002, 13).

Consciousness-raising groups among white women that started with activists in the student movement and among women of color in the civil rights movement, where women forged new feminist social and political identities—and the slogan that the personal is political—are other clues to unpack the interface between the personal and the movement (Morgan 1970; Silliman et al. 2004). Charles Payne (1995) and Doug McAdam (1988) write about how activists created a "beloved community" among participants in the 1964 Mississippi Freedom Summer and the extraordinary energy, courage, and sense of belonging it generated in a movement, even among people far from Mississippi. They, too, home in on the ways in which those activists shared their lives and fashioned them into social and political identities that explained the meaning of what they were doing. More recently, Miriam Ching Yoon Louie has chronicled the personal and political transformation of immigrant women garment workers from sweatshop workers to "sweatshop Warriors" (M. Louie 2001).

These books all describe a kind of "nuclear fission" that took place when participants in these movements connected their quests for personal and meaningful relationships to the world in which they lived to the activism in which they were engaged. The explosive energy was personal, a sense of liberation, of infinite possibility that gave individuals the courage to do things they'd never dared or thought themselves capable of, to connect to others in ways they'd not dreamed possible, and to dream of changing the world so everyone could live their lives in equally meaningful ways. The explosion became a social phenomenon as participants' liberation and sense of meaning captured the imaginations of a wide audience and drew them in. This intensity, connection, vision of infinite possibility, and energy a movement releases are all fragile and fleeting, and these authors and participants in these movements know it too well. But they are onto something that is deeply important, namely the internal structures of meaning and purpose that release this extraordinary movement energy and magnetism, and, most important, broad ownership of its identities and ideas.

That is what this book explores. The social justice movement in Los Angeles and the nation may become more or less enduring, more or less powerful in the coming years, but it did have something of this explosive energy and excitement during the 1990s, and it did have an enduring impact on popular perceptions and political sentiments.

I seek to understand, first, how a movement creates emotional energy and an open sense of possibility within people, and second, how that personal sense gets translated into political ideals and organizational forms that spread more broadly. My hunch is that energy comes first from people giving birth to themselves as political beings, individually and collectively. This process involves the creation of new political subjectivities with new visions of possible worlds that resonate with and become owned by large numbers of people. The book is about the process by which activists give birth to those new selves and new visions, and begin to invent the political practice that allows more people to undergo their own political transformations.

This is a little too lyrical for my comfort. So let me try to be more specific. To learn about a movement's political subjectivity, I will focus on how those who gave birth to new selves experienced their own politicization process. More concrete still, how did activists come to be activists? What social relations and cultural meanings supported their rebirth? What made the process meaningful and exciting—what were their epiphanies? What messages and perspectives did they bring to the world? Who did they speak to? for? In short, this is a study of political identities, how they are made, and what they are made from.

POLITICAL IDENTITY

Anthropologists and kindred others offer several theoretical resources for studying political identity. They have shown that activists speak to, through, and for particular constituencies in complex ways, presenting to the public a collective political subject or identity in whose name action makes obvious sense. However, they also show that internally, the mix of activists and constituents is much more heterogeneous and contentious than its public and strategic presentation (Bernstein 2002; Holland and Lave 2001; Joseph 2002; Pardo 1998; Pulido 1998; Stephen 1997). Their analyses allow us to ask, how do people construct political identities in the first place? I don't mean labels, like worker, immigrant, or woman. I mean rich, textured understandings of oneself as a person linked to families, neighborhoods, jobs, schools, and particular histories that explain in personally meaningful ways why and how one must act politically in order to live a meaningful life.

A second strand of work connects activists' personal constructions of meaning and actions to other people through local cultures. Rich theoretical support comes from a multiplicity of studies across disciplines for the idea that people create selves and social movements from a repertoire of local knowledge, experiences, practices, and beliefs that they share among a wider circle of that movement's potential constituents. (Evans and Boyte 1986; Kaplan 1997; Kroskrity 2000; Payne 1995; Polletta 2002; Stack 1996; Brodkin Sacks 1988). If personal stories are culturally rooted, then it makes sense to ask whether and how activists' stories reflect on and transform the meanings of cultural beliefs and practices into new political subjectivities. One meaning of the truism that all politics are local is that social movements reinterpret aspects of local cultures in ways that infuse them with new political meanings, and create new political perspectives. As important, the ways activists interpret local cultures resonate with members of those cultures, transforming personal identities into broadly social ones, and draw whole groups of people into social movements.

Dorothy Holland and Jean Lave's (2001) concept of "history in person" brings these strands of analysis together in a useful framework. They analyze ways that people construct themselves as social beings in a context structured by what they call locally contentious cultural practices, which are in turn nested in a wider context shaped by enduring, institutionalized political struggles. The particularly useful part is that they flag all levels—personal, local, and wider society—as at once mutually constituting and internally contentious. The internal struggles at any level are both shaped by and in turn shape those of other levels. It is a particularly good framework for thinking about how the personal is the political and the political is the personal, locally and on the scale of a wider social movement.

This framework meshes well with Antonio Gramsci's idea of ideological struggle as ongoing, part of the fabric of daily life, and critical for those who would transform society to take seriously. He argued that the practices and meanings of local and political cultures are always undergoing interpretation and contestation, and are therefore always potentially at the center of ideological struggle. Gramsci argued that those struggles are about making revolutionary interpretations of widely shared experiences, dispositions, and structures of feeling those of the majority so that they will join the revolutionary movement. Making political meaning is ultimately a battle to shape the discourses, categories, and assumptions that people spontaneously think with because these shape how and what one can think, and therefore do (Gramsci 1997; Hall 1988, 1996; Sassoon 1980; Williams 1973).

I will use this framework to guide my exploration of connections among personal stories, local cultures, and social movements. My goal is to make sense of who is contesting what and what the contestations tell us about how activists are reinterpreting local cultures, how the reinterpretations inform the emerging politics of the movement—and reciprocally, how their own activism shapes activists' views about their particular cultures. More specifically, the goal is to show these three interconnections: (1) how the ways activists analyze their own politicization process connects them to the social movement they seek to build—its political actors, practices, organizational forms, and goals; (2) how their cultural communities shaped their politics and political selves; and (3) how their politics in turn have led them to challenge prevailing internal and mainstream views of their culture and to strengthen alternative internal perspectives.

There is a certain irony to the fact that something as public and palpable as the energy a social movement unleashes has flown under our analytic radar screen. How can we study the structure and process of the nuclear fission that makes a social movement? I take my lead from Morgen (2002), Payne (1995), and McAdam (1988), who direct us to look at the activists. How does their activism give their lives personal meaning, and reciprocally, how do they transform personal meanings into a social movement? How do personal meanings become shared and collectively owned? Is there a new political subjectivity and who owns it? How do events and sharing stories about them become movement ideals and practices?[2]

To answer these questions, I went to Los Angeles activists who came of political age in the most visible sector of this social justice movement, labor and immigrant workers' rights, during the 1990s. I asked these kinds of questions in open-ended interviews with thirteen activists. Tritia Toyota, who was working on her dissertation on new Asian-American activism, interviewed another three activists (Toyota 2004).

These sixteen activists are the book's narrators in the sense that their words are the core of the argument I build. These narrators come from a variety of backgrounds, but most are children of immigrants from Asia, Mexico, and Central America. Two are white women, one is an African-American woman. Most were also college students, and became political while in college. Two became activists as rank-and-file workers who became organizers. As a volunteer participant in a variety of labor and community-based organizations during this decade, I also had many informal conversations about the issues.

Why so many college students (fourteen of sixteen, to be precise)? As it turns out, the labor and immigrant workers movement is full of ex-students (Ganz et al. 2004; Rooks 2004). They have a very large presence, especially among organizers. Recruiting student organizers—over rank-and-file workers—has been a long-time labor pattern nationally, and, as we see in chapter 2, Los Angeles is no exception.[3]

More germane here is who these college students are. Like the great social movements of contemporary U.S. history—labor in the 1930s and the civil rights movement of the 1950s and 1960s—the college students who loom largest are those from the same backgrounds as those movements' constituents. In the thirties, many were college-bound children of Southern and Eastern European immigrants; and in the 1950s and early 1960s, many were African-American college students. In the 1990s, college-bound children of immigrants—Latina/o and Asian in Los Angeles—began turning away from careers that define mainstream success and gravitating to the new labor activism in significant numbers. Twelve of our fourteen college-origin activists are children of Latina/o and Asian backgrounds.

As students of color, they have a special fund of not-always-welcome personal experience with ideological struggle that has given them both a critical angle of vision and a healthy appreciation for its importance for social movements. As college students from marginalized communities, and among those the mainstream has anointed the "best and the brightest" and candidates for social leadership, they are in the crosshairs of a race-like and a class-like struggle, often objects or prizes in a society-wide battle for their allegiance. On whose behalf will they lead? They are the pride of their families and communities, repositories of their hopes for a better life. To the mainstream, they are the proof that

America is a meritocracy. And to the powerful, the hope is that they will persuade "their people" that the status quo is socially fair and is what the good life looks like. Their dilemma is whether to represent the poor and racialized and be a force for change, or to carry the arguments of the powerful to their communities by succeeding in the world as it is.

I've focused on activists who are organizers. The nature of that job, especially in labor unions, places them in the middle of a different kind of ideological struggle. Organizers are not in positions of institutional leadership; they do not negotiate with other organizations, nor do they lobby power holders. That is what institutional leaders do. Rather, the job of an organizer is to be what Belinda Robnett, who studied black women organizers in the civil rights movement, calls "bridge leaders." That is, they bring the organization's message to potential constituents and members, and bring potential constituencies' perspectives to the organization's leaders (Robnett 1996). Their job is outreach and recruitment of masses of people to their group's message.

But organizers are particularly well placed to learn popular understandings, priorities, and desires among potential constituents. To carry out their job of mobilizing and organizing requires educating, encouraging participation, and developing leadership. Not surprisingly, Robnett found that the black women organizers she studied tended to represent constituents' views to their organizations more than the reverse, and that organizing was a radicalizing experience, making them instigators of democratic radicalism—or at least of more democratic programs and practices that connected to potential constituencies. In this view, organizers, already committed to social justice, are most likely to understand potential constituents and what their movement should look like in order to resonate with their needs and aspirations.

College students, children of racialized immigrant communities, labor organizers. Each of these social statuses contains its own mix of experiences with being in privileged and subordinated positions. This ensemble of what critical theorists call multiple marginalities encourages a great deal of socially critical reflection and political analysis. As we shall see, their insights and reflections, together with those of white, college-origin organizers and rank-and-file-origin organizers of color, have met the analytical challenge of articulating the process by which they have made themselves into political subjects who are members of working-class ethnic communities, and are creating new forms of democratic politics from those perspectives. Their narratives show a structure of events and insights through which they connect personal meanings to cultural and political communities and to wider democratic practice. And, most important, they show vividly the excitement of discovery, the epiphanies, and the energy they create and communicate to those they organize.

I suspect that these narrators are not that different from others in their cohort, and perhaps nationally. If so, their collective portrait may well be a glimpse into a more general behind-the-scenes process by which are born the political subjectivities, meanings, and organizational forms of what many see as a new kind of democratic social justice movement. My hope is that this book will add to the small but growing effort to analyze the many strands of progressive politics within and beyond Los Angeles.

ORGANIZATION OF THE BOOK

Chapters 1 and 2 set context for the study. Chapter 1, "The Context of Labor and Immigrant Workers' Rights Activism in Los Angeles," describes the key changes in the economy and demography of Los Angeles since 1965, the year of the Watts uprising and the dramatic rewriting of U.S. immigration policy. Deindustrialization and deunionization combined with large-scale immigration from Asia, Mexico, and Central America radically transformed the ethnic composition of the city's working class. The interaction of deindustrialization and immigration with a racist and xenophobic political backlash shaped the city's landscape of activism in the 1990s.

Immigrant worker activism helped spark a rebirth of unionization. Unions, together with a broad spectrum of interconnected organizations, took on with considerable success the assaults of ethnic, racial, and economic backlash politics. These efforts schooled a generation of young workers and college students in political activism, and inspired a cohort to seek a life of full-time social justice activism.

Chapter 2, "Narrators and Narrative," sets out the landscape of labor and immigrant workers' rights organizing, and where the sixteen organizers who serve as the book's narrators fit in it. Labor and immigrant worker organizations form a coherent domain of activism with issues, organizations, and activists joined together in networks and organizational coalitions. These organizations and their members have ties to other progressive issues and organizations, but they are less-tightly connected and more episodic. I suggest that the book's narrators are part of a generational "nineties cohort" of labor and immigrant workers' rights organizers that are tightly networked together. The narrators, like young labor organizers generally, are mainly children of immigrants from Mexico, Central America, or Asia, and more women than men. This generational cohort of various ethnicities cuts across organizations and issues with diverse constituencies in community-based and issue-based organizing, but their closest political ties are with others in labor circles. The chapter also looks at the value of personal narratives for showing how people come to see social and political life in ways that are radically different from ruling ideology. Becoming the author of one's own life is part of becoming a political actor. Narrators chronicle the process, analyzing personal experiences, how they came to reinterpret their meaning, the personal and political transformations they stimulated, and the meaning of political practice to their sense of self.

The third, fourth and fifth chapters are the narrators'. They analyze the process by which they gave birth to themselves as new political subjects embedded in working-class and ethnic communities, and the nature of their democratic practice and visions.

In chapter 3, "Political Identity Starts at Home," they reflect on their parents' contributions to their socio-political selves, offering retrospective analyses through the lenses of full-time activism. We see their parents enlisting them in the difficult project of crossing social and national borders as a way of improving their lives, and in the larger project of changing and reinterpreting, but also reinforcing, their new versions of cultural identities. They are proud of their parents' success and deeply connected to their families and communities. But in their stories based on experiences shared by many new immigrants, the interpretation shifts so that barriers to success appear as institutional, and success becomes less an individual property, less the results of a person's or family's hard work and more a collective struggle against the racialization and xenophobia that holds back the whole community. Success becomes an achievement of the group. And, not least, they create counter-stereotypic models of womanhood and manhood in the process.

Narrators analyze the ways their experiences created a pre-political sense of themselves as unable or unwilling to fit themselves into the social boxes of an alien and unjust society, longing for a place to call home, but seemingly destined to move back and forth between inhospitable social places, and by so doing, to know more about social injustice than they wished at a young age.

In chapter 4, "Making Identities Political," narrators describe the processes by which they transformed their childhood experiences into a political identity. Where the previous chapter described the impact of being moved across borders by their parents, in this chapter they analyze their own choices of borders to cross and how those choices helped them create what Gloria Anzaldúa and Cherríe Moraga called a borderland social space and a political identity they share with others in it (Anzaldúa 1999; Moraga and Anzaldúa 1983). They describe their efforts to find home places, often in ethnic studies programs, in colleges where they feel out of place. From these bases they became involved in a variety of campus activities with "other others," where they drew upon earlier skills at dealing with difference to create a wider political framework of groups and issues with which they felt kinship. They came to see a variegated "us," made up of a multiplicity of the marginalized. In their activism, they came to "put the margins at the center," as bell hooks put it (hooks 1989). And finally, involvement in successful campaigns crystallized their sense of political agency, that by acting in concert they can make a difference in the world.

Not least, they reinterpret the widely shared experience of being racialized and racially marginalized in a way that makes multiracial coalitions rather than single ethnic solidarity the central site of democratic practice. Politics becomes a practice that, though rooted in ethnic identification, takes them beyond this zone of comfort into identities and coalitions across differences. Political practice becomes in part a process for negotiating conflict and differences.

Chapter 5, "Democracy and Political Praxis," takes up the political practices, goals, and visions that narrators have created in the course of their political activism. It places narrators within a heritage of activism that shares two key principles: organizing is about building the personal capacities for democratic leadership among those they organize; and movement-building involves practicing the democracy and social justice it envisions for the future. The chapter examines what organizing looks like in narrators' interpersonal political practice. It then examines the organizational aspects of their visions of democracy. Narrators work within, and have helped to build, a landscape of organizational structures, practices, and cultures that include a mix of small, relatively non-hierarchical immigrant worker organizations and much larger and more hierarchical labor unions. By working in and with both kinds of organization, narrators have developed a few clear ideas about what democracy looks like—and should look like—in the institutional practices and cultures of very different kinds of activist organizations. Those ideas include ways of restructuring social movement jobs and rethinking the place of social movement work as part of creating models of more democratic work-life balance more generally.

And at least as important is the imperative of changing institutional practice and culture so that it speaks to the priorities of workers of color and women, and reflects them in organizational leadership. Finally, in their narratives and in the organizational forms they are building, they are coming to theorize what has been called "the working class" as itself more as coalition-like, a work-in-progress, than as a unity with prior and self-evident shared interests.

The conclusion of the book returns to the big questions of identities and democracy that the narratives raise. The first question asks what kinds of ideological work narratives perform in shaping a social movement. Narrators have created a range of counter-hegemonic social subjects that make up the public face of a movement. But narrators also want to create a movement that deals with multiple forms of marginalization. I look at the silences and differences in the narrators to suggest some of the challenges and unfinished business of such a movement. The second question, which asks where narrators fit in the heritage of democratic social movements, focuses on why cohorts have been such important incubators for generating social movements, their identities, and understandings of democracy. I suggest that difficulties in intergenerational continuity may be a possible downside to the vitality of cohorts.

CHAPTER 1

The Context of Labor and Immigrant Workers' Rights Activism in Los Angeles

THIS CHAPTER DESCRIBES THE BACKGROUND to labor and immigrant workers' rights organizing in Los Angeles during the 1990s, and situates the book's narrators and their cohort of activists in that arena. First, I discuss how demographic and economic changes in the Los Angeles region made new immigrants from Latin America and Asia the core of the city's working class. Next I discuss the political climate of anti-immigrant and more general racist backlash in the 1990s and the broad-based mobilization against it. I focus on the organizational landscape of labor and immigrant workers' rights activism that played a key role in combating it. Revitalized labor unions and immigrant workers' rights organizations catalyzed a synergistic growth of activism that took on class, racial, and ethnic oppressions together. Indeed, Los Angeles for a brief moment looked like a poster child for what a broad-based social movement might look like.[1] College students and young workers were inspired and enabled to become full-time organizers, and activists.

THE DEMOGRAPHIC AND LABOR FORCE CONTEXT

The roots of the story go back to 1965, when Los Angeles was a very different city. Prior to 1965, Los Angeles was overwhelmingly white and white ruled. Despite the fact that it had once been part of Mexico, Los Angeles's Mexican-origin population was dwarfed by the stream of white immigrants from the midwestern United States. During and after World War II, Los Angeles became the industrial center of the West Coast, and home to a large, and largely white, unionized work-force. Los Angeles was also a very segregated city, residentially as well as occupationally. Mexican-Americans, African-Americans, and Asian-Americans had virtually no political representation; public facilities such as beaches, swimming pools, and schools were segregated, as was hous-ing. Police brutality was a major problem for all communities of color.

The Watts uprising, or riot, and changes in U.S. immigration law, both in 1965, set the stage for a transformation of Los Angeles from a segregated and white-ruled city to the most multiracial and multiethnic city in the country, with hotly contested and complex racial politics. The Watts uprising by black Angelenos in the face of intransigent institu-tional racism marked the beginnings of a major challenge to the racial status quo and gave birth to social movements that began to rethink politics from a variety of nonprivileged perspectives. Over the next decade, activism by students of color to gain access and representation in the curricula of higher education, and activism by black and Mexican workers to gain access to unionized industrial jobs, had a fair degree of success in ending de facto segregation in workplaces and in higher education.

Nineteen sixty-five was also the year that the United States rewrote its immigration laws in a way that allowed significant numbers of people to migrate from non-European countries. By the 1970s, Los Angeles was becoming a magnet for large-scale immigration from Asia and Cen-tral America that reshaped the city's ethnic and racial demography in general, and that of its labor force in particular. By the 1990s, new immigrants had joined African-Americans and other U.S.-born peoples of color in pursuing ethnic and racial justice in the political arena.

Demographics

The class composition of migrants from Asia and Latin America dif-fered in significant ways. Professional and middle-class migrants were a large part of the immigrants from Asia, while those from Mexico and Central America were predominantly rural and working class. Chinese, Korean, and Filipino businesspersons and professionals facing economic uncertainty and political restrictions found attractive the new law's high quotas for business entrepreneurs, managers, and those with training in a variety of professions, and found Southern California a desirable destination. As a result, the city drew large numbers of well-educated and middle-class immigrants from Hong Kong, Taiwan, China, Korea, and the Philippines. Where Chinese and Filipino migration built on earlier streams of largely working-class migrants, significant Korean migration began only after 1965. Large numbers of political refugees—from both middle-class and peasant backgrounds—from the Vietnam War and from Pol Pot's regime in Cambodia also settled in nearby Orange County and Long Beach, respectively.

The 1965 immigration laws had a very different impact on migrants from Mexico and Central America. As with the Philippines, this region—especially Mexico—had a long history of working-class migration, and the forces that produced an exodus of low-income rural and urban working-age people from Mexico persisted. But the new law put quotas for the first time on Mexican immigration and on immigration from other Latin American countries. Those quotas were far below normal migration from Mexico alone. With the rise of war and repression during the seventies and eighties in Central American countries, many more refugees attempted to enter the United States than were stipulated in the quotas for these countries. Although there were provisions for political asylum and refugee status for people fleeing communist countries, refugees fleeing repressive dictatorships of the right, like Guatemala, El Salvador, and Honduras, were not granted the same refugee status granted to Vietnamese, Laotians, Cambodians, or Cubans. A significant consequence of these policies was to make large numbers of Mexican and Central American immigrants illegal. As a result, many in the new Latina/o immigrant communities were undocumented, stigmatized, and particularly vulnerable.

However, the class bias of the 1965 immigration law also worked against working-class Asian immigrants. A large but indeterminate number of working-class Filipinos, Chinese, and Koreans also immigrated for work, but without documents. They, too, were illegal, and vulnerable in the same ways as their counterparts from Mexico and Central America.

By the 1990s, Los Angeles had become a city of immigrants and refugees. It is now the most nationally and ethnically diverse U.S. urban area and home to 4.8 million immigrants (31 percent of its population), the largest percentage of immigrants in the country (Allen 1997). Documented and undocumented, they come in greatest numbers from Mexico, Central America, China, Korea, the Philippines, and Southeast Asia.

More specifically, by 1997 Los Angeles County had become a county of predominantly Latino immigrants, mainly Mexican. The combination of longstanding patterns of migration for work and the new streams of political refugees from the wars in Central America supported a sharp increase in the numbers of Mexican and Central American immigrants. By 2000, 44.6 percent of the county's population was Latina/o. Today, Los Angeles can claim to be the second-largest Mexican city and perhaps the largest Salvadoran one as well. Only about 31 percent of its residents were Anglo whites, followed by Asian/Pacific Islanders (11.8 percent), the fastest growing population, and a shrinking population of African-Americans (9.5 percent) (Davis 2000, 2–7; Southern California Association of Governments 2001).

How New Immigrants Changed Los Angeles

In the last three decades, new immigrants have changed the ethnic patterns of the city's residential landscape across the class spectrum. They've also revitalized decaying business areas of the city, reorganized old industries, and created new ones.

Chinese businesses and developers transformed the predominantly white suburb of Monterey Park into the hub of a bustling business and residential center for new Chinese immigrants. As Chinese have passed Filipinos as the largest Asian ethnic group in Los Angeles, they have expanded their businesses and residence outward from Monterey Park, across the San Gabriel Valley.

Korean immigration is most visible in small grocery and liquor stores, dry cleaners, restaurants, and garment-making subcontractors. Korean small businesses have replaced white stores that left African-American and Latino communities, and have rebuilt a declining mid-Wilshire business district into Koreatown, a vibrant commercial center of small businesses set in a neighborhood made up largely of new Central American and Korean immigrants. Korean garment subcontractors, employing largely new Latina/o and Southeast Asian immigrants in small shops scattered through central and south Los Angeles, have been key to Los Angeles's emergence as the nation's largest apparel producer.

Mexican and Central American working-class immigrants have sought housing in lower-rent neighborhoods across the metropolitan area. They are transforming South Los Angeles's African-American neighborhoods and have already transformed formerly all-white working-class cities of southeast Los Angeles County into Latina/o cities.

The Labor Force

In the sixties and early seventies, largely as a result of post-Watts political activism, black workers gained access to unionized public sector employment and black and Chicana/o[2] workers gained access to unionized industrial and service sector jobs. By the late seventies, the United States economy was beginning to hemorrhage manufacturing jobs, especially in industries that were heavily unionized. In Los Angeles, as last hired and thus those with least seniority, black and Chicana/o workers suffered a disproportionate share of these job losses as auto and other heavy industries shut down in the course of the seventies. Beginning with the Reagan administration in 1981, big cuts in public sector jobs have whittled away at African-American gains here as well. The jobs that did grow in numbers during the eighties were nonunion service-sector jobs in cleaning, care giving, and tourism. In the seventies, many of these were union jobs. However, as the service sector expanded in the eighties, these jobs became de-unionized, declined in pay and benefits, and simultaneously became occupational niches of new immigrants.

By the 1990s, working-class Los Angeles was a city of low-wage workers. The large-scale industrial economy and unionized labor force that had sustained a middle-class quality of life for hourly workers in the sixties has been replaced by nonunion service jobs and by small, scattered subcontracting shops in manufacturing, and a declining number of public-sector jobs. Post-1965 immigrants, especially those from Mexico and Central America, are at the center of the service and manufacturing economy in Los Angeles, and largely in these low-wage, sweatshop, and nonunion jobs. A quarter of all families in Los Angeles in 2001 were considered working poor. In California, almost 60 percent of such families were Latina/o (California Budget Project 2003).

Job slotting on the basis of race, ethnicity, and gender are long-standing features of the U.S. labor force, and Los Angeles is no exception. Latina/os, along with Asian refugees from Vietnam and immigrants from China and Southeast Asia, make up the core of the garment industry labor force. Los Angeles is home to the nation's largest garment industry, and that industry also employs more workers than any other manufacturing industry in the city (Ong, Bonacich, and Cheng 1994). Health care and elder care rely heavily on Asians, especially Filipinas, and on Latinas. Tourism, child care, manufacturing, and construction likewise depend upon an immigrant labor force. Although not all new immigrants work in low-wage jobs, the large majority do so, including many professionals (Scott 1996; Waldinger and Bozorgmehr 1996).

Organizing at Work and in the Community

Patterns of cross-ethnic and racial contact at work differ from those in neighborhoods. Patterns of job slotting bring together Latina/os and Asian-Americans in the workplace, but also frequently separate them from African-Americans. However, working-class Latina/o immigrants and working-class African-Americans are likely to share neighborhoods, especially neighborhoods that were black or black and Japanese-American in earlier decades, and to be separated from Asian-Americans (Allen 1997; Lipsitz 1998; Waldinger and Bozorgmehr 1996; Waldinger and Lichter 2003).

Two important organizations, the Community Coalition and AGENDA, a multiracial community-based group, bring together African-American and Latina/o constituencies. They train significant numbers of young community organizers, and serve as mentors of young community-based activists. The Community Coalition has a large and thriving program of political education and organizing for high school students. They in turn are part of a multiracial coalition of county-wide organizations that work with high school students. The most visible community-based struggles have been those spearheaded by high school youth, especially the passage in 1997 of Proposition BB, a $2.4 billion bond issue for repair and improvement of schools, as well as ongoing movements against racism in the criminal justice system against youth of color, most notably by the Youth Justice Coalition and Families to

Amend California's Three Strikes (FACTS). Their campaigns to reform mandatory life sentencing for those convicted of three felonies have garnered widespread support.

Working in heavily industrialized cities in southeast Los Angeles County with concentrations of recent immigrants from Mexico and Central America, Communities for a Better Environment (CBE) organizes against toxic dumping in communities of color. With the high school student organization, Youth for Environmental Justice, they prevented the reopening of a highly polluting oil refinery and blocked the construction of a very large gas-fired power plant in 2000, despite the electricity shortages produced by deregulation.

Wider patterns of workplace and neighborhood segregation and mixing shape the ethnoracial composition of organizers and issue areas. Latina/o and Asian-American organizers tend to be concentrated in labor and immigrant worker activism. There are many Latina/o and Asian-American, a fair number of white, but few African-American organizers in the most actively organizing unions. This seems to be in part because black Angelenos are concentrated in existing public sector unions, where, given the push to privatize public services, there are few opportunities for expansion or new organizing. It is also in part because of de-unionization of service-sector jobs that had been predominantly African-American. With de-unionization and wage cuts, they subsequently became jobs held by new immigrants. And unions' efforts to increase their strength have focused on the expanding nonunion private-sector service industries where new immigrants are concentrated (Waldinger and Der-Martirosian 2000). Reflecting residential ethnoracial patterns, African-American and immigrant Latina/o activists come together to organize working-class community-based politics, environmental justice, and high school students. Here, key issues are public-school quality, job programs, and ending police and prison abuse.

THE POLITICAL CLIMATE AND ORGANIZATIONAL LANDSCAPE

If the Watts uprising gave birth to a militant and class-conscious racial politics, the 1992 Los Angeles uprising showed the need for a significant update to such politics. The Black Panther Party, followed by kindred Asian-American, Native American and Chicana/o movements, put people of color at the center of its analyses of class issues, and began to show how racial and class oppression were linked. These perspectives remain important. But the largely black-white racial dynamics in Watts contrast with those of its 1992 counterpart, the so-called Rodney King riot. Here, African-American outrage at the acquittal of four white policemen, whose videotaped and nationally televised brutal beating of motorist Rodney King sparked a major riot. Its racial and class dynamics were much more complicated than those of Watts (Kwong 1997; Waldinger and Bozorgmehr 1996). Patterns of looting, in addition to demonstrating the anger in African-American communities against institutionalized white racism, also revealed their deep ethnic and class anger toward small Korean businesses in South Los Angeles. Less publicized, looting patterns also revealed anger by new Latina/o immigrants against Korean and white businesses. There was also anger in the Korean community against white racism demonstrated by the lack of police and city protection of their businesses. And Latina/os understood the mass arrests and deportations of Latina/os without documents in their possession as governmental racism. The 1992 uprising made clear just how complex are today's fault lines of race, immigration, ethnicity, and class,

Following the uprising, but fueled also by a major recession and the beginnings of recurrent state budgetary crises, California saw a sustained assault on the rights of both immigrants and U.S. citizens of color. Five high-profile backlash voter initiatives were directed at immigrants and young people of color between 1994 and 2000. On the ballots in 1994 were propositions for mandatory life imprisonment for three felonies, popularly known as "three strikes" (Proposition 184), and another to deny health and educational benefits to undocumented immigrants (Proposition 187). Both passed, although the latter was declared unconstitutional. Then in 1995 the Regents of the University of California passed two measures that ended all race, gender, and ethnicity-based affirmative action at the university. The following year, California voters passed Proposition 209, which made such affirmative action illegal anywhere in the state. Bilingual education was outlawed in 1998 (Proposition 227); and in 2000, voters passed Proposition 21, which allows juveniles to be tried as adults. Although the focus of the right-wing backlash was against people of color, the homophobic so-called Defense of Marriage initiative, Proposition 22, was also passed in 2000.

As in the aftermath of Watts, new organizations and new politics developed to combat the xenophobia and racism of the 1990s. Activist opposition to the backlash voter initiatives introduced a generation of high school and college students to political activism in new groups that sprang up to educate youth and the adult public. The labor movement in Los Angeles was also changing, responding in part to the anti-immigrant backlash and in part to the centrality of immigrant workers in the labor force. Activists of color of the sixties and seventies generation came into leadership positions in the County Federation of Labor and several key unions, where they initiated ongoing organizing drives among immigrant workers. And immigrant workers themselves undertook a number of stunningly successful organizing drives that brought national attention to Los Angeles. Justice for Janitors succeeded in unionizing office cleaning in much of Los Angeles; largely immigrant Mexican workers independently organized a huge strike of all drywall installers from San Diego to Los Angeles; and immigrant workers unionized an automobile wheel plant on their own (Lichtenstein 2002, 247–256; Milkman 2000; Waldinger et al. 1997).

Campuses as Cradles of the 1990s Political Cohort

As a result of all this activism, high school and college students in Los Angeles during the nineties found themselves going to school in a highly politicized climate, one that opened the possibility of considering a life in social justice organizing. The narrators in this book are part of this cohort and were in college during these years. They took their first steps toward activism in the many opportunities for labor and antiracist involvement on their campuses during this period. They tended to circulate among a variety of issue-based organizations and coalitions that brought different constellations of people together. The outcome of this rich climate of issue-based politics was that it stimulated student activists to develop a more integrated political understanding of the links between issues, and the links between their constituencies—in short, to connect a lot of dots.

For example, UCLA, not normally an activist campus, generated a great deal of activism around racial/ethnic, class, and economic issues. These years were marked by the politicization of ethnic and women's studies student organizations and the campus ethnic and feminist newsmagazines, as well as the Community Programs Office. This office became a home for students of color, especially African-American students who sought activist and community service opportunities. A number went on to become community organizers in South Los Angeles.[3] Student responses to state politics of racial backlash and to cuts in the educational budget created an activist climate that began to link class, race, and human-rights issues. Although key issues and the most visible leadership came from students of color and the ethnic studies student organizations they built, student activists at UCLA spanned the ethnic and racial spectrum.

Activism began early in the decade. In 1991 there was sizeable campus opposition to the first war against Iraq. In 1992 students protested moves to charge undocumented students out-of-state tuition. That year also saw the first of California's budget crises, with cuts in state funding to education and sharp fee increases at public universities. Over four hundred demonstrators protested at the installation ceremonies for a new University of California president at UCLA and held a teach-in against fee hikes and staff cuts in the face of high administrators' salaries and raises. That movement joined graduate and undergraduate students in sustained activism. The following school year, 1992–1993, saw protests and demands for withdrawing university support from fraternities when the racist and sexist lyrics of a fraternity songbook were published in the campus feminist newspaper.

The biggest protest of the decade however, was the Chicana/o Studies ten-day hunger strike and tent city in the middle of campus in spring 1993. Centered on the demand for a Chicana/o Studies department, it galvanized much of the campus and produced widespread support from students and Los Angeles's wider Latina/o community. So, too, did the subsequent Chicana/o student takeover of the faculty center, and student opposition to the invasion of the campus by the Los Angeles Police. This struggle was ultimately won by building a large, strong, and often contentious coalition that included Chicana/o students, other students of color, feminists, faculty, a broad range of local groups in the Chicana/o community, and key political leaders across the progressive spectrum (Russel y Rodriguez 1994; Youth Power Change Web site).

In 1994–1995, students mobilized against Proposition 187, which denied health, education, and welfare benefits to undocumented immigrants. Some two hundred students demonstrated at the Federal

Building, and a larger demonstration on campus demanding that the chancellor refuse to implement the proposition resulted in arrests of twenty-six students. In early 1995, students again rallied against University Regents' moves to outlaw affirmative action at the University of California and against the anti-gay policies of campus ROTC. By the following year, a multiracial coalition of progressive students ran a successful slate called Students First for student government. That year was marked by activism against proposition 209, which outlawed affirmative action in California. These demonstrations brought together a wide spectrum of opposition from law students, the graduate student union, campus unions, MEChA, Justice for Janitors, the African Student Union, the Asian Pacific Coalition, the Muslim Student Association, Samahang Pilipino, and the Gay and Lesbian Student Association. A demonstration of eight hundred participants at the Federal Building culminated with thirty-four arrests of people who sat-in in the middle of Wilshire Boulevard.

In 1995–1996, a long-simmering student effort to get the university to offer language courses in Vietnamese and Tagalog flowered into a demand for a Southeast Asian Studies program. This was also the year that longstanding organizing efforts to unionize graduate student teaching assistants came to fruition. That year's graduate student unionization drive was supported by Justice for Janitors, which was then a young and vibrant union of commercial building cleaners.[4] After the passage of Proposition 209, the student government organized a "Death of Education" campaign promoting awareness of the consequences of that voter initiative on admission of students of color, with support from students who had been active in many of the above efforts (UCLA Yearbooks; UCLA Archives, Box 15: Students of UCLA, Student Activism Collection). However, campus activism dropped off sharply after the passage of Proposition 209 and the ensuing plummeting numbers of African-American and Latina/o students at UCLA.

During this decade, immigrant workers and their supporters built a very visible and dynamic social movement in the streets and workplaces of Los Angeles. Their struggles inspired and engaged activists at UCLA and other Los Angeles campuses. In part this was because new organizations dealing with the plight of immigrant workers revealed the impacts of xenophobic policies and practices and linked the struggle for workers' rights to the wider spectrum of struggles for racial and ethnic justice. These organizations, which will be described more fully later, also developed dynamic new ways of organizing. The Justice for Janitors, or JfJ, campaign to unionize office and building cleaners on the west side of Los Angeles brought the situation of immigrant workers directly to the public and pioneered dramatic ways of bringing their message to residents of Los Angeles through huge demonstrations of red-T-shirted workers supported by clergy in full liturgical dress, sometimes tying up traffic at busy intersections.

Immigrant workers' struggles on their own behalf stimulated a great deal of campus interest in labor issues. The Asian Immigrant Workers Association, a new community organization, initiated a statewide campaign against sweatshop practices by clothing manufacturer Jessica McClintock. In Los Angeles, UCLA students in Asian American Studies spearheaded that campaign. And a campus and community support group at UCLA and UC Riverside, Common Threads, soon sprang up in support of garment workers' efforts to unionize the Guess clothing company (Common Threads Artists 1998). They all followed JfJ's strategy of delivering their message directly to the public through street theater, demonstrations, posters, and humor.

The narrators who were UCLA students at the time had contact with, and often circulated among, different issue-based groups. For example, Roxane Auer was initially interested in environmental issues, something she attributed to her white upper-middle-class background. But this interest quickly led her to learn about the ways that corporate exploitation was implicated in human rights abuses in East Timor and Burma, and to issues of environmental justice and human rights in the Environmental Coalition. Roxane also helped to found Common Threads. Aquilina Soriano also became involved in the Environmental Coalition, but by a different route. She joined the Filipino student club in search of a place to learn more about her Filipino heritage when she first came to UCLA. Her earlier interest in environmental justice activism focused at UCLA on toxic dumping on Indian reservations. Then, in part because there were other Asian-American women involved, she joined the Environmental Coalition. But she was also involved in activism against xenophobic Proposition 187, and worked with the hotel workers' union on organizing New Otani Hotel workers.

The shift in Michelle Mascarenhas's trajectory in 1991 lets us see some of the ways that an activist climate opened up new opportunities. In the late 1980s she entered school as an engineering student, and was not an activist. The 1991 Gulf War and campus activism around it led Michelle to change the course of her life. Her parents are from Goa, but they had lived in Kuwait before coming to the United States. Having heard family stories about Kuwait's undemocratic social order motivated Michelle to join the campus opposition to the war. This experience led her to rethink her choice of engineering, and she took a year off to work in the Peace Corps in South Africa. She returned to UCLA right before the Los Angeles uprising of 1992. She changed her major to history and women's studies, organized VOICES, a very active women's studies student group focusing on issues of women of color, and also became involved in the Jessica McClintock campaign and Justice for Janitors community-support work. In graduate work in urban planning at UCLA, she became president of the graduate employee union.

Even activists whose efforts remained more focused on one issue nevertheless found themselves working with a wider spectrum of activists. Thus Stephanie Monroe focused on issues of sexism while at UCLA. She was the editor of the campus feminist magazine that published the racist and sexist lyrics of a fraternity songbook. That exposé began a major campaign against a fraternity subculture of racism and misogyny that brought together feminist and Chicana/o Studies students and faculty across the race and gender spectrum. Quynh Nguyen's family fled Vietnam, living first in Montreal, before settling in Los Angeles. Quynh focused her activities on an effort to get courses in Vietnamese taught at UCLA, initially because she wanted to take Vietnamese. But that campaign widened to include students who wanted courses in Tagalog. And the process of critiquing Eurocentrism in language offerings led to a campaign to establish a Southeast Asian Studies program, and a wider process of coalition building.

Narrators who attended UCLA were not unique in their campus experiences. At Yale, Joann Lo's initial interest in the Taiwanese student club broadened during a year in Australia to include indigenous people's rights, and, in the context of the Yale clerical workers' unionization effort, to labor and gender issues. Suyapa Portillo at Occidental College first gravitated to a campaign for racial equity for faculty, then to an internship working on a hotel-worker organizing drive among immigrant workers at a building where her mother and other Central American immigrants worked.

Narrators often felt overwhelmed by the endless number of specific issues that needed attention—war, affirmative action, ethnic studies, fee cuts, sweatshops, human-rights abuses. Roxane Auer recalled wishing at the time for the apparent simplicity of the late sixties when the Vietnam War was, at least in her father's stories, THE issue that united everyone. Yet, like other UCLA narrators who circulated from group to group and issue to issue, she also began to make larger political connections and to develop a more integrated political analysis. Thus, the seeming fragmentation that came from the multiplicity of issues competing for attention had the paradoxical effect of stimulating activists to think in more integrated political ways. Political integration was also helped along by opportunities afforded by a rich stew of activism to meet and talk across racial and ethnic lines that might otherwise separate students. At UCLA, student activists built a number of multiracial coalitions, including a progressive slate that won election to student government in 1996 on a broad platform of racial and social justice.

Thus, narrators who attended colleges and universities in the nineties became politicized mainly for the first time in this rich stew of issues, organizations, and campaigns. Shared experiences of circulating among activist groups and building a variety of coalitions no doubt contributed to the emergence of a politics that connected the dots of race and class, labor and immigration, environment and human rights. Among this cohort, global capitalism tends to be the line that connects the dots.

Why Labor?

During the 1990s activist labor unions, living-wage community groups supported by these unions, and a new body of immigrant-worker advocacy and education groups became identifiable domains of social-movement organizations, and the city's most consistent hot spots of political activism. Local efforts were supported by changes in the leadership of the AFL-CIO, which created a national Organizing Institute and supported a variety of ethnic, women's, and lesbian/gay caucuses.

The Asian Pacific American Labor Alliance (APALA) and the Organizing Institute recruited and trained organizers who came to Los Angeles. Their active recruitment efforts on college campuses brought a new cohort of campus activists to union locals in Los Angeles. Many of these new recruits were children of Asian and Latin American immigrants, and had their own vision for union organizing. Joann Lo, for example, was inspired to relocate to Los Angeles because she wanted to organize immigrant Asian and Latina/o workers: "I felt like working in the union would be someplace where I could do some good, where I could make a change, and have more of a chance as a person of color to help kind of push and change unions to organize Asian-Americans and other people of color. And so I decided that what I wanted to do was to work in the union."

In this manner, labor and immigrant rights organizations in Los Angeles came to employ a large number of the narrators of this book, part of the "nineties cohort." As we'll see in this chapter and subsequent chapters, they constitute a cohort in more than a generational sense. They circulate among the different labor and immigrant workers' advocacy organizations in the course of their work, and these organizations themselves regularly cooperate with and support one another. In these ways they create an identifiable domain of social activism, and an identifiable network of "nineties cohort" activists within it. The next two sections of this chapter describe labor and immigrant workers' rights activism as a domain of activism in Los Angeles that is defined institutionally and by social networks.

KEY ORGANIZATIONS

Institutionally, this domain of activism is defined by a number of closely cooperating organizations of different types—labor unions, independent worker organizations, and community labor-support organizations—and by the formal coalitions they create with one another. Social networks that specifically tie the nineties cohort organizers together locate narrators within this broader landscape and provide the basis for thinking of their politics, which are explored in the rest of the book, as representative of a broader political generation.

In the 1990s, Los Angeles saw a concurrent growth in union activism among immigrant workers and unions that sought to organize them, and the expansion of efforts by existing immigrant rights organizations to include the rights of immigrants as workers. In this respect, Los Angeles is part of a larger national pattern of growth of new forms of worker organizations, progressive activism within a number of unions, and cooperation (albeit sometimes uneasy) between these kinds of organizations. By the 1990s, the independent worker organizations were beginning to change the face of worker organizing nationally and in Los Angeles (Louie 2001; Mantsios 1998; Milkman 2000; Milkman and Wong 2000; Tait 2005; Tillman and Cummings 1999; Wong 2001).

Their ongoing organizing projects provided opportunities for young activists to volunteer and to become paid staff. The following thumbnail descriptions are designed to sketch the landscape of the organizations engaged in labor and immigrant workers' rights activism in which narrators participated. It does not include all groups operating in this landscape, but it does include those of major interest to this cohort.

Unions

Three unions have very high profiles of public activism and employ the bulk of young organizers: Justice for Janitors, organized as Local 1877 of the Service Employees International Union (SEIU), the Hotel Employees and Restaurant Employees International Union (HERE, Locals 11 and 814, since merged into UNITE HERE Local 11), and the hospital and nursing home organizing of then-SEIU Local 399. These unions have expanded the scope of their union drives beyond the workplace. They regard outreach, education, and organizing in the public arena—community-based organizing efforts—as important parts of successful unionization. There are certainly other actively organizing union locals in the Los Angeles area, but these three have been particularly salient to the nineties cohort of young organizers.

It is important to recognize that the union locals where most organizers work or have worked, HERE and SEIU locals, are keystone institutions in the organization of labor and immigrant workers' rights activism in Los Angeles. Most obviously, they train and recruit organizers, and bring new activists to Los Angeles. They also act as financially stable centers, allowing activists to circulate through them on their way to or from other forms of activism that employ fewer paid staff at any given time or that may have shorter life spans. Thus, although only six of the sixteen narrators in this study were union organizers at the time I interviewed them, eleven narrators worked in unions at some time before, during, or after the interview. Unions offer activists opportunities to stay involved in organizing and to remain in the area during the inevitable periods of quiescence that characterize the waxing and waning of social movements and groups dependent on insecure funding or volunteers.

These unions are also important places where young organizers meet one another and form friendships and political networks across race and ethnicity. Thus, unions facilitate the creation of dense political and social ties among young organizers. The relative density of young organizers in these unions has allowed these activists to form a cohort that shared a student background, linked by shared experiences, social ties, and shared perspectives, as we will see below.

Finally, these unions provide opportunities for stable employment with health benefits for activists who want to make a living by being politically engaged. Indeed, three of the four narrators who had children by 2004 were working for unions: John Delloro continues to work for SEIU, but for Local 1000, the California State Employees Association, as staff director for Los Angeles; Javier Gonzalez is state political director of SEIU Local 1877, Justice for Janitors; Norma Martinez moved from Californians for Justice, a political education group focusing on high school students of color, to become an organizer for the California Nurses Association. One parent, Quynh Nguyen, moved from organizing with the United Food and Commercial Workers to become national organizing director for the Asian Pacific American Labor Alliance (APALA).

Activist unions have also supported creation of a cohort of young activists by local and national recruiting. Their continual need for organizers helps bring young activists to Los Angeles. Unions also feed other groups active in immigrant workers' issues indirectly because the possibility of union employment allows them to remain and stay politically active in Los Angeles, and to build political community there even during slow times.

Justice for Janitors (JfJ) is the name of a national campaign launched in 1986 by the Service Employees International Union to unionize the largely immigrant Mexican, Central-American, and African-American workers who clean commercial buildings in Los Angeles, Atlanta, and Washington DC. Vanessa Tait credits much of JfJ's dynamism and SEIU's willingness to organize janitors to earlier decisions by locals of the community-based independent United Labor Union (ULU) to affiliate with SEIU. ULU locals in Boston, Chicago, and New Orleans were among the earlier efforts to create new forms of worker organizing in the 1980s. They were run by, and successfully organized, low-income workers of color in jobs that unions deemed un-organizable—home-health-care workers, cleaning, and hotel workers (Tait 2005, 150–158).

The first and perhaps most dramatic effort of JfJ took place in Los Angeles when janitors of the office buildings in Century City held a peaceful rally and were attacked by the Los Angeles police. The ensuing film footage of police beating demonstrators drew widespread community support for the workers, including that of many local and national political leaders, and their victory put Los Angeles and immigrant worker organizing on the national map. Again in preparation for their contract negotiations in 2000, JfJ turned out massive demonstrations of red-shirted workers, clergy in their full regalia, and a variety of public officials, and garnered a huge outpouring of spontaneous community support. Here, too, significant gains in wages and benefits resulted.

JfJ pioneered two tactics that have become part of the repertoire of activist unions in Los Angeles. The first was a move away from bargaining individually with each employer (in this case janitorial contracting firms, who in turn worked for building owners) toward bargaining for a large swath of the industry—here Century City and downtown office buildings. The second was a strategy to portray their fight as one for social justice and fairness, and to invite public support from a wide swath of Los Angeles's constituencies.

For activist-oriented college students in Los Angeles in the early nineties, JfJ was an important first contact with a labor movement that reached out to them and welcomed their support. It was also a union that repaid that support when graduate student teaching assistants tried to unionize at the University of California. But relatively few college students are organizers for this union, which has developed its own corps of organizers from among its ranks and from among Central American activists (Gottlieb et al. 2005, 87–94; Fisk, Mitchell, and Erickson 2000). Their efforts to democratize their local from within by running an independent multiracial slate led to conflict with SEIU, and ultimately to receivership and reorganization (Tait 2005, 251–252).

HERE, the Hotel Employees and Restaurant Employees International Union, merged with UNITE, the Union of Needletrades, Industrial and Textile Employees, in 2004 to become a single national union, UNITE HERE. Earlier in the 1990s, HERE Local 11 in Los Angeles undertook unionization campaigns that were very visible in downtown Los Angeles and on the west side, both locales with a concentration of large luxury hotels. A larger number of college students have become organizers for HERE, and HERE has been a training ground for them. However, the majority of HERE organizers are drawn directly from the ranks of hotel workers.

HERE has engaged in three bitterly fought, high-profile struggles with some, but not outstanding, success during the 1990s. For most of the early 1990s, they engaged in a long, protracted, and ultimately unsuccessful campaign to unionize the New Otani Hotel in Little Tokyo. Its greatest success was in unionizing workers at the Ambassador Hotel, which was owned by the University of Southern California. For the latter part of the decade, HERE has waged an uphill struggle to unionize the multinational corporate luxury hotels in Santa Monica's beachside tourist zone, with some very solid community support and limited success. However, those struggles have borne fruit since then, with many of the beachfront hotels becoming unionized. Then in late 2004, HERE in Los Angeles participated in the union's national campaign to synchronize contract negotiations with the major hotel chains across the nation, and won synchronized negotiations from key Los Angeles hotels.

Despite its limited budget, HERE has probably been the most innovative of the activist locals. Like JfJ, it sees itself as practicing community-based organizing. It has pioneered "card check" elections, a practice of voting for unionization that is supervised by community leaders, religious and civic, instead of using the cumbersome and anti-labor machinery of the National Labor Relations Board. This has meant additional struggles with employers who are opposed to a practice that brings community leaders into the process. HERE Local 11 has put a great amount of effort into building ongoing community-based organizations in support of living-wage ordinances (see next section). Finally, in the late nineties, HERE Local 11 and SEIU Local 1877 mounted a joint unionization drive among workers at all airport concessions. They combined this effort with a successful campaign to extend the living-wage ordinance to airport workers at Los Angeles International Airport (LAX).

SEIU Local 399 is a very large local that has engaged in three health-care-worker unionizing drives in the Los Angeles area. The first was a long, bitter, and very successful drive to unionize workers at all the hospitals of the Catholic Healthcare West chain in Southern California. They began an even broader drive to unionize several hundred nursing and extended-care homes, but this has now been shifted to another SEIU local. Its current drive, a statewide drive, is an even more ambitious one to unionize all Tenet Healthcare workers in California. Tenet is the state's largest hospital chain.

Local 399 does not have the kind of high community involvement in its campaigns as Justice for Janitors and HERE, but it does serve as a training ground for a very large number of college student organizers (as well as a fair number of organizers recruited from among the ranks of workers). Its Tenet campaign brought many organizers from across the Northwest to Los Angeles. Local 399 has been important for bringing college activists from other parts of the country to Los Angeles, where many of them remain after leaving Local 399.

Living-Wage Groups

HERE, with support from other locals, helped create and sustain community-based organizations that work in city and county politics to improve workers' conditions through living-wage ordinances. These are laws mandating wage minimums and health-care benefits that are high enough to live on without the need for welfare or food stamps to supplement them.

HERE Local 11 took the lead in creating the Los Angeles Alliance for a New Economy (LAANE), the community-based organization that spearheaded a drive for living-wage and health-care benefits for employees of all businesses that contracted with the city or county of Los Angeles. LAANE succeeded in building a very broad coalition, which in turn persuaded the city and the county of Los Angeles to pass laws requiring all businesses contracting with them to pay hourly wages above

California's minimum wage, and to include contributions toward some form of health-care coverage. These victories led Local 11 to help organize Santa Monicans Allied for Responsible Tourism (SMART), which has waged a long campaign to establish a new version of a living-wage ordinance. Theirs calls for a living wage and health care to be paid by *all* medium and large employers in Santa Monica's luxury tourist zone. This ordinance has voter support, but employers have mounted a sustained legal and public-relations challenge to it. Both SMART and LAANE employ organizers of the nineties cohort in their campaigns.

Immigrant Workers' Organizations

Not all immigrant worker activism has been union based. Beginning in the early 1990s, a whole new type of organization that focused on the issues facing immigrants as workers and workers within an ethnic enclave economy grew up as part of the wider activism of the decade. Concern for immigrant workers' rights found organizational support from immigrant community-based organizations and from college campus organizations. The two are often closely linked. Their common denominator is to meet the needs and vulnerabilities of immigrant workers. These new organizations are less focused on unionization of low-wage workers than on facilitating workers' self-organization in whatever forms seem appropriate. They put a strong priority on education and leadership training. Their methods mix assistance, education, and organizing campaigns and groups among immigrant workers. In Los Angeles, this strand of nonunion, specifically immigrant-worker, organizing can be traced back to 1991, and it broadened over the decade.

The Korean Immigrant Workers Alliance (KIWA) was founded in 1992 in the wake of the L.A. uprising. When the government offered little help for Koreans who were burned out, a Korean business group organized relief for business owners. KIWA was born from a successful campaign by progressive activists to obtain relief for the many Latina/o and Korean workers in Koreatown businesses who were also economically devastated by the uprising and who were ignored by business owners. KIWA focuses on the conditions facing workers in Koreatown businesses—wages and hours, immigration problems, and employer threats. KIWA went on to work with restaurant workers, many of whom were paid less than the minimum wage or owed back wages. KIWA moved from filing claims on workers' behalf to outreach and education, and most recently formed the Restaurant Workers Association of Koreatown (RWAK), which had grown from 75 to 150 members by 2002, and was run largely by restaurant workers. KIWA's current focus, the Market Workers Justice Campaign, involves education and organizing among workers in Korean-owned markets and supermarkets. Their goal in this campaign is to gain decent wages and proper treatment for workers at the large Assi supermarket in Koreatown. (See www.kiwa.org/e/homefr.htm.)

The Pilipino Workers' Center (PWC) formed in 1997 with the sponsorship of KIWA. It works largely with Filipinos who face workplace and housing issues. It has formed the Association of Filipino Workers and is in the planning process for an organizing campaign among Filipino home-health-care workers, as well as having formed a church-labor working group. (See www.pwcsc.org/organizing.htm.)

Garment worker unionization drives early in the decade generated the formation of campus and community support groups. As those drives failed, activists began to create new forms of immigrant worker support groups. Modeled on San Francisco-based Asian Immigrant Women Advocates and its successful campaign to gain back-wages for Jessica McClintock workers, Asian-American college students began to create kindred groups, and drew very broad support (Lopez-Garza and Diaz 2001; Louie 2001). They created a climate of awareness about the illegal conditions under which immigrant workers in Los Angeles's largest industry labored, and prompted calls by public officials for improved oversight. The discovery of enslaved Thai garment workers in an El Monte sweatshop in 1995 (Su and Martorell 2001) caused a public outcry. Some seventy-one workers had been brought to the United States with false papers and under false pretenses, and were imprisoned in a house that served as both sweatshop and living quarters. After many months of imprisonment in a sweatshop that existed since 1989, a worker managed to pass a note to a neighbor, who in turn notified the police. The building was raided and the women were freed. At that point the Asian Pacific American Legal Center took on the prosecution of the owner and securing legal status for the women. Together with the Korean Immigrant Workers Alliance (KIWA) and the Coalition for Humane Immigrant Rights in Los Angeles (CHIRLA), and with support from UNITE, the garment workers' union, they formed the Garment Worker Center (GWC) as a drop-in center for garment workers in January 2001. Today that organization shares offices with Sweatshop Watch, a kindred project that monitors sweatshop origins of brand name fashions. From 2001 to 2004, garment workers of the GWC initiated and sustained a national boycott, and, with the Asian Pacific American Legal Center, a successful lawsuit against dirty and dangerous working conditions at sewing factories that produced Forever 21 clothing (Downs 2005; Ito 2005; Louie 2001; Sweatshop Watch 2005).

CHIRLA was created in 1986 to advocate, educate, and organize for immigrant and refugee rights. In 1991 Chicana/o and new Latina/o immigrant activists in Los Angeles formed the Institute of Popular Education of Southern California (IDEPSCA). In the 1990s, it joined with CHIRLA to create three immigrant worker self-organizing projects. One of these, the Day Laborers Project, was organized to defend day laborers from police harassment and improve wages.[5] They have also organized a day laborers' association to govern wages and to get the city to provide recruiting centers for construction day laborers. They have succeeded in gaining permanent worker centers at a number of sites around the city. Here they offer education about workers' rights and social services available to immigrants, and offer assistance in getting employers to pay wages and overtime owed.

With the election of John Sweeney as president of the AFL-CIO, that formerly moribund body took a turn to supporting organizing. Labor historian Nelson Lichtenstein writes (2002), "The agenda of the Sweenyite leadership was not far different from that of those who revived the labor movement in the 1930s; open the door to the cadres of the Left, welcome the new immigrants, carve out a distinctive political presence somewhat independent of the Democrats, and, above all, 'organize the unorganized.'" Under Sweeney, its Organizing Institute (OI), beginning with the Union Summer program in 1996, began an aggressive program of recruiting college students into the labor movement. The OI is now a regular recruiter on college campuses. In its efforts to recruit a diverse spectrum of young organizers, the AFL-CIO gave some support to ethnic, women's, and gay and lesbian caucuses.

APALA, the Asian Pacific American Labor Alliance, formed as a national caucus within the AFL-CIO in 1992. It became increasingly active under Sweeney's administration in recruiting Asian-Pacific students to the labor movement, especially in California. It organized several national Organizing Institutes of its own to recruit Asian-American college students to labor organizing. Because of its labor activism and the large number of Asian immigrant workers, Los Angeles became a draw for Asian-American activists trained by APALA.

LINKS AMONG ORGANIZATIONS

Unions have helped to create self-sustaining organizations, like the living-wage groups LAANE and SMART, that are homes for a wider age spectrum of organizers. They work cooperatively with independent workers' groups like KIWA, PWC, and GWC, and with labor caucuses like APALA, which attracts mainly young Asian-American activists, and CHIRLA, which attracts mainly Latina/o activists of a broader age range. Although these are ethnic-based organizations, they operate in a multiethnic political field. As part of the multiethnic organizing landscape, these groups in turn create new forms of organization for their immigrant worker constituencies, which are alternatives or complements to unions: a domestic workers' cooperative; a day laborers' association to govern wages and to get the city to provide recruiting centers for construction day laborers; education about workers' rights and social services available to immigrants; assistance in getting employers to pay wages and overtime owed. Key to all these efforts is building leadership among immigrant workers and new forms of organization in which they can exercise it. Living-wage and immigrant-workers' organizations help to create new political constituencies around their focal issues. Additionally, APALA also offers union organizers a supportive environment that brings together Asian-American union organizers and organizers in immigrant workers' organizations to strategize about ways to build democratic practices within unions.

Finally, this cohort of activists in immigrant workers' groups are also tightly networked in formal, issue-specific coalitions. Thus, PWC, KIWA, GWC, the Domestic Workers Association, and the Day Laborers Project are all part of the Multi-ethnic Immigrant Workers Organizing Network (MIWON). And the Coalition of Immigrant Worker Advocates (CIWA) includes KIWA, CHIRLA, Sweatshop Watch, and the Maintenance Cooperation Trust Fund (MCTF). This last is an effort by SEIU Local 1877 (in which Justice for Janitors participates) and unionized building owners to monitor wages and cleaning subcontractors. Issue-specific coalitions like these bring in union organizers as well.

One example of such cooperation was MIWON's leadership in organizing demonstrations in Los Angeles as part of the statewide campaign to get driver's licenses for undocumented immigrants, which unions strongly supported as well. Another instance of broad coalition building was MIWON's successful effort to have the Los Angeles City Council endorse a resolution on December 18, 2001, the UN-declared International Migrants Day, supporting the Immigrant Workers' Platform. This included, in addition to principles of decent work and fair pay, and access to adequate healthcare and education, the more controversial demand for access to driver's licenses. Eight non-MIWON immigrant-rights and community organizations, as well as the SEIU, sent representatives to the council meeting, and another seventy-one church, community, and ethnic associations, immigrant and poor people's advocates, social service, student, and legal groups, and labor unions endorsed the action. In this case, the list of "usual subjects" reveals that there is a sizeable, dense network of mutually supportive organizations capable of mobilizing at some level for the rights of immigrant workers (Refuse and Resist 2001).[6]

The shape of the organizational landscape in which young activists operate is something of a mix. In day-to-day operations, there are many independent organizations with separate but related missions and constituencies that operate in a complementary manner and engage in formal coalitions from time to time. The interpersonal networks of young activists buttress these ties by informal support. "We support each other's actions" was a phrase I heard often from narrators. This portrait of a relatively egalitarian organizational field reflects narrators' political ideology, where many issues are important, rather than each organization seeing its issue as intrinsically more vital or a keystone for making large-scale social change. As we shall see, among this cohort of activists the prevailing view seems to be that in particular situations one issue or one group's agenda may be deserving of broad attention from other groups. These are the circumstances under which groups support one another's actions. I tend to think of cooperation among groups as like a solo and chorus form of organization, where different organizations "sing lead" in the sense of taking leadership on particular issues and call upon the chorus for backup, and then return to the chorus, doing their own work and providing support to those who take the lead on other issues.

However, it is also clear that activist union locals serve as a critical center in this landscape. They have financial and organizational resources far greater than do other organizations in the field of labor and immigrant rights, and directly and indirectly use those resources help to support the existence of these organizations. They provide jobs when budgets of smaller organizations get tight; they provide funds and other forms of support to smaller immigrant workers' rights groups.

This network of people and groups—unions and newer groups with newer approaches to organizing around labor and immigrant rights—is strategically innovative and engaged in building complex coalitions in their organizing. They hire significant numbers of full-time young organizers who cut their teeth in campus and high school struggles during the nineties; they nurture a new generation of leaders; and, as we'll see later, they are a force for more democratic politics within unions and the political process more generally. The dynamism has its roots in the perspectives and practices of the current generation of labor and community leaders, who were themselves activist organizers in the 1960s and 1970s. They are sponsoring and sometimes mentoring the new generation of activists in these organizations, as well as supporting new organizations that work in concert with them (Ho 2000; Louie 2001; Louie and Omatsu 2001; Wong 2001).

CHAPTER 2

Narrators and Narrative

BY THE LATE 1990S, THE VITALITY of immigrant-worker organizing in Los Angeles, its impact on the labor movement, and its ripple effect on campuses had begun to attract serious analysis. It was clear that new ways of organizing, new coalitions, and new political sensibilities were in the wind. I felt it, too. For about four years, I had been a community volunteer in campaigns of the hotel workers union (HERE) and the service employees union (SEIU) as well as in the living-wage campaigns both unions supported. I had a UCLA connection to some of the narrators, whom I knew as students or as friends of students I knew. I also met other students and community activists in Common Threads, a community-based anti-sweatshop group we organized, and through participation in Sweatshop Watch's campaign for back-wages for Jessica McClintock workers (Louie 2001).

This study grew out of my interest in the young organizers I met during the 1990s. They seemed to be thinking in innovative ways, but it wasn't altogether clear to me what they were. I wanted to learn about their visions of democracy and social justice, their sense of the issues, goals, and the social groups who had a similar stake in them. I also wanted to know what it meant to *them* to be an activist, how they got there, and how they saw their journey as connecting them to or separating them from others. These were all questions of meaning, of what Dorothy Holland and Jean Lave call "history in person," or in this case, how the political is personal (Holland and Lave 2001).

I began a series of extended interviews with organizers around these questions to help design a larger study. As I began reading the interview transcripts, it became clear that the interviews were part of a wider conversation not only with me, but also with one another, and with a wider public of potential constituents. That conversation was about the nature of political actors, and their practice and visions of social justice, but it took the form of political life histories.

This chapter introduces the narrators and explains what we can learn about their politics and practice from focusing on their political narratives. The first section, "Narrators and Their Cohort in Labor," sketches the shape of what I'm calling a nineties generation of activists in Los Angeles and situates the sixteen narrators in it. The second section, "Why Narrative?" makes a case for what we can learn about emerging political ideas from closely attending to activists' reflections on their own political journeys.

NARRATORS AND THEIR COHORT IN LABOR ORGANIZING

The question I address here is whether there is a cohort that came of age in the 1990s that links together younger activists within a distinct circuit of labor and immigrant workers' rights institutions. If there is, and if our narrators are part of it, then there is also reason to think that the ways they think of themselves as political actors and the political visions, goals, and philosophies they express are representative of a wider political generation. I return to the question of political generation in chapter 5 to suggest that this generation of Los Angeles activists in labor is part of a wider generational cohort that includes neighborhood organizing, environmental and racial justice movements, and movements across the ethnic and racial spectrum in Los Angeles. Further, there are indications that they are part of a national political generation that is building similar organizational fields from which they develop similar conceptions of what democracy looks like.

Sixteen activists narrate this book. In their backgrounds, they are more or less like those of their age group who are labor and immigrant workers' rights organizers in Los Angeles. This is a fortunate accident, because I interviewed people by snowball sampling—asking interviewees to introduce me to others I might interview. Narrators' social networks are also similar to and connected with those of their wider cohort. This suggests that there is an identifiable cohort of organizers in labor and immigrant workers' rights that is tied together both organizationally and by interpersonal ties to constitute an analytically identifiable domain of social movement activists.

Thirteen, or just over three-quarters, of the narrators are children of immigrants and refugees, or new immigrants themselves.[1] Thirteen narrators are Latina/o and Asian-Americans (appendix B, table 1). Seven came to the United States as young children, four of them as undocumented immigrants from Mexico, El Salvador, Honduras, and Vietnam. The other six are U.S.-born children of immigrants from Korea, China, Taiwan, the Philippines, Mexico, and Goa. Twelve are women, drawn from across these ethnoracial groups. Four are men, three Latinos and one Filipino. Two are white women and one is an African-American woman. Class backgrounds also vary; five organizers identify themselves as growing up in somewhat middle-class or affluent circumstances, while another eight identify their households as working class or poor. Nine interviewees were married or in domestic partnerships at the time they were interviewed, two had children and another was pregnant. One is a single gay man and two are lesbians who are also life partners. Thirteen of our narrators graduated from college; two became full-time organizers a few credits shy of graduating, and two did not go to college but were recruited from their workplaces to become organizers. In short, these organizers are predominantly women of color, Asian-Americans and Latinas, who grew up in working-class or lower middle-class families, went to college, and who are the first generation in their family to grow up in the United States.

I compared narrators' backgrounds and social networks to those of their age cohort, thirty and younger, who were staff organizers at SEIU Local 399 and the combined HERE Local 11/814, as well as to LAANE/SMART. Together these groups employ ninety organizers, the largest concentration of young organizers in Los Angeles. For this reason and because most narrators had been affiliated with at least one of these organizations at some point in their organizing careers, it seemed like a reasonable reference group (see appendix B).

The two groups were demographically fairly similar, with a few exceptions. Narrators' demographics reflect the preponderance of women and of Latina/os and Asian-Americans among organizers in the city, as well as the very low percentage of African-American organizers. But there are no white men among narrators, and there is a significant percentage in the wider sample. Narrators also under-represent Latinas and over-represent Asian-American women. Although the numbers are too small to be more than a rough guide, a larger majority of narrators (75 percent) than of the larger group (60 percent) are children of immigrants or immigrants themselves. More narrators (88 percent) than the larger sample (about 69 percent) attended college (appendix B, table 2).[2]

NETWORKS LINKING UNIONS AND IMMIGRANT WORKER GROUPS

Not surprisingly, the relatively dense personal networks of narrators and their counterparts in the larger sample of organizers are centered on the staffs of unions and immigrant workers' rights groups, suggesting that these groups form a distinct arena of political activity in Los Angeles for this cohort of activists.

Narrators are tied to each other and to other staff in unions and immigrant workers' rights groups in a dense web of generation-specific personal ties. Narrators in unions and immigrant worker groups tended to know one another, while the two narrators who worked in organizations outside this circuit knew significantly fewer of the other narrators. Within labor, there seemed to be two sub-networks among narrators that come from working on the same union campaign and from ethnicity. Asian-Americans and APALA members had the densest ties with one another, and knew narrators in immigrant workers' rights groups and in SEIU, which had recruited many Asian-American organizers for its hospital campaign. Likewise, narrators in LAANE/SMART and HERE, which worked very closely together, knew one another well, as did those across ethnicity who participated in SEIU's hospital campaign. But since most narrators moved around in jobs and campaigns, they were also connected indirectly to still others through mutual friends. Thus of twenty-five jobs and organizational memberships held by narrators, seven were in HERE, five each in APALA, SEIU, and immigrant workers' rights organizations (KIWA, CHIRLA, GWC, PWC), and one each in organizations that were not work-based but were based in immigrant workers' working-class communities—Food Security Project, Californians for Justice, and AGENDA (I return to these in chapter 5).

Suyapa Portillo's trajectory illustrates the kinds of ties made by a narrator who grew up in Los Angeles. She came to the United States from

Honduras as a young child with her mother. Working in Central American communities remained her political priority. I met her just after she left the SEIU union campaign at Catholic Healthcare West hospitals. Her brother worked for CHIRLA/IDEPSCA's Day Laborer Project. "My brother had told me about the day labor position that was open, but I decided that I didn't want to work with my brother because he would be my lead. It's too close and I would rather just be family. But I did hear about this other position opened at CHIRLA, because they collaborate a lot on the day labor project so they will know what is going on all the time."

Joann Lo came to Los Angeles from the east, recruited by an APALA organizing institute. Her ties, like many other narrators, center around the workplace and link her to people in unions and immigrant workers' rights organizations. From working on the SEIU Catholic Healthcare West drive, Joann became friends with Suyapa Portillo, Eileen Ma (whom she knew from the Organizing Institute), and John Delloro. When she moved from the hospital drive to a joint HERE-SEIU Local 1877 airport campaign, she met six other narrators, three of whom worked for LAANE/SMART, which was also involved in that effort. Most of Joann's closest friends several years later still came from organizers she met in these two campaigns. Through one of the narrators who moved to Justice for Janitors and another who is on the board of the Pilipino Workers' Center and still works at SEIU Local 399, she keeps up her ties to these organizations.

The density of union and immigrant workers' rights activists as political friends of the organizers I surveyed at SEIU, LAANE/SMART, and HERE is broadly similar to the pattern I found among narrators (appendix B, table 3). Like the narrators, the organizers came to their current positions from a background of earlier political activism in labor, living-wage, immigration, and antiracist activism. Their closest political friends were drawn from among their coworkers and from organizers in affiliated groups, as well as among clergy who worked closely with these groups. HERE and LAANE/SMART organizers also had a scattering of friends across a wider range of Los Angeles human-rights, community, and peace groups. Among the SEIU Local 399 organizers I surveyed, many had recently relocated to Los Angeles from SEIU locals in Washington and Oregon. Consequently they had fewer friends who

were local activists, and these tended to be with other union and immigrant workers' rights organizations.

It thus seems that narrators' political friendship circles are similar to
those of other young union organizers, and that their densest ties are
with organizers in other unions and in immigrant workers' and immigrant rights' organizations. We can therefore think of immigrant work-
ers/labor as more than an organizationally identifiable domain of social
activism. Within this domain there is also nineties generation cohort of
organizers who are tied together by workplace and friendship ties.

In sum, demographically and in terms of their college backgrounds,
narrators resemble their counterparts in unions and immigrant workers'
rights organizations. Narrators are also representative of their cohort
of labor organizers in their friendship and political networks. Indeed,
young labor and immigrant workers' rights organizers seem to know
one another and to have their densest personal networks with people
in a circuit of these organizations, all of which suggests that there is
an identifiable activist domain of labor and immigrant workers' rights
activism, and a nineties generational cohort within it.

WHY NARRATIVE?
Activists as Narrators

First a caveat. I would like to say that I consciously chose to ask narrators to tell their political life histories because I understood that there
were important connections between constructing political selves and
political perspectives that emerged clearly in life history narratives. But
that's not the case. I simply fell into it. My interaction with the interviewees shaped their narratives in specific ways. The way I organized
my questions and topics for interviewees gave a life history form to the
interviews. Most obviously, questions like "What were your earliest
memories of . . . ?" and "Did your parents ever tell you stories about
political involvement?" or "Were they activists themselves?" prompt
people to construct their analyses as political biographies. In response to
those questions, activist narrators produced stories and analyses that offer
a retrospective account of the birth of their political selves, and show
how they interpret the wider political landscape from that social perspective. In short, they created political life histories, in part because
I took it for granted that life histories were the natural or commonsense
way to learn about the nexus of the personal and the political.

However, the forms and conventions of narrative are culturally specific. They exist apart from and prior to the specific narrator and narrative. There is nothing natural or universal about telling one's life story as a form of interpretation or theory building. I was not the only one to slip into a life history form. So did Tritia Toyota, who participated in this study and interviewed three activists, and so, too, did most of the interviewees. I infer this from the ways interviewees structured their narratives, such that I often did not ask my prompts because narrators anticipated them as key to their explanations. I believe this was so because life history is a popular narrative form in the United States—in literature, cinema, and psychological therapy, as well as in consciousness-raising and coming-out stories. These are known forms for storytelling across the political spectrum and across class and ethnic lines; and they have great didactic, explanatory, and expressive possibilities.

More immediately, I believe the reason life history seemed so natural is that most narrators and I participate in a political and academic subculture where life history is an important form for constructing and explicating political theory. Many of the narrators have taken college courses or majored in ethnic or women's studies. They are familiar with this literature on political identity. Some of the most influential theoretical works about political identity and social change rest upon and are written in the form of personal testimonies (P. G. Allen 1992; Anzaldúa and Keating 2002; Asian Women United of California 1989; Christian 1988; Kennedy and Davis 1993; Lorde 1982; Moraga and Anzaldúa 1983). These writers have adapted popularly known forms and brought them into the academy to create new theories and critiques by using personal testimonies that are designed to communicate especially with a student and activist audience.

In the interviews, narrators were necessarily giving retrospective analyses of their experiences and their meanings in light of who they are today. My sense is that many of the questions I asked were also questions they had already asked of themselves, so that the quality of these answers was of sharing stories narrators had already told themselves and perhaps others as part of their constructions of political subjectivity, of explaining who they were and why they chose the road less traveled (Brodkin 2003). Some interviewees have published their narratives (Delloro 2000; Wong 2001). Many, but not all, interviewees found the life history form useful and appropriate for describing the nature of their own political identities and how they connect to a wider social landscape through it. They assumed, rightly, that by explaining their personal transformative journey and what they learned from it, they would effectively be able to communicate to me their understanding of the political landscape, past, present, and future, and their place in creating change.

Narrative

Before turning to their narratives in the next chapter, it is worth a small analytic detour to make explicit the nature of the work that political narratives and the narratives in this book perform. Political narratives articulate new and usually oppositional political philosophies about what political actors and democratic political practice might look like, and how they are rooted in wider historical traditions. Narratives are also a communicative form that has played an important organizing role for social movements by building social relationships among potential movement constituents.

The political philosophy of narrators in this book took shape as a political life history. In this respect, the activists in this book are part of a wider tradition. Thus, among activists in the Central American sanctuary movement in the 1980s, one aspect of the credibility and effectiveness of testimony is its combination of personal experience and the depth of meaning given to it by the narrator. For this reason, Lynn Stephen (1994) notes, testimony is regarded as intellectual work, and the ability to tell one's personal story is the mark of an intellectual.

The first principle of these political philosophies is that ordinary people are actors capable of having an impact on culture and history. To create a narrative is to exercise personal agency, to act upon society. Narrators create plots and social characters, not least themselves. Being the interpreter of events makes the narrator an active agent in constructing the world. In their political narratives activists construct themselves as oppositional political actors and analysts. They show the historical circumstances that shaped them, and show how from this vantage point they have developed a critical analytic perspective on the state of the world. Their life history provides the evidence for why they think and act as they do in a way that makes activism a commonsense trajectory.

Narratives also reveal the daily life of ideological struggle. Oppositional perspectives are not self sufficient. They live in complex and interdependent relationships with those they seek to supplant. Even the most oppositional narrators are creatures of mainstream culture. Peacock and Holland (1993) argue that to tell an effective story, narrators must use cultural forms and symbols, plots and personas that are accessible to their audience. Their ability to communicate new interpretations, views, and personas is paradoxically linked to the fact that they are embedded in mainstream ones. Peacock and Holland (374) argue that narrators are at once "creators and creatures" of their culture and social relations. The mainstream can be a conceptual or emotional starting place for political narratives, the tension around which the plot of coming to an oppositional position unfolds. Historian Luisa Passerini (1998) reminds us that even the most counter-hegemonic memories have been shaped and constrained by narrators being embedded in the mainstream.[3]

Struggles over history and memory are important dimensions of activists' political narratives. Those tasks involve articulating and reclaiming submerged histories that offer traditions that are alternatives to the mainstream. One consequence of the episodic histories of democratic social movements is that so much of their histories and contributions have been appropriated by the mainstream or erased from public discourse (Ho 2000; Horne 1995, 1996; Louie and Omatsu 2001). For example, speaking of memories of feminism in the grassroots women's health movement of the 1970s and 1980s, Sandra Morgen (2002) describes some of the consequences of those erasures for our current understandings of feminist history: "I saw how little attention was being paid to the role of grassroots activism in the dramatic changes in women's health care over the two previous decades. I noticed (how could I not?) that the heroic and innovative campaigns against AIDS and breast cancer were presented as if they were spontaneous and unprecedented, as if they had no connection with and owed none of their successes to the women's health movement."

To the extent that the victories by women across the ethnic and racial spectrum are appropriated as mainstream progress, or erased altogether, so, too, are the histories of feminist womanhoods and the possibility of connecting to these wider traditions. Struggles over historical

memory are part of the ideological battles. As we shall see in the next
chapter, cultural constructions of gender loom large in this effort.

As the Popular Memory Group put it in thinking about struggles to
reclaim submerged histories more generally:

> The formation of a popular memory that is socialist, feminist and
> anti-racist is of peculiar importance today. . . . As Gramsci argued,
> a sense of history must be one element in a strong popular socialist
> culture. It is one means by which an organic social group acquires a
> knowledge of the larger context of its collective struggles, and
> becomes capable of a wider transformative role in the society. Most
> important of all, perhaps, it is the means by which we may become
> self-conscious about the formation of our own common-sense
> beliefs, those that we appropriate from our immediate social and
> cultural milieu. These beliefs have a history and are also produced in
> determinate processes. The point is to recover their "inventory" . . .
> in order that, their origin and tendency known, they may be
> *consciously* adopted, rejected or modified. In this way a popular his-
> toriography, especially a history of the commonest forms of con-
> sciousness, is a necessary aspect of the struggle for a better world.
> (Popular Memory Group 1998)

Personal testimonials of Central American refugees, especially
through the sanctuary movement, are familiar to many Los Angeles
activists and offer points of connection to cultural and historical lineages
of opposition. Central American testimonials are simultaneously collective and personal documents. They are collective in that they tell the story
of "a community of collective memory" that was built as part of a political movement.[4] The goal of testimony in the sanctuary movement was
to create for its audience a new perspective based on new knowledge,
and a will to act on it. In the language of liberation theology, from
which it developed, testimony is part of the "conscientization," or a
consciousness-raising process, for North American audiences and
Central Americans alike (Stephen 1994; Westerman 1998).

Los Angeles activists wage similar struggles in their narratives when
they rediscover and reclaim these and other submerged cultural as well
as historical traditions as part of creating robust political selves. Their

political narratives create actors who are not only shaped by culture and history, but who reshape it not least by reclaiming and carrying on submerged historical and cultural traditions. In so doing, activists' testimonies offer an alternative spin on the world as it is, and connect themselves to a history of efforts to make it better.

Political narratives are also communicative events among activists who weave their personal narratives into a collective political philosophy, and between activists and audiences as relationship-building efforts. Here the narrative form becomes central. Where philosophy's rhetorical style tends toward the didactic—"it is," or "one should"—that of these narratives is testimonial—"I experienced" or "I think."

As communicative events among activists, narratives create shared webs of cultural meaning that are at once personal and cultural. For example, Central American activists and refugees socialized, shared stories privately and in oral testimony to North American audiences, and in the process created a popular memory and a "traditional" structure to their testimony (Stephen 1994; Westerman 1998). In a parallel way, beginning in the late 1960s, young women came together in consciousness-raising groups to tell stories from their lives. In the process, they taught each other how to tell a political life story. Through co-creating personal stories, they also created a collective political actor, and a story that explained the birth of feminists, the nature of feminist consciousness, and of feminism as, actually, several social movements (Cade 1970; Morgan 1970). Elizabeth Kennedy made a parallel argument for the creation of a working-class lesbian oppositional culture in the 1950s through storytelling and making claims to bars and public space (Kennedy 1998; Kennedy and Davis 1993).

Between speaker and audience, narratives encourage an interaction that fosters active engagement. The act of telling one's story to interlocutors or to an audience is an act of building personal relationships. The testimonial form invites both similar and different testimonials; it opens conversation.[5] For example, in the Central American sanctuary movement, Stephen argues, the intimacy of the form encourages personal identification and helps create a new political perspective in the audience that communicates across lines of power, culture, and language (Garcia 1994; Stephen 1994).

In a parallel way, KarenMary Davalos (1998) argues that activist Chicana/o scholarship uses narrative creatively to critique hegemonic constructions of Mexican and Chicana/o culture and society, and to create counter-hegemonic understandings of these cultures across generations. Moreover, because much of this work comes from collaborations between scholars and community people, often in activist endeavors, their understandings come from and are owned by a wider constituency.[6]

Far from least, their narratives are another form of bearing witness, which as we saw earlier is a form of political critique in which the narrated life embodies the negative consequences of the social order, and performs the intent to change it. Narrators of personal testimonies construct themselves as unique and specific beings but in relation to collective social and political selves through explanations of how they came to their present politics. The idea of bearing witness through personal testimony combines life history and social activism in that the telling of a life is done intentionally to create an empathetic bridge to an audience to persuade them to share in the perspective of the narrator.

Narratives, then, are powerful weapons in what Gramsci referred to as ideological struggle, where opposing political forces do battle over how to interpret important experiences, emotions, and perceptions so that they "naturally" and self-evidently support quite different courses of action, alliances, and political programs (Gramsci 1997 [1971]; Sassoon 1980). These struggles take place at many levels, from mundane conversations to the clashes of organized political groups. Ideological struggles for hearts and minds are the inner workings of politics.

I've suggested that personal narratives are sites where activists create themselves as political actors. Their narratives let us see the everyday lives of ideological struggle as they reinterpret familiar experiences in counter-hegemonic ways and create collective political actors with their own points of view from these experiences. Narratives let us see how creating political agency is part of a wider politicization process. Narratives and oral histories are personal windows on struggles around ideology and identity and how they shape (and retard) counter-hegemonic *collective* popular memories and subjectivities and connect them to wider cultural traditions and historical lineages of opposition and social justice. These narrators think deeply about political identities and how they shape action. Their understandings and meanings are important because they come from daily praxis and because narrators as organizers are located in positions to make them matter a great deal. I treat their analyses as those of experts in the field, about how a cohort of activist thinkers understand the world as it is and its relationship to the world as they would like it to be.

CHAPTER 3

Political Identity Starts at Home

BORDER-CROSSING FAMILIES AND
THE MAKING OF POLITICAL SELVES

> I think my family's struggles had a very subconscious
> effect on me. I didn't grow up thinking of social
> justice. I just let myself in with a latchkey from the
> time I was five. We did garment work on the floor
> of the apartment and I thought it was fun. I prepared
> myself for poor treatment for being a foreigner. But
> I also absorbed my parents' pain and anger and
> stubbornness that this isn't the way it's supposed
> to be.   —Quynh Nguyen

QUYNH NGUYEN SPEAKS TO the hardships faced by so
many refugees and immigrants, but gives them a particular interpretation: "This isn't the way it's supposed to be." In this and the following chapter, I will be suggesting that these narrators are constructing
counter-hegemonic interpretations of mainstream portrayals of "the"
refugee or immigrant experience. Through their narratives, here of
childhood and in the next chapter of coming into their own as adult
political actors, they are speaking about events, feelings, and perceptions
that are very widely shared among today's immigrants. But they reorganize them in important ways.

The United States has a long tradition of interpreting cultures and
communities of immigrants and native-born peoples of color negatively.
At one extreme are nativist and racist ideological portrayals. But many
assimilationist and liberal arguments for better treatment or more
resources for those that society discriminates against also embed some
variety of deficiency theory. For example, anthropologist KarenMary
Davalos pithily characterized mainstream anthropology's stereotypical

treatment of Mexican-Americans as "an oppressed luckless group with no language, no culture, and no motivations" (Davalos 1998, 34). In such views, people somehow need fixing so they can enter the mainstream. Mainstream approaches to upward mobility, education, and immigrants' adaptations to life in the United States often organize these experiences as wounds or cultural traits in need of cultural remediation or cure.

In her study of college-age Chicanas, Aida Hurtado captures well how scholarly versions of hegemonic ideology organize everyday experiences of immigrants and other people of color, and affect the ways they see themselves—even those who know better (2003, xiv). Delighted but surprised about the richness and honesty, strengths and willingness to be vulnerable with which these young Chicanas responded to her study, she also worried that

> I too, in spite of my best efforts to fight against it, had succumbed to the view that "we couldn't be that good" [like the young Chicana respondents in her study], that we must have some "hidden injuries of class" . . . suffer from "stigma vulnerability" . . . and experience "acculturation stress" . . . as we moved from predominantly working-class Chicano environments and families into predominantly white institutions. The social science literature, often repackaged in the popular media, had partly convinced me that . . . we are forever in psychological "limbo" . . . unable to fully integrate our "multiple worlds" . . .

Hurtado focuses on the point that she experiences herself as being defined as an inadequate "other" by the mainstream, and her emotional internalization of it. It is an important moment because it captures the impact of the dominant culture, and becoming conscious of that impact. Being able to create a counter-hegemonic and empowering narrative from the same experiences that hegemonic culture weaves into a story of deficiency depends on this double recognition. When scholarly and activist narratives revisit widely shared experiences to name the disempowering narrative and replace it with an empowering narrative, they become powerful forms of politicization.

Scholarly confrontations between mainstream ways of interpreting subordinated cultures from the outside and potentially counter-hegemonic ways of defining them from within are much like the political contests in which testimonios and political narratives are engaged. Both challenge who can act as an interpreting subject and the nature of what counts as a legitimate interpretation. Indeed, the fields of ethnic, women's, and queer studies came into being around precisely that political mission, and have used artistic and scholarly personal narratives to create new social actors who interpret the world from those points of view. As with political testimonios, Davalos argues, referring to Chicana/o scholars, those projects are also engaged in telling counter-hegemonic stories whose "profound bias [is] to empower the people under investigation" (Davalos 1998, 37; see also Acuña 2000, 448).

This chapter is about narrators' recognizing mainstream spins on emotionally powerful experiences for what they are, and beginning to retell in counter-hegemonic ways experiences of stigmatization and oppression that are widely shared in immigrant communities. They take on three hegemonic stories about immigrants.

First, and most broadly, they challenge the ways that hegemonic stories stress the divisions between children of immigrants and their parents around assimilating into the mainstream—parents can't or won't, but children can and will. The subtext of that story is that assimilation is the natural goal of immigration and that immigrants are welcome in the American mainstream. It speaks to the hardships parents undergo in search of better lives for themselves, and especially for their children, and to the separation this quest creates between parents and children. It claims that children become at home in the new society and alienated from their parents and culture.

Narrators offer a counter-narrative to this story that unites them with their parents and with their communities and cultures. They identify with their parents' quest for a better life and with their feelings of not being "at home." Most narrators' parents came to the United States as political refugees or in search of safety, security, and better economic opportunities. They made the choice first to cross national and then social borders in search of education and employment, knowing that this would be socially difficult and often painful for themselves and their children. In doing so, they experienced distorted and stigmatizing reflections of themselves in the words and deeds of white America's institutional gatekeepers. They enlisted their children in crossing social borders, going to schools with affluent whites, or to college. Narrators tell powerful stories about childhood experiences they share with many other children (the next section in this chapter): crossing the border into the United States; crossing language and social borders in school; and making friends as children across social borders. In all these accounts they emphasize the shock of seeing themselves as "other." The dominant emotional theme in these childhood stories is of nonacceptance by mainstream America. At best, there is conditional acceptance, but the conditions of assimilation demand rejecting important parts of themselves, families, and cultures, which they refuse. They grapple with the difficulties of living simultaneously in more than one world and on different sides of power and privilege borders, while at the same time fully inhabiting none and feeling out of place in all.

Narrators also challenge the mainstream gender story that immigrants come from "traditional" cultures that subordinate women. Here, the implied contrast is that "modern" American culture does not. Instead, narrators reflect deeply on their family members as at once grounding them in new versions of their ethnic communities and doing so by modeling ways of being adult women and men in them (the second section in this chapter). When they analyze these connections, narrators describe family members as exemplars of ideals they wish to follow—both in their willingness to take the hard road for what they believe and for a self-respecting sense of self. The events they highlight are less about their parents' political views than about the ways parents or other family members modeled ethical values and ways of being women and men in the world.

Finally, narrators take on mainstream constructions of "the immigrant dream" as striving, Horatio Alger-like, for material and individual success in the land of opportunity. Instead, their narratives show their families and communities as helping to shape a sense of self and belonging in a social world where reciprocity and responsibility to others was paramount. Here, success becomes defined in collective and communitarian ways. Instead of deficiency, they see caring, resourcefulness, and courage as part of being a woman and a man in this community. Instead of people bound by "tradition," the narratives show women and men living cultural traditions creatively and resourcefully.

These are counter-narratives, explanations of the experiences that set the narrators on the path to becoming the political activists they become in the next chapter. Together, both chapters show the narrators constructing themselves and their families as socially competent actors and members of a cultural community with their own non- or counter-hegemonic perspectives on society and culture. These counter-narratives, then, are part of an ideological struggle about how we understand ourselves and the possibilities for a just society.

CHILDHOOD AND THE MAKING OF POLITICAL SELVES

When I met Suyapa Portillo, she had already had been a hospital-worker organizer with SEIU Local 399's Catholic Healthcare West campaign, done a short stint as an organizer for the Screen Actors Guild, and was then working on welfare reform at CHIRLA, the Coalition for Humane Immigrant Rights in Los Angeles. She was born in Honduras. She grew up in Los Angeles and went to Pitzer College there, where she first became involved in political activism addressing racism. For Suyapa, her mother's fear for the safety of her politically active son was the catalyst to radically change her own life and Suyapa's.

> I was born in Copán, Honduras, Central America, and when I was about seven years old, I was a regular kid growing up in a little town. My dad was a teacher in the school; and he would get the newspaper every day, and all the newspapers from the region. One day looking through the newspaper he noticed my brother's picture in the paper saying that the students were taking the university, and that the military was surrounding the place. So of course, that evening we got on the bus and headed to the university in the capital; we lived pretty far from the capital. And I think that's when it clicked to me that my brother was involved in these issues. He is my brother and was the one who played with me all the time when I was little; he is twelve years older than me. That it was the first time I became aware of what students were doing.
>
> Ever since then our lives took a different turn in the sense that our parents divorced—there were a lot of family problems. My mom decided to leave the country after that, maybe a couple, three years

later, leave my dad for personal reasons, and leave the country because she wanted to take my brother out of the environment because she was very afraid for his life.

Then, when the opportunity came, this guy was transporting people to the U.S. for $2,000 U.S., she borrowed the money and we began our journey. We left the little town and went to the city where my mom worked as a secretary. She never left me. My brothers were already in college, so I was the youngest one. She figured out how to get to the U.S. and together we came by land.

We got caught by immigration, so we were detained for a month. And this is in 1983 when the worst of the Central American bloodbath was happening. When they were interrogating my mom they thought she was a Nicaraguan Sandinista or something, so we were taken to interrogation separately, off from the group. There was a group of people detained and interrogated all night. I didn't know what was going on. I just remember the guy trying to figure out where my mom was from because she was trying to pass as a Mexican so if we got turned back, we wouldn't have to go back to Honduras, but Mexico.

They didn't believe her, and they put us in a holding cell. Then they transferred us to Chula Vista and then we were transferred to a place we used to call Hotel Cortez—Cortez Hotel like the conquistador. What it was is a detention area in San Diego for families, elders, mothers, and children.

Suyapa Portillo analyzed the process of crossing the border as a transformation in identity. When she left town with her mother, she was a "regular kid growing up in a little town." By the time she reached San Diego, she had been detained, seen her mother interrogated, and gotten the message that they were less than welcome "others" in the United States.

The United States-supported war in El Salvador divided Milton Pascual's family. Like Suyapa, Milton grew up in Los Angeles. He began hanging out at HERE Local 11 while he was still in high school. The Pascual family is a force in the local, as two of his uncles are organizers. Milton did not join them immediately, but instead went to California State University, Los Angeles.

Milton's parents came to the United States when he was a baby. Milton was raised by his uncles and grandparents in El Salvador until his mother came to fetch him.

> I never got to see my parents until I was eight years old. I would see them by pictures, but I would never talk to, see them, be face to face with them, until my mom went to El Salvador and picked me up, which was really hard for me to accept, that she was my mom. The people that I looked up to were my grandma and my grandpa and all my uncles and my aunts who took care of me for eight years.
>
> So I went on this journey of coming to this country, illegally like most of us do, as Hispanics do. My mom first took me to the main city of Mexico which was Mexico City. I was really afraid, first of all, because I didn't know—I couldn't trust her as much as I would trust my grandma, even though she was my mom, my full-blooded mom. It was really hard, you know, it wasn't my position. I was a little kid. I was only eight years old.

Milton's first social sense of himself came during a dangerous journey with a mother who had not been his active parent. As a "little kid," he experienced himself in this context as a pampered child and felt ashamed.

> So I was in Mexico City. At the time I was so pampered. Because I was the first grandson, the first nephew, the first everything— so everything was given to me. What happened was that, when we were in Mexico City, at eight years old, I couldn't even tie my shoes. I was so pampered. And what happened was that I started crying when I couldn't tie my shoes because we were supposed to get up the next morning and catch another plane to Tijuana, and I started crying, and my mom goes "what's wrong," and I tell her I can't tie my shoes.
>
> And so to this moment it's kind of embarrassing saying it, but I'm very open, and I could tell anybody, so I told her about my shoe, and, you know, she tied it for me, and then I started having a little bit of confidence. So she took me to Tijuana and she left me with a coyote there. She got back on the Greyhound bus to come to the United States. She was already a resident, and I was out there, an

eight-year-old boy, with a coyote by myself, going underneath a pickup truck, underneath with some other guy and trying to cross the border and I was really scared. By the time they opened the truck, I was already in San Diego. And from there I got in the car and they took me to my house.

In Milton's story of crossing the border, his fear of a frightening family transition was made even more frightening by a very dangerous journey. Milton's sudden sense of himself as pampered expressed the extraordinary shift of self demanded of him. From being an ordinary kid who could rely on his family to protect him, he was suddenly expected to leave them and trust his life to strangers. That Milton's mother accepted him as the kid he was did give him confidence that his mother loved him, and one base of nascent security.

For Milton, and for Quynh Nguyen, their first experiences with going to school in a foreign country—the United States for Milton, Canada for Quynh—were their most powerful senses of the meaning of crossing a national and cultural border.

Milton's first day at school brought an assault on his sense of self:

When I started third grade, I didn't know the language. It was really hard starting elementary. I remember my first day at school, that I was in line, and they were taking roll call. What was happening, they were calling everybody's names. And at that time I didn't know my name was Milton. Everybody used to call me Uardito, short name of Eduardo. And then they told me from now on you're Milton. And I was like, I come here and you change my name all of a sudden. And it was like, that's the way you have to go. I was there by myself. I didn't know anybody. And then they said Milton Pascual and I didn't know what to say. Everybody was saying "here, here" but I didn't know what that was. And they were calling roll. And all of a sudden they repeated it twice and my friend— my best friend still at the moment, he was next to me, and he is like, "Aren't they calling you?" in Spanish. He was talking to me in Spanish, and I was like, I guess. And then he said, "He's here." And from that moment on, him and I built a great relationship since the third grade, and we still see each other, and we still talk to one another.

School was also Quynh Nguyen's first experience with being stigmatized as an alien. Her family, among "the first wave of the Vietnam refugees, the boat people," went to Montreal, Canada, in 1975–1976. Quynh was a campus activist at UCLA involved in efforts to create a Southeast Asian Studies program. While she was wondering what to do with her life, HERE, looking for a Vietnamese-speaking organizer, recruited her. When I met her, she was working as a community organizer for the United Food and Commercial Workers union, having already done a stint as an itinerant organizer in Texas.

> Ironically, I went to a French school but the first English words I ever learned [were] "boat people," hurled at me by French-speaking students as an insult. It's like, wow, I didn't know what it meant. I only knew that it was bad. I also had a cousin who was in second grade; it got so bad we ditched school. How many kindergartners do you know who ditch school? We didn't tell our parents. We were home from school and almost burned the apartment down. When we told them what was going on, they complained to the teacher. They intervened and it got better.

Both Milton and Quynh described painful "othering" experiences in school. But they do not describe themselves as fully alone. Another student translated for Milton and guided him, and they became lifelong friends as a result of that experience. Quynh's parents protected her from taunting students by intervening with the teacher.

Border-Crossing at School

Narrators' parents understood that they had chosen difficult paths by crossing national and social borders, but they believed that they could improve their lives by so doing, and encouraged their children to cross race, class, and status borders. Education loomed large in their efforts. Parents worked hard to make sure their children went to good, safe schools, either by enrolling them in distant schools or by moving to predominantly white suburbs with good schools.

The parents of Norma Martinez, John Delloro, and Milton Pascual all found ways to get their children into what they saw as good schools even though they were far from their working-class neighborhoods. Norma Martinez grew up in South Gate, a working-class, predominantly Latino city in heavily industrialized southeast Los Angeles County. Local school officials told her mother about a busing program for integration to better schools on Los Angeles's heavily white and affluent west side. She enrolled Norma and two of her sisters in the west-side program, while her older brother went to a school in the San Fernando Valley and her older sister remained in South Gate.

Norma was an organizer for Californians for Justice, a statewide group that does political education and activism with high school students of color. Norma was half of the Southern California staff. She focused on issues of educational equity in Long Beach and the heavily immigrant cities of southeast Los Angeles County.

> When my parents used to go to a function at our school, they were really grateful that we could get this education. They didn't know about the education we got. They just knew it was good because the neighborhood was so good and all these houses, and everybody was white, so they knew it had to be better than where we were because it looked different. So they were just happy and my mom was happy that I could hang out with these rich people who gave me something that she couldn't.

John Delloro's parents enrolled him in a Catholic school in Granada Hills for some of the same reasons. In the last chapter John appeared as part of the UCLA network of activists. As a student he had organized the campaign against Jessica McClintock's sweatshop practices, and, like Quynh, had been recruited by HERE. But he went to Las Vegas to organize casino workers before settling down with SEIU's Local 399. In John's junior high school years, his family moved from New Jersey to Los Angeles, where his father

> started a little meat company, Pocono Sausages, in Highland Park. When we moved we lived right above the factory, so it was a small room above where the factory was. And I remember the majority of employees were Mexican and Filipinos, all of whom were undocumented, I remember, and were just newly immigrated. We used to work a lot in the factory, too.
>
> But we would go to school in Granada Hills, because my parents are very religious and wanted me to go to Catholic school. I think,

like a lot of other families, you want your children to go to a very good school. So before we moved into California, they looked for schools and they found a great school, St. Euphrasia, in Granada Hills, which was Catholic. They wanted us to be raised in a Catholic school.

Milton Pascual's parents were concerned for his safety.

At the time that I was in high school, I used to come from high school, from the [San Fernando] Valley all the way to Los Angeles because I lived at the Coliseum in South Central [Los Angeles]. The reason that I wound up out there was because my parents, my whole family thought there was so many gangs and stuff, that I was going to fall into that atmosphere. So since junior high, they said, we are going to bus you out to the Valley. Every day getting up at five o'clock in the morning and every day riding the bus and coming home at five.

Norma, John, and Milton found that crossing class and racial barriers from a position of racial stigmatization could be very stressful. For Norma Martinez especially, being offered acceptance in a "first-class" white world as an "exceptional" student constituted conditions that disrespected her community and was particularly painful.

I have never told [my mother] that I would have rather not gotten bused because I know she did it because she wanted the best thing for us. And I mean sometimes she said, "I felt bad that you had to wake up so early and get home so late and really do homework and go to sleep and then wake up and go back to school." But she wanted the best for us and she did it because of that. And she is very proud of all of us—all of us have done different things in our lives, but she is very proud.

I went to University High School in West L.A. I got bused all my life to the white schools. My younger sister and I were the ones that continued through. I think throughout we were considered—in elementary school we were considered gifted students and both my sister and I, along with other people got bused. But very few other people, and they put us in all these special classes.

For myself, when I got to junior high school, a lot of my friends were friends that I used to get bused with. I saw that they didn't—it was also like the students who were in these classes didn't want to get associated with the regular students who weren't as smart as they. So they wouldn't get invited to all these things that I would. So I thought it was really unfair. My friends that I used to get bused with thought I was not wanting to be their friend. But the people that I was around most of the day were these people that were from the west side because they were in my classes. So when I went to high school, I didn't want to be in these classes. I had AP Biology and I failed out of AP Biology because I didn't want to be there. I used to ditch with my friends that got bused with me. And I didn't do as well academically as I could have, I think because of that. I didn't want to—you know, I didn't—I wanted to be with my friends who I got bused with.

John Delloro felt some of the same pressures as Norma. But where Norma rebelled against the conditions imposed on her for acceptance into the white world of academic success, John did not.

My dad would drive in a pickup truck and do his deliveries, and we would be in the pickup truck, and he would drive us early in the morning all the way there. I remember it was so early because of traffic to go from Granada Hills to Highland Park. We would get there and we would get off. And the thing about Granada Hills and Euphrasia, it gets pretty dramatic to go to an area that is predominantly white and a lot richer and everyone had BMWs. And I remember my brother was really mostly struck by that more than me even though he was younger than me. He would feel kind of ashamed, he told me, when my dad would come and drop us off because everyone was driving those BMWs and stuff in that area. And my dad would come in the beat-up pickup. We would always be picked up late, too, because he was coming from far away. And we were the last to be picked up, too. So even more you start to see those, but you're still not able to fully articulate it.

When I first went in, I stuck out like a sore thumb. Maybe I didn't, but I felt like it. I had a really deep New Jersey accent. It's all gone now. I don't know what happened to it. And I remember being teased about it, and I just remember everyone looked old to me, really old. Everyone dressed really nice. It's different from a small town and you go to Granada Hills, a suburb, and a lot of blond hair blue eyed, even more so. The part of New Jersey I was from it was Polish and Italian.

And it was, yes, it was sort of like I didn't feel like I fit in anyway. So it's not like I felt—I think in retrospect, I don't think I would have felt the same way as my brother. I think he was trying to fit in, very honestly. He was a lot younger. I kind of went in already not expecting to fit in myself at all. It was just very different, very, very different. I was glad to be different because I kind of felt like I was starting anew basically. I really felt that way when I was there because in New Jersey I felt, if I stayed there, you know, there's expectations of you that will always remain with you as you're growing up. They will always remember you a certain way, and then here no one knows me. It was like a big vacation basically.

And I eventually became friends with this one other guy in the class who was really into the punk scene and brought me into that scene.

Embracing a punk social identity helped John make a close friendship with a white student. He describes later on how, well into college, he constructed himself in ways that at once bridged and avoided confronting race.

Michelle Mascarenhas's family comes from Goa, a state in India. Michelle was also part of the UCLA network described in the previous chapter. I knew her as a women's studies major who organized Voices, a student organization for women of color. She also was a founder of Common Threads after graduating. She went on to build the Food Security Project, which organizes in immigrant and U.S.-born working-class communities of color to improve food quality, jobs for community members, and community decision-making about what is served in school cafeterias, as well as working with local farmers and farmers' markets (Mascarenhas and Gottlieb 2000; Paul 2004).

Her recollections of a fragmented self in high school resonated most strongly with Norma's understanding of conditional acceptance.

There weren't very many Indians in my suburb, Covina. It was mostly white at the schools that I attended, and there was a growing Latino, mostly Chicano second, third generation Mexican-Americans. And so especially in my early childhood, I felt like an outsider. I still don't really have any close friends from high school that I would consider to be so close. I think that was because I wasn't really sure of my place. I played really different roles in different places, and—how do you say it—held back a lot of parts of me. My friends didn't come over to my house very much, and I didn't talk about myself as Indian per se, or I didn't recognize myself—I didn't want to recognize myself as from a different—or having certain attributes that were different in my family or in my culture. In many ways we were very westernized so there wasn't that big of differences.

Milton Pascual also kept his worlds separate. On the one hand, he played junior varsity football for El Camino Real High School and developed cross-racial friendships, but he passed lightly over this part of his years in our interview. On the other hand, he spoke passionately about his after-school involvement with HERE, the hotel and restaurant workers union.

During high school, I was like captain of my football team . . . I played football there for four years and I graduated, and I couldn't go to college right after high school. The reason I couldn't go to college was because I wasn't a resident.

Going into the Valley, it's a different atmosphere than what is it in Los Angeles. Most of my friends in the Valley were white people, were people that—it didn't matter to me what color they were, but they were people that I learned to deal with, that I learned to talk to, that I learned to have relationships with.

So I was bused out there, and you know, during high school, I started being more involved with the union. My uncles will tell me, look why don't you just come to this action and see how you like it, do picket signs. And I was fifteen, sixteen years old, and that's when I met Keren Linsurian who has been my buddy. He's in charge of computers. I learned so much from him; he would show me what to do with picket signs and how to make banners and I loved that. I loved getting into actions, screaming for people's rights. And every time after school, after high school, the bus would drop

me off on Third and Bixel and I would make a turn and go to Local
11 and be just like, "Keren, what are we going to do today?" And
then [not] go home until eleven o'clock in the [night]. And then get
up at five o'clock to the catch the bus at six-thirty in the morning
again.

In contrast, Stephanie Monroe found that crossing class and racial
borders from positions of privilege was a liberating experience from the
gender restrictions of white upper-middle-class girlhood. At about age
five, Stephanie went from living with her mother in a working-class
African-American neighborhood in northern California to San Diego
to live with her father in an affluent white neighborhood. She was part
of the network of UCLA activists, editor of the campus feminist newspaper, and, when I interviewed her, an organizer for LAANE, the
living-wage campaign to create legislation that provides living wages and
health-care benefits to workers at businesses that contract with Los
Angeles City and County.

> I think part of it also was growing up as the youngest daughter
> with three older brothers. My dad likes us to be competitive, and
> so our family was very competitive, and I had an immediate kind
> of chip on my shoulder about being the youngest and being a girl,
> and was really clear about being left out because I was a girl and
> because I was the youngest. And also I grew up being really tough,
> and because we were on our own with my mom, we all kind of
> bonded.
>
> So I think there's some intersection between gender and class in
> some of those ways that sometimes women are thought to be little
> more "floofy" or more mannered, or not get your hands dirty. I
> think also that I automatically felt more alliance with my friends at
> school who were more like me, who just didn't have all these kind
> of—I don't know how else to say it, mannerisms and rules. And
> I remember people in my neighborhood, for example, would take
> these ballroom dancing classes and their parents made them—some
> of them made them take ballroom dancing classes. And I hated all
> the people in my neighborhood; I didn't feel like I fit in. I felt
> rowdier and lower class. And so my friends who were women
> friends were tomboys and were all different.

Stephanie attributed crossing color and class lines and her cross-racial friendships at school to making her critically aware of her racial and class privilege. However, unlike Norma and John, Stephanie did not have her class and racial self reflected back to her through a negative lens. Underscoring the power of institutionalized whiteness—most proximally the whiteness of schools as institutions—she did not experience herself as a stigmatized other, nor did she find school to be a place of conditional acceptance.

Negotiating Friendships Across Social Borders

All these activists made school friends across class and racial lines. Negotiating these relationships was socially complicated, but narrators developed the skills to manage them. But they also handled them quite differently. The differences in their strategies for managing friendships across social borders emerged most clearly around visiting one another's homes.

Norma's (and perhaps Michelle's) strategy was to protect her family from knowing the feelings of inadequacy and marginality that she felt by keeping her Bel Air friend away from her home.

In elementary school, my best friend was Linda Berg,[1] who was from South Africa. She was white, and she was my best friend. It was like leading a double life. I used to go spend the night at her house and she had a maid. She lived in Bel Air. We lived in a one-bedroom house with five of us and my mom and my dad. It was Linda Berg and Katy Smith and I who used to hang out. Katy was biracial. She was black and white. I think growing up it was difficult like that because I kind of had to visit and then go back to my small house, and see all these people with so much money, all the kids and their parents so rich.

[My parents] wanted me to experience that because they couldn't give it to me. So whenever my friend Linda would invite me to dinner or to spend the night at her house, my mom was really glad, and happy that I could; it was something that she couldn't give me that I could live it somewhere else.

I used to lie about the bedrooms that we had. I used to lie about that in elementary school. I used to. I mean I didn't make my house as big as theirs, but I was embarrassed. I was ashamed of living in a one-bedroom house with seven of us. So I never talked about that, and she [Linda] used to want to come [to my house] but I wouldn't want her to come.

John Delloro's closest friend was the boy at St. Euphrasia with whom he shared a kind of marginal punk identity. That marginality, John's parents' acceptance, and his friend's family situation facilitated their friendship.

But every day after school we were at the company anyway, and I remember the friend when I was in grade school, he would actually go with us to work in my dad's factory with us. And the workers would laugh at him a lot because he had a 'hawk and spikes, so when he put the hat on, it went on his head, and so they would always laugh about that and point at it. And they pretended to hang sausage on it as a joke. So, yeah, we mostly hung out together in that area.

He was looking for work, and my dad said, oh, you know, come with us. And he did it a few times because his mother—he came from a single-parent household. His mother, I remember, was so involved in the church he never saw her anyway, and so he had all this time. So that sort of—that kind of just fit in. He was like almost part of the family. He like slept over and ate with us and very much was part of the family.

Stephanie's girlfriends from school were tomboys and were all different—ever since I was in first grade. In first grade my best friend—one was Vietnamese and one was Latina, Mexican-American. When I went to Eileen's house, I took off my shoes and I got to eat egg rolls, and when I went to Yvonne's house, we had tortillas, and I kind of learned.

KB: Did they come to your house?

SM: That is an interesting question. No one hung at my house because my stepmom was very, very clean. Her family is German, and they are just—it was no fun. It was just—you had to be so particular. The only reason we would go to my house was to use the pool. You could be as rowdy as we wanted in the pool area. But inside the house, just our room. It was either in my room or at the pool, but everything else was like, breakable.

KB: So did your two best friends come out to your house?

SM: Yes. And one of them was the daughter—I didn't realize until I was in high school. I didn't even think about it. I realized that one of them was the daughter of a person who came and cleaned our house once a month. And I didn't even realize that. She remembered, and I didn't remember, which I thought was interesting.

Stephanie saw in retrospect that she had not recognized her position of privilege, but that her friend whose mother cleaned for her family was quite aware of their unequal social status. Stephanie also did not experience anything resembling the conditional acceptance that was so painful in Norma's recollections, nor Norma's or Michelle's protectiveness of their families' from the negative stereotypes they experienced in their wealthy white schools.

To sum up, between immigration and school, John Delloro, Norma Martinez, Suyapa Portillo, Quynh Nguyen, and Milton Pascual all had painful childhood experiences, shared by other narrators of color, where they went from being unmarked, normal kids to having a powerful set of state institutions tell them they were members of a racial group that was far from being the norm. Michelle Mascarenhas experienced the feelings of marginalization without a vivid experience of going from normal kid to stigmatized other. Narrators experienced themselves as having (at least) two conflicting social selves, even though they responded differently. At opposite poles, John found a certain freedom in embracing a nonracial marginal identity, while Norma refused to abandon her friends and hence rejected the conditions under which her school was willing to accept her. As good students, their school experiences granted them all as individuals ambivalent acceptance that was contingent on their social skills at performing well within the white middle-class values of their schools, their friends, and their friends' families. Stephanie Monroe's analysis underscores that crossing borders from a position of privilege can insulate one from the pain, and also from the knowledge of structured inequality. Early on, they all developed skills at forming social relationships across socially structured power differences, even if they decided to manage them in different ways.

WOMANHOOD AND MANHOOD AS POLITICAL AGENCY

The gendering of political agency emerges most clearly from narrators' reflections on how they see their mothers and fathers as "actually existing" models for being women and men in powerful and non-stereotypic ways. In my initial analysis of the interviews, I was especially surprised to discover how important were narrators' descriptions of their mothers. This was so because I'd been struck during the interview process at what seemed to me like gender blindness. By this I mean a relative absence of feminist consciousness in that few narrators discussed issues of gender equity in their political practice or as significant politicizing forces in their lives. In retrospect, I realize that I was expecting feminist consciousness to look the way it did for young white women in the sixties—focused on creating egalitarian social and intimate relationships with white male peers. But most narrators are women and men of color who are shaping their own feminist consciousnesses in today's very different racial landscape.

Narrators' unconditional identifications with their families anchor and connect them to ways of being in the world that are grounded in specific ethnoracial heritages. I was struck by the admiration and respect narrators expressed for their parents—their skills at reinventing themselves, their strength, their solid sense of identity even as they crossed and recrossed national and social borders, and their abilities to deal with socially structured differences and dimensions of inequality.

Several narrators reflected at length on the ways that family members provided them with a repertoire of self-respecting ways of being women and men that resisted external and internal racial and ethnic stereotypes, and that provided respectful models for gender relations. Not surprisingly, since most narrators are women, mothers were especially prominent.

Suyapa Portillo described her mother's personal and political transformation from the time she decided to leave El Salvador and her father, continuing with their journey to the United States.

[While they were interned by the INS] my mom figured out a way, you know, notary publics would bring information and put it by the phones so people, if they wanted to contact their family to get them out, would know who to call. My mom called this one number, and it happened to be this woman, a notary public, that lived in Echo Park. And my mom said, I have no money. We were stripped of all our money in TJ [Tijuana], all our family belongings and everything, so we had nothing. My mom was determined to make it to the U.S., so she made an agreement with the notary from Echo Park. For every case that my mom referred to her, the notary would credit $25 to her account until we reached the $1,500–$2,000 we needed to get out.

Basically my mom would wait early mornings for the shipment of people that would arrive at five in the morning. Between the middle of the night and five in the morning, my mom would stay up and wait, and when the first people arrived she would have information to give people or she would give them the number, call this number, this woman can help you, and tell them that I told you, it was very important. So that is how we got out. A month's worth—my mom needed about $2,000 to get out. I think it was $1,200 for her work permit process and then about $500 for me. So it was close to $2,000. And so she worked really hard day and night, and basically referred people to this woman in Echo Park. And, when we got out, this woman put us up for one or two nights. We were in San Diego. We got out and then the woman figured out how to help my mom get to L.A.; and basically the woman gave my mom a job as a secretary because my mom was sort of fast with the typewriter and the phone, so gave her a job as a secretary but paid her only $100 a week, which at that time was, I guess, somewhat good, but not enough to send home and not enough to live.

And then my mom ended up finding additional income, which was cleaning houses or at that time cleaning a hotel where Hondurans used to work called the Embassy Hotel, which is now owned by USC [University of Southern California].

My mom ended up becoming a member of HERE Local 11. She was able to organize. She organized with Maria Elena Durazo that took over [from the previous leadership], and was part of the reform of that union. So my mom was one of the workers among many who were able to help her. And now my mom sits on the executive board of HERE Local 11. So through that experience, I think I started to see the transformation of my mom and to understand politics a little better. Once I got to college, there was an opportunity to do internships, one at KIWA and also at HERE local 11, and that's how I learned about union stuff and was excited by it.

So it was sort of a process for us, and to see my mom go from somebody who would fight all the time with my dad for freedom, basic freedom, you know what I mean, to smoke a cigarette or to wear something she liked, to someone standing up to the boss and organizing other workers. I don't know if you have heard, but the whole deal with USC [the university's recognition of HERE as the workers' bargaining agent] right now, she has been very involved in that whole process getting people involved—so it was an amazing transformation that changed my life.

The relationship between her mother and father had an important influence on Norma Martinez's construction of womanhood and expectations for her own marriage. Her mother struggled to escape poverty in Mexico, married her father, and migrated with him to the United States. Like others, they both worked factory jobs, doing shift work—her mother worked nights and her father worked days—so someone would always be with the kids.

I think my mom was probably mostly responsible for most of everything. But I mean one of the things that my mom prided herself on was my father really helped out a lot, and it was really unusual and so, [speaking as her mother] "you probably won't get a man as nice as your father. So watch out, don't think that this is the way it is." They pretty much shared everything, and my mom pretty much ran the household, but everything was pretty equal. He cooked if he was at home, and he did a lot of stuff at home and if she couldn't do it. But she didn't think that that was the way that it was—like that wasn't the norm, she didn't think—so she wanted to warn us and save us from that.

I think that the personal stuff has helped with advancing my work, too, because, when I was twenty years old, my boyfriend moved to Berkeley, and he wanted me to go live with him. And she said, yeah, and if you don't like it, Norma, you could always come back home. And I think it says a lot, especially with my family, because a lot of families, like my cousins, if you leave with a man, you could never come back—that is it. And she always said, well, no, you could always come back home and if it doesn't work out it's okay. And just little things that sometimes people say she spoiled us. But she always said you guys don't have to do anything at home. I will clean for you guys because, when you get married, you might marry this really bad man and if you do you might have to do all this work at home. And if you can't really do anything about it, well, then that's going to be your situation. But as long as I can help, you don't have to do. But we didn't marry anybody like that. All of us have really equal relationships with our partners.

Like other narrators, Norma reflected on the complex ways that her mother modeled womanhood for her. Neither she nor her mother expected Norma to be the same kind of woman as her mother. Both acknowledged that the norm was not what they wanted, and in that respect, they shared a counter-hegemonic perspective on Mexican womanhood. Indeed, the point of crossing all those national and social borders was to open up new possibilities for her daughter to be a woman. Norma's mother modeled less a pattern of specific roles than expectations that relationships with intimates needed to be structured around mutual respect and agency. Further, what Norma took from her mother's messages—intended and unintended—was that giving and demanding respect and agency for herself was also a specifically Mexican way of being a woman.

But I guess she didn't realize that by raising us that way we were already not going to choose that. We weren't going to choose that because she gave us so much freedom and choice that we weren't going to choose that, but she was doing it because she thought that that was what we were going to do—not so much that she thought that men are mean, but that's just the way it is. Women do the work. And I don't want you to do all the work. I think that you shouldn't do all the work. And I think her thinking about it isn't as clear— it's not like as radical—women shouldn't do—because she is very much, I think—she is still very much thinking like you should clean, you should do this. But she just wanted us not to do it so much, or she wanted it to be easier. But by doing that we realized that that was not the kind of life that we wanted so that we wouldn't do it anyway and none of us do it anyway.

Norma's partner was also an organizer, and they have a young child.

I made a conscious decision that in—when he decided to move here, that one of us had to mellow down our work, and he decided that it would be him. So he's doing stuff at teaching so he could do lot more of the housework and taking care of our daughter, because if we were both out, then it would be a lot more difficult. So he stays home and watches the baby. And when I go away on the weekends, he watches her. My mom helps out some. But he bathes her; he cooks for her.

Liz Sunwoo reflected on the ways that, even though her parents seemed to be like what she thought of as traditional Korean women and men, they were strong in unexpected ways that influenced her deeply. Liz grew up in the Los Angeles area and went to small, mainly white Wheaton College in Massachusetts, where she became active in on- and off-campus issues of racial justice, and with students doing famine relief for North Korea. She returned to Los Angeles for graduate work in journalism at the University of Southern California, and joined the staff of Korean Immigrant Workers Alliance (KIWA) after she graduated, which is where she was at the time of her interview with Tritia Toyota. Here, she describes her mother's strength after her father's death.

I was very young and my mom never really worked in America before; and my dad was the main income, and there she was. My mom is a good example of a strong woman. Even though she is a Korean mom, she did some untraditional things with her life, raising two kids on her own for a long time was one of them. She went to go to work and we had to be on welfare for a while and do the food-stamp thing. I didn't know what was going on. I was so young, but she told me that she could not afford to give us lunch money, and she would cry and cry.

Liz also attributed her activism and political outlook to her parents directly. Part of their influence came from the way that they were religious: "Looking back, I think definitely a lot of my activism is rooted because of my parents. With my parents [religion] was always [about] doing what is right and just loving all people. [My father] always brought that to our family."

Explaining that her father and mother were both deeply affected by atrocities and disasters beyond the United States, Liz continued: "That's the kind of thing that I remember. You know they are really people who gave of themselves for something greater. And looking back I think it really influenced me. I don't think they intentionally set out to do that. I think consciously they wanted us to be good people, though."

But the Los Angeles uprising in 1992, when Liz was a sophomore in high school, was a major politicizing event. Not only were her parents taking political action, but her mother was modeling new and strong ways of being a Korean woman—in a context where many women and men were doing the same.

> When I think about [activists], I think of people who are very strong and passionate and put themselves out there. I never thought of my parents that way because, they have never been confrontational until—and I know every Korean-American says this—but when the riots happened, I think that struck a nerve with my parents and took them to a different level of activism. I mean that was a very tumultuous time for my parents. A lot of our family and our family friends were involved and were living in L.A. [They] had their stores burned down and stuff like that. They all worked near Koreatown, and they couldn't go to work, and they would stay home and watch TV and get phone calls from our family and their friends.
>
> Then there was a point where a lot of—I don't know who organized it, but the Korean American Society started to organize these peace rallies. And they would all be wearing white with headbands that say peace. And then my parents were like, "we are going to go to L.A." When the riots were officially kind of ended and I was still scared that they would start up again, they took me and my cousins and my brother out to L.A., and we participated in the peace rally. I was really shocked that my parents would want to because they are so—I think even in American standards they

weren't confrontational. But at that point I was really stressed. I was a sophomore in high school, and at that time, I was just really shocked that my parents would do that.

I think before that I was always, not introverted, but kind of fearful. And I think since that time, when I saw my parents—I think it was really weird for me—I think seeing them being so free, like they didn't worry about me walking off, and stuff like that, and they were holding hands with people that were singing "We Shall Overcome." That was stuff I have seen in class, and it was very surreal to see my parents, who I always felt would be very non-confrontational, and also not able to stand up for themselves because of language or whatever. And when I saw them in the rally, I was really shocked, like, they are taking a stand for something. They pushed me out there to hold a sign on the street for peace, and then they were wrapping the banners around my body, and it was really emotional, a traumatic turn in my life. I think for young Korean-Americans my age, one way or another the rally has affected us. For me that's when I really felt empowered, and that's when I first heard the Korean-American women's [voice] and I was like, wow, and my mother was a speaker and she paid to be a strong woman.

Yes, it really changed the way I thought. I think it really changed the way I thought of being involved in the community, and how to impact a community wider than our little community in Torrance. Just to see masses of people out there, especially working for something like peace, the people were doing something about it and the people would see it on TV, and they would feel like there was hope, and I kept reading about it in all the Korean-American publications and the L.A. Times.

Quynh Nguyen emphasized both parents' extraordinary resource-fulness in reinventing themselves in order to survive as refugees. Some of that involved working many jobs at once, but some of it involved the value they placed on helping others in the refugee community and in creating the kinds of relationships that build communities. For Quynh, resourcefulness, hard work, and responsibility to others in the Viet-namese refugee community are important ways of being a Vietnamese woman as well as a Vietnamese man. In this respect, political and personal agency appear as ungendered at the same time as they are also specifically qualities of Vietnamese women.

But Quynh's reflections on her mother's life also convey an understanding of her mother's particular kind of Vietnamese womanhood that embodied a strong sense of personal agency independent of family relationships, which is also a central theme in Quynh's life.

> My parents lived more of their lives in a country at war than at peace. They have uprooted three times. They were born in North Vietnam and fled south as children when the country split. Then they had to escape at the end of the war and ended up in French Canada. Then they came to the U.S. as undocumented immigrants and had to learn English. And so it gives you a sort of fatalism, but it also makes you strong. Survival becomes everything. Survival *is* success.
>
> I think my mother relied a lot on her wits and strength throughout her life. She worked when her family discouraged it, rather than marrying young. She met my father when they were both teachers. After they married, he studied law and fought his way up to being a judge. She also studied law while she was pregnant with my brother and raising me. She earned her law degree right before we had to escape Vietnam. Then we had to start all over in French where their Vietnamese education was useless. As long as I can remember, after we came to Canada and the U.S. they were always working two or three jobs, and taking classes at the same time, either English or typing or another skill to improve our lot and maybe get some respect.
>
> My mother was a particular driving force in the family. She engineered each of the moves and was going to do whatever it took to make our lives right. Like a lot of immigrant parents, they sacrificed a lot for us and wanted us to become doctors. One time I asked her why—I thought it was about the money—but she also said something like, "If there's another holocaust or if the U.S. empire is at war, doctors will be needed the most." It's her war-born adaptability and survival instinct. Stability has always been her dream for us, more so than riches or fame.

At one point I listed all the jobs my parents and I had worked since emigrating, and it came out to thirty-four different job categories! My father had worked as a baker's assistant, security guard, Chinese food deliverer, hospital orderly, school janitor, translator, refugee assistance, fraud investigator, bookkeeper, you name it. My mother has done manufacturing, data entry, clerical, coat checking, electronics assembly, manicuring, social work, on and on . . . always looking for stability and respect.

Some of these jobs are very typical for Vietnamese immigrants. Every family has someone who's done garment work, nails, electronics assembly. Many of these jobs are considered women's work but men do it too. For a few years in Canada they tried running a small business, considered a step up. It was a milk and wine store in the front room of our apartment. I helped with the cash register and deliveries. Ironically, my first job was as an eight-year-old cashier and now I'm working for the Retail Clerks Union. They barely got by, but my mother got to work with the kids nearby. They sold the store after four holdups and the gunmen came back to the apartment where the kids were.

I think I must have absorbed their feeling, fighting for control over their lives. They worked so much and yet work was so frustrating, personally and financially. They faced discrimination daily. A lot of parents take these frustrations home to their children, who may not know that it comes from the workplace. But now I know. It was very hard.

My family had a much deeper political influence on me than just making me angry. I got the strongest example of social responsibility from my parents. While they were not politically active, they were always helping people in some way. There was always a friend or stranger at the kitchen table getting help, whether it was with their family problems, finding a job, sponsoring their kids from Vietnam, or trying to understand their IRS forms. I would be told to translate for them, writing letters to landlords, or going to Social Security hearings. I still get calls to translate documents for friends of relatives. My parents always gave me a sense that no matter how little you have, you always have something to help with.

It is important for Quynh that her parents understand that her work as a union organizer rests on what she's learned from them, and that it is related to their struggles, even though her work is more about collective than individual paths to security and dignity in work.

> My parents have also participated in my organizing, especially when I'm involved with Vietnamese workers. They help me translate, proofread; I seek their advice all the time. I sometimes seek their contacts and friends for community outreach to support worker campaigns. My mother especially had a sense of what I do during the Farmer John campaign. She knew every blow because she and I translated every leaflet. We bonded over political language and thoughts I never knew growing up. I think she has definitely accepted my work.
>
> For years, my father told his friends I was working for unions to get experience so I could be a labor attorney. But more recently, the Coalition of Labor Union Women had a banquet where they presented awards to labor organizers past, present, and future. I received the award representing the future, and I invited my parents. They were for the first time proud of my work, and so that was a breakthrough. I wasn't so marginal. There is a place in this society for what union organizers do.

Roxane Auer is also part of the UCLA network. With Michelle Mascarenhas, she was a founder of Common Threads. Her reflections on gender as someone who is not from an immigrant background, but from a white and upper-middle-class family, add another thread to counterhegemonic constructions of gender. Her mother's feminism and its importance to her offer a critique of mainstream discourses of modern gender equality. Having to give a speech on feminism was the occasion that forced Roxane to reflect on her mother's influence on her own, non-stereotypic, but also non-hegemonic way of being a white and a middle-class woman.

> Vivian Rothstein invited me to speak at a feminist event on feminism, and it made me think of something that I haven't thought of too much. I just talked about myself as a feminist and realized that one of the things that made me probably strong in deciding that

I needed to take a stand or doing something more significant with my life was the fact that my mom worked my whole life and fought very hard for independence from the norm of what a housewife was supposed to be—very vocally with my father for that kind of independence. And while that is something that goes on in countless households, I just know that I grew up with a sense that I had to figure out what it was that I needed to do with my life and that getting married wasn't it. I mean that ran through my head. But that definitely was a start. And education. You had to be a strong person, had to speak up for yourself, how to get on the phone and ask for things. She was always forceful about, "You're going to have to learn how to do this sometime. Get on the phone and do it," that kind of a person.

She is political. I got her to admit at one point on a road trip once, if she analyzed all her social beliefs she was probably a socialist, and has always supported everything I have done. She's a wonderful person that way and definitely political. Definitely supports me. She was a union flight attendant for years. Didn't get more education about that until I started working for unions. She would say, yes, absolutely I think what you're doing is important with unions you know. [speaking for her mother] "No way would I have had the wages I had if I hadn't been union."

And what I really loved hearing, the stories that she told me about that was "there's no way we would have gotten to stop having to wear high heels and wearing makeup and put our hair up without the union." And as a young woman that story was really inspiring to me of what a union can do for women. That's not often what unions talk about, but it's another example. You know, they had rules how much you had to weigh before they could hire you. And it was skinny, beautiful, young people. And to me that was outrageous. So I'm sure that had an influence, a big influence.

And I hadn't thought about it so much in concrete terms until we had this event. And it was great, and I talked about it and invited my mom to the event and introduced her to everybody.

John Delloro was also very clear that his mother stood up for herself and taught her children to do likewise. Like Quynh, John's model for selfhood also applies to women and men both. By focusing on his mother, though, he develops a model of specifically Filipina womanhood that puts political agency at its center.

My mother and father are very strong, especially my mother. She's a very—she's a health-care worker. By coincidence, she is right now organizing to get a union, and that happens to be on this campaign [SEIU's campaign in Los Angeles to unionize hospitals run by Catholic Healthcare West]. So by coincidence. And she actually has been a very strong role model.

To give you a sense of what my mother is like, she moved here to the U.S. when she was nineteen years old as part of the nursing programs. She came in 1968, right around the day after Martin Luther King got shot. So she arrived in this country, assuming it was all going to be beautiful, and she arrived in Newark, New Jersey, as a nurse when buildings were on fire. So she has always sort of had an edge to her, being nineteen and growing up on the East Coast.

And I remember this one situation that sticks in my mind where there's a head nurse, a supervisor, entered the room that they are working in. And she's an RN in critical care, and the head nurse says, "What are these beds doing here? Why aren't they moved?" And my mom said, "Well, no one said anything to us. We were not aware of that." The supervisor gets on the phone, and she's like, "These people don't know what they are doing." And all the nurses are Filipino, and my mom took real offense to that. My mom turns to her while she's on the phone and says, "Listen, I'm a professional, and no one told us to move these beds." And what happened next was the woman just ignored her.

My mom was very upset about that, being referred to as "these people" and being treated like that. And so she demanded from the woman an apology, and the woman ignored her and walked off. So my mom went above her and went to her boss and complained. And so she called and complained every day for three weeks, and then finally at the end of the month, the supervisor finally went up to my mother and apologized. And she wouldn't give up until she got that apology, so I think that made a big difference having someone like my mother and my father, who very early on stressed that we should

stand up for ourselves, which actually kind of conflicted with my
Catholic upbringing a bit, to turn the other cheek. Things get very
difficult. And my mother was like, "You don't let them push you
around. You hit him back." And to agree with both of these things
was a bit of a struggle. At the time I couldn't fully articulate what it
was my family was teaching me.

John did not talk about standing up against injustice as a gendered
quality. It was something both his parents subscribed to, and that he
understood as appropriate for both women and men (Delloro 2000,
n.d.).

Stephanie Monroe also understood independent thought and action
as something for women and men both. However, her father's message
gave it a strong gendered dimension, that white and middle-class girls
and women could be as smart and assertive as men.

We [my father and I] have to have continuous struggle. And the
issue of privatizing the schools. We have this huge, these real
struggles, but we enjoy the struggles. I think he also says to me that
he's so proud to be able to—two sources of pride when he has these
discussions with me, one is that I can beat him but he likes having
an intellectual conversation and I can hold my end and I can convince him; and the second one is because I'm his daughter and I can
do all that. And so he's really—through my whole life has always
respected me as a little person, and he thinks I'm really intelligent
and he loves to introduce me to all his friends, as his daughter the
union organizer. He thinks that is so funny. And he likes all the discussion that it creates, and I'm like oh no, I have to go through
another one of these discussions. He's very proud of me.

Stephanie's stepmother modeled a very different version of white
middle-class womanhood. Although, like Roxane, Stephanie saw it as
an awful model, her father approved it in practice, making it clear that
there was more than one way of being a white woman. Stephanie's reflections on these messages during high school led her to construct assertive
and independent womanhood through the lens of her father's working-
class background as white working-class and as similar to non-white
forms of womanhood. At college, she sought out feminist groups at

UCLA that provided models for white and middle-class women to be intelligent, independent, and assertive.

Narrators talked less about fathers, or men, as specific positive models. More often, like Quynh Nguyen and John Delloro, the positive qualities of their fathers were somewhat taken for granted because they conformed to shared understandings of what is appropriate to men. However, Milton Pascual's description of the men in his family and the meanings of manhood he learned from them are the sharpest illustrations of the ways that close kin offered positive and self-respecting ways of being men in ways that clearly counter external and internal stereotypes. Narrating the breakup with his girlfriend during college, he says:

> At that point I didn't know what I was going to do with myself. So I called my dad, and I tell him—I was crying on the phone. I was like, "Dad, this is going on. What can I do? Give me suggestions" because at this time me and my dad were really close. And he is like, don't move an inch. I will be right there in like ten minutes, and he got there in five minutes, and I guess at the same time that he hung up with me he called my uncles. And they came to me and they aided me, and they said to me, "Look, you're too young, you're only twenty-two. You have your life ahead of you and plenty of women out there that really will appreciate you as a person." So Fred was telling me this to make me think positive.

During his college years at California State University, Milton worked for UPS. He worked there during the big strike.

> [During the UPS strike] my parents—my dad would tell me, "Here's a check for $500" so I could pay my rent. And I would tell him, like, no, dad, I don't want it. He was like, but how you are going to pay your rent with this. And I was, like, I don't want it. To tell you the truth, I want to feel how people survive with minimum wages and how they struggle to survive with kids. I want to know how that feels. In my life I had a silver spoon. Everything had been given to me and I want to know how that feels, I told him. And I would rip the checks. I would leave them, and I would tell him, I love you, I have to learn. I have to be a man.

Milton went on to describe how he did the same with his strike funds during the UPS strike in which he participated: "I lent people mine, and they were at the facility that I worked in at UPS. And that opened my eyes. That made—that hit reality. That strike opened my eyes and I felt what people felt when they are on strike. I know how it is to suffer. I know how it is to make tough decisions and they made me stronger and made me pull out of my childhood, made me be a man."

What Milton valued in his father and uncles was much like what he liked in his elementary school friend. Speaking of that day when his friend came to his aid, "I thanked him because, you know, a person wouldn't do that. That means that you have good manners, you have a great heart, first of all, and I thanked him for that, for being there for me, for being a friend to me, I really appreciate that. I still bring it up to this day, and he knows. You and I are always going to be friends no matter what happens in this world."

For Milton, being a man meant being responsible to and caring for others. His uncles and his father cared for him, let him know that he had the possibility for a better, more mutually respectful kind of relationship in the future. Being a man also meant being able to take care of himself, but even more important, it also meant being responsible to and supportive and caring of others—intimates, friends, and coworkers.

CONCLUSION

In these narratives, parents enlisted their children in challenging barriers and in giving positive meaning to their ethnic identities. Narrators' stories show their families' successes at crossing national and social borders, and show how their successes were themselves challenges (however painful) to the ways that mainstream social institutions wished to define them. The parents of these narrators showed them repertoires of skills for defending themselves, reinventing themselves, and protecting their families in social contexts where they were stigmatized and disadvantaged.

In analyzing their histories, narrators have created political identities for themselves in which ethnic identification has a central place. In the previous chapter I suggested that narratives perform ideological work, and as they do so, they also reveal the daily life of ideological struggle. Even the most oppositional ideology gains its traction from engagement with widely shared experiences that have supported mainstream views, but interprets them differently. The personal narratives in this chapter are weaving their strands into a larger, collective narrative that began with feminist women of color who were activists and theorists some thirty years ago. Narrators' strands and the tradition to which they contribute perform three ideological tasks. They redefine gender and success, and claim for their communities and cultures full entitlement to society's rights and responsibilities.

Gender

Narrators interpret their cultures' constructions of womanhood and manhood in counter-stereotypic ways. The ideological mainstream in the United States tends to stereotype all nonwhite cultures as adhering to "traditional"—macho and patriarchal—gender ideologies and practices, against which it celebrates an American modernity of gender egalitarianism. It is an ideology that has some resonance inside many ethnic communities as well. Narrators challenge these stereotypes in the ways that they identify as part of their communities through identifying with their mothers, especially, but sometimes fathers as well. Narrators celebrate their mothers' strength and core commitment to social justice, and fathers' caring and support. Suyapa Portillo's mother's journey from wife to member of the executive board of HERE Local 11, and John Delloro's mother's standing up to a hospital supervisor's racism are one kind of model for womanhood in their communities. Liz Sunwoo's parents' religious outlook of giving "of themselves for something greater" was another. The two models came together when her parents took her to a Korean-American demonstration at which her mother spoke after the 1992 uprising. And Roxane Auer's mother's participation in the struggle of flight attendants to end sexist airline practices modeled strength and a commitment to social justice as a way of being a white and middle-class woman. It also called into question the "modern" gender egalitarianism that mainstream ideology claimed for itself.

Mothers like those of John and Suyapa stood up to racism and triumphed. The mothers of Norma, Roxane, and Liz wrote their own kinds of gender scripts. They loom large as catalysts to activism in the young organizers' retrospective analyses of the kinds of gendered agents they made themselves.

Counter-stereotypic models of manhood include Norma Martinez's father doing housework and Milton Pascual's father and uncles modeling manhood as emotional support and responsibility to and for others.

Narrators' parents also modeled a repertoire of ways of being specifically Mexican, Honduran, Salvadoran, Filipina, Korean, Vietnamese, and middle-class white women and men that were neither the dominant society's stereotypes nor dominant internal ideals, but were rather new and self-made ideals that their children embraced.[2]

If narrators who were children of immigrants saw their mothers and sometimes fathers offering them counter-hegemonic and culturally-rooted ways of being women and men, white women narrators emphasized their family experiences that challenged the white mainstream notion that America was beyond sexism. By connecting to her mother's feminism, Roxane became aware of the dependency inherent in the white and middle-class ideals of womanhood she grew up around. Stephanie's connection to an alternative to that womanhood came through her father and nonwhite friends.

Narrators are creating their own ethnoracially grounded models of egalitarian gender relationships and women's agency that run counter to mainstream practices and discourses that subordinate women. It is important to underscore that these are counter-stereotypic models— they differ from stereotypes of Latina/os and Asians in the dominant white mainstream, and they differ, too, from gender stereotypes that circulate within those communities. They may also reinterpret existing community constructions of gender in new ways. In a social context where racist gender stereotypes and racist discourses about "personal responsibility" are marshaled to justify cutting social programs for the poor, we need to recognize the importance of the ethnoracially specific ways that these activists are redefining gender, for they constitute a conceptual, discursive, and more democratic lived alternative. (Glenn 1994; Solinger 2001).

When narrators connect to their families around ethnically specific but progressive and counter-stereotypic womanhoods and manhoods, they are reorganizing hegemonic narratives of immigrant experiences into something at once more reciprocal and more political. In these tellings, narrators portray themselves and their parents as working together against hegemonic constructions of "traditional" gender norms, both those that prevail within their ethnic communities and those stereotypes that are imposed by the dominant society.

Are these visions confined to the politically converted? That is, do these interpretations of widely shared experiences have any purchase in a wider population? The question is, to what extent are these goals widely shared? Or at least to what extent is the project of challenging internal and externally imposed gender stereotypes shared? Aida Hurtado offers a strong affirmative (Hurtado 2003, 271; see also Bernal 1998 for a similar, earlier construction of Chicana womanhood). She interviewed Chicana college students, at least in part to see "whether the writers [of Chicana feminism] just barely a generation before them had 'gotten it right.'" She found that young, non-activist Chicanas, like these narrators, "see in their mothers unnamed feminists and unsung heroes," and, too, their relationship to their mothers was "overwhelming in its solidarity in political struggle" (10).

Success

Embedded in narrators' constructions of their families is a challenge to the ways that the mainstream imagines immigrant dreams of success through hard work as an individual goal of material well-being. Narrators' described the hard work in detail. They also show their families crossed the border in search of a better life and enlisted them in the quest by sending them across social and class borders in search of a good education. Woven into accounts of their family's hard work for economic survival were stories of helping and being helped by others in the community, taking responsibility for one another by sharing material and social resources, and by a more general ethic of caring—for example, Quynh's parents enlisting her in helping other Vietnamese write letters to government agencies. When she and other narrators described the qualities their parents modeled for them, caring for others, more general concern for human rights, and social fairness joined hard work. Womanhood and manhood demand responsibility not only to intimates, but also to a wider community.

But it is also important to acknowledge that it takes effort to persuade parents to see this as narrators do. For example, Quynh described her efforts to get her parents to understand that her union organizing is another form of their work. It wasn't unusual for narrators' parents to hope they would be doctors or lawyers. What is important here is that the narrators show them another form of success they can connect to.

Narrators emphasized their family's emotional, material, and social interdependence with others. Individual economic success was less important than what they perceived as a more interdependent or collective understanding of success in creating the circumstances where members of the community were treated fairly, so that their hard work could bear fruit. The idea that success is a collective enterprise and that it is measured as improvement of a community is nascent here, but it will become amplified in subsequent chapters as narrators describe the goals of their own activism.

Narrators' rejection of assimilation into the mainstream is implicit in their interpretation and embrace of parents as models. They are deeply attached to their families, communities, and cultures, but also willing, like their parents, to go to work and school in mainstream institutions, however painful it is. Doing this has given them a personal consciousness of the ways that imposed social organization forces them and their families to fragment themselves into selves (and life-course decisions) that are at war with each other.

Cultural Citizenship

Finally, these narratives replace cultural deficiency ideologies with a vision of cultural citizenship. This is a concept first developed by Renato Rosaldo. Speaking of Latina/os, Flores describes "the process by which Latinos form community and claim rights as cultural citizenship. Cultural citizenship can be thought of as a broad range of activities of everyday life through which Latinos and other groups claim space in society, define their communities, and claim rights. It involves the right to retain difference, while also attaining membership in society. It also involves self-definition, affirmation and empowerment" (Flores 1997, 262).

Narrators work with many of the same themes about the experiences of being an immigrant in the United States that are found in mainstream literature, from conservative to liberal. Their counter-hegemonic interpretations of these experiences are part of building a counter-hegemonic way of seeing the world that is built into the political identity fashioned in these organizers' narratives. They deal with pain and disorientation at finding themselves socially marginalized and at being on receiving end of the institutional racism and ethnocentrism of the economic, health, educational, and justice systems. The also have to negotiate differences in perceptions and knowledge between themselves and their immigrant parents even as they share the drive to a better life that impelled their parents to migrate. Mainstream perspectives explain these experiences through stories and theories of immigrant differences or deficiencies, whether as arguments for xenophobic or conservative policies, or as arguments for more liberal or fairer policies. Narrators' feelings as children and college students that they, their families, and cultures were not quite right, not quite good enough in the white world come from inside the dominant ideological organization of immigrant experiences by mainstream ideology.

But their narratives transform these elements into a very different story about community entitlement. They talk of their parents' very hard work for little pay or respect, the racism they and their parents endured and fought, their growing awareness of institutional racism in schools, the labor force and the city's geography, and respect for their parents' perseverance. They show us their paths to their clearer knowledge about the inherent unfairness of government and corporate America to a broad working-class racialized and ethnic spectrum of the nation's populace without whom neither Los Angeles nor California would run. This is an explanation of ideological opposition, the beginnings of a counter-hegemonic political ideology. Part of that ideology entails basing claims for cultural citizenship on awareness of their importance to U.S. economy and society.

In claiming cultural citizenship, redefining success as collective and about fairness more than getting rich, and by creating more egalitarian ways of being a man and a woman in their ethnic communities, narrators are creating a political ideology that contains a vision of an alternative to prevailing ideas. That vision is rooted in diverse practices and daily values of a variety of ethnic communities. Identification with one's ethnic community or culture is the foundation upon which most narrators build political ideology and gendered working-class political subjectivity.

The success of social movements rests heavily on the ways that their internal culture and repertoire of practices resonate with the daily culture and practices of potential constituents. The work that these narratives have performed, with some success, has been to reinterpret those everyday cultural practices in a political way (Brodkin Sacks 1988; Naples 1998; Payne 1995; Polletta 2002; Flores and Benmayor 1997). Rejecting mainstream expectations that they will change to fit the status quo, narrators are poised to begin articulating a politics of how society needs to change to fit them, and to root that politics in political reinterpretations of gendered immigrant working class experience. The next chapter turns to how narrators made this transition to reshaping their worlds through political activism.

CHAPTER 4

Making Identities Political

Narrators' border crossings have made them acutely aware that they inhabit a social landscape whose contours were not designed to accommodate them or their families. They have experienced themselves as marginalized, stigmatized, and conditionally accepted, most centrally on the basis of their racial and ethnic background. As a result, they have come to perceive themselves as people out of place, as lacking social places where they fully and unconditionally belong. Where hegemonic ideologies would organize these experiences and feelings to emphasize the pain and deficiencies produced, we have seen that these narrators have begun to reorganize them into a counternarrative that creates a new and more complex center of belonging.

In this chapter narrators describe the process by which they came to create political home places, a kind of liminal social space premised on accommodating difference, from which to act and to create a political praxis. They describe the reorganization and politicization of their identities as personally liberating, exhilarating, and life changing. It produced an emotional high, the nuclear fission that comes from the meeting of many personal transformations in shared activism, that generated a sense of infinite possibilities for making change.

Narrators' new home places have much in common with Chicana feminists' concept of a borderland, or *la frontera,* as a social location which can give birth to new and liberatory politics (Anzaldua 1999; Moraga and Anzaldua 1983).[1] Chicana feminism has its origins in multiple social movements of the sixties, as Chicana activists found themselves "challenging stigmatization on the basis of sexuality, race and ethnicity, class and gender . . . From the beginning, many Chicana feminists have not been concerned with reaching consensus or avoiding disruption . . . as they voice their condition as women, lesbians, members of ethnic and racial groups, and predominantly members of the working class. [As a result] they confronted their internal diversity earlier than many other groups, including the white women's movement" (Hurtado 2003, 3).

The idea of a borderland was born from this feminist political practice of internal difference among Chicanas. At its center is the idea that many different people inhabit a particular kind of social space within which they constitute themselves in new ways. This perspective looks inward to suggest that interrelationships among some constellations of multiple identities create a new kind of sense of political identity. They create new identities linguistically—by using Spanish and by creating and voicing their own discourses and perspectives, including those of sexuality and gender. People who inhabit borderlands experience multiple and crosscutting forms of subordination and marginalization from the mainstream. Through language they overcome their erasure in the mainstream and in other movements. Part of the reason the concept of a borderland or living with multiple marginalities is so useful is that it describes and conceptually links together situations experienced by virtually all people of color and immigrants, and also to some extent by working-class white men, women of different classes, and out gays and lesbians.

Chicana feminism resonates strongly with African-American feminist theoretical perspectives. Bel hooks's idea of putting the margins at the center, thinking about the world critically from the various perceptions and experiences of a wide circuit of oppressed people, is quite similar to a borderlands consciousness (hooks 1989; for an Eastern European counterpart see Penezic 2005). So, too, is veteran civil rights movement activist Bernice Reagon's analysis of the experience and necessity of coalition politics. For Reagon, coalitions are a kind of home, but not a home place of likes, not a place where you feel "at home." Rather it is a place of creative dissensus, diversity, and democracy where new ideas and possibilities can be born (Reagon 1986). Indeed, Hurtado, in her analysis of major themes in Chicana politics, argues that the importance of coalition politics rests upon understanding identities as social and historically constructed useful vantage points for envisioning paths to social justice. Borderlands social spaces and political coalitions are powerful ways to bring one's different identities together rather than to be torn apart by their contradictions, as she and other theorists argue (Hurtado 2003). It is an alternative to hegemonic views, and I believe a more robust way of thinking about what many people *do* when confronted by these complex sets of assaults and marginalizations. It highlights the ways that people succeed in integrating and using their experiences to develop new and useful spaces and discourses for seeing the world and being women and men in it.

Most of the book's narrators share this sensibility. They've learned it by crossing many social borders, often painfully. These experiences and the understandings they engender are the stuff from which narrators construct their sense of political agency as one that expects to find big differences among politically kindred souls and allies. They expect to find themselves and their allies sometimes receiving or expecting some kinds of gender, class, or race privilege even as they participate in groups fighting against these forms of socially structured subordination. They expect that dealing with such differences and the perspectives they generate is part of the territory of social movements. However much they may sometimes dream of a political "home" where everyone agrees, they suspect it's unlikely, and they have had a great deal of practice dealing with socially structured differences in political perspectives.

In this chapter, narrators continue their narratives of political radicalization, from a search for home to the creation of borderlands and coalitional political spaces. As they came into adulthood, most narrators chose paths where they would continue to cross social and national borders, despite the fact that their choices might well lead them to uncomfortable places. Sometime in their college years, narrators began to transform feeling out of place and a sense of social inequity into a political consciousness. Most narrators as children excelled at school. Some went to white schools, and they and others continued on to mainly elite, white colleges, where they were in a racial or class minority. Some returned to their parents' homeland or studied abroad as part of their search for a home place, only to discover that was not home either. In their journeys back and forth between the worlds of the powerful and the worlds of their families, narrators transformed their sense of personal marginalization and social unfairness into an astute awareness of the racial and class structures of power and privilege within and beyond the United States.

Narrators who are children of immigrants emphasized their journeys across social borders toward politics more than did white or African-American narrators. Both groups describe somewhat different processes of immersion. Both describe the same combination of gradual, step-by-step involvement and life-changing epiphanies. But narrators of immigrant families described less a linear process of greater involvement than a moving from place to place or group to group—not necessarily even as activists or in activist groups—in which they experienced themselves differently.

Latina/o and Asian-American narrators spoke of four distinct steps in the development of their political identities, although they did not necessarily take them in the same order: First, narrators searched for, created, or found social homes, organizational contexts like ethnic studies or women's studies programs where they did not feel like ugly ducklings or racially marginalized people. Here, they most often connected with their heritage, and people's histories of struggle against oppression.

Second, they connected with "different others" who also felt marginalized, and developed a sense of kinship beyond race, ethnicity, or gender. Many narrators traveled to their home countries, which broadened their sense of kinship as transnational; many broadened their sense of kinship across racial, class, gender, and sexuality lines within the United States.

Third, as part of an identity that spanned national and social borders, they began to analyze the world and to create a meaning and value system that was reflective of their social identities. These facilitated developing a shared consciousness and vision of social change and themselves as change agents. Narrators described transforming their consciousness, or politicizing their identities, as one kind of empowerment.

Fourth, they experienced a powerful sense of political agency through successful collective action. For some, being willing to take action was a conscious test of their new perspectives and identities. Others had these experiences thrust upon them, or were thoughtful spectators to successful mobilizations. Collective action underscored the possibility of making a change in the social fabric so that the marginalized were at home in the center. It was a dimension of empowerment.[2]

Successful actions were empowering in another way, in that they forced those who had constructed narrators as second-class "others" to acknowledge in deeds as well as words those narrators' understandings of themselves and society.

Yet, each of these narrators had very different epiphanies—points they mark as the beginning of a new consciousness or a political sense of themselves. For some it was the discovery that collective action could make a difference; for others it was recognition that they had been on the receiving end of racism; and for still others the realization that they could make life decisions without constraints they had previously taken as inevitable.

The Quest for Home Places

Narrators' efforts to feel like swans instead of ugly ducklings, to experience themselves as belonging, were quests to find or create social contexts where they felt at home, and where they were not forced to fragment themselves. For most, the search took them to places where their race and ethnicity were valued. Identity clubs, like MEChA, and ethnic studies programs loomed large as safe havens, especially in white and elite environments where narrators of color felt marginalized. Narrators who were workers or who attended more racially and class-variegated colleges or community colleges found complex identity homes. Still other narrators consciously shopped around, looking for explicitly political contexts where they might feel at home. In all, of the fourteen narrators who attended college, all but three found ethnic or feminist identity homes.

A number of narrators who attended elite white colleges found their first welcoming places in identity clubs, ethnic studies programs, feminist groups, or coalitions of students of color. Tori Kim went to the Korean Club. Coming from a heavily white high school, Quynh Nguyen was glad to find so many Asian-American students: "As with many Asian-Americans who end up at UCLA or many of the UC schools, I saw more Asians than I'd seen in my life. You know, coming from schools where we were much more of a minority, it felt great."

Stephanie Monroe joined UCLA's feminist newspaper staff. Roxane Auer gravitated to the environmental movement, which she identified as an issue comfortable to her as a middle-class student: "I think environmentalism was always for me the most comfortable of activisms, coming from an upper-class white background, taking trips in nature."[3]

Identity clubs and ethnic studies programs were some narrators' first contact with analyzing race and ethnicity from a political perspective. As the daughter of Taiwanese immigrants growing up in Ohio, the Taiwanese-American Club and the Asian-American Students Association at Yale were Joann Lo's first political exposure. Support work for the Yale clerical workers' strike in 1996 introduced her to labor activism, which continued through her college years. Joann came to California after college because she was inspired by a talk at Yale given by Kent Wong, the head of the Asian Pacific American Labor Alliance (APALA). She attended an APALA three-day Organizing Institute, and then took an organizing job with SEIU Local 399 in Los Angeles. When I met her, she was working on the joint SEIU-HERE campaign to organize workers at concessions at Los Angeles International Airport.

While she was a student at Yale, her first political involvement was with the Taiwanese-American Club.

> Just learning about Taiwan's history first opened my eyes to oppression because, I don't know if you know much history on Taiwan. But the Nationalists lost, so they took over Taiwan. Previous to that it was Japan that controlled Taiwan for fifty years until the end of the World War II, and they lost. Supposedly Taiwan was under the auspices of the UN, but the Chinese took it over. And they massacred political leaders, teachers, doctors, all the educated people, to take over. And also there were aborigines, indigenous people in Taiwan who were pushed out into the mountains. So learning that kind of history really helped for me to understand oppression.

It also helped her to see her own family's history in the context of a wider struggle against their oppression.

> When the Nationalists took over, they were just kids. But people in their generation grew up right under this oppression. And I mean, in the schools they couldn't speak Taiwanese anymore. They had to speak Mandarin. No one could—you couldn't own any books about Communism, read anything about that kind of stuff. And anyone who was thought to be subversive or trying to organize against the Nationalists, they were kidnapped and tortured. And so my mom

even told me that one of my dad's uncles was kidnapped, just disappeared one night, and years later came back a totally different person. And so my parents actually grew up thinking, don't get involved in politics; don't cause trouble, because of that sort of atmosphere. But there are people in my parents' generation who grew up trying to organize and fight back and who ended up being blacklisted, and they came to the U.S. For many years they couldn't go back to Taiwan; that has changed now.

Douglas Marmol found a home place in HERE, only in part because it is a predominantly Latina/o union. Douglas wasn't demographically marginal by race or ethnicity at work because as a food service worker at Los Angeles International Airport, he worked with many other Latina/o workers. Douglas is Salvadoran and from a political lineage. His uncle is Miguel Marmol, Salvador's most famous revolutionary. Douglas came to the United States as a teenager and went to work in a series of food-service jobs. He encountered HERE when he worked at one of the airport food concessions. Already familiar with unions and the benefits they offered, he became active in the union drive, and ultimately the union asked him to be a worker-organizer. This is a position that HERE has negotiated in its union contracts. Workers may take a six-month leave from their job to work as a union organizer, after which they return to their job. Worker-organizers can take multiple organizing leaves. While on leave, their salaries are paid by HERE. When I interviewed him, he was on his third leave to work for the union full time.

However, the union became truly a home place for him when it explicitly welcomed him as a gay Latino man. Even more important, that acceptance was the catalyst for becoming an activist in a way that allowed him to bring together struggles for economic and sexual justice. I asked him about how his family and childhood might have contributed to becoming an organizer, and, as I'll discuss later, these were not the roots of his activism.

> KB: So let me ask you a different question. I mean I could say what made you an activist, but I could also say what made you—why do you think that you took it to heart?
>
> DM: Because I knew—I'm not thinking just about me, because me personally, because I got involved in the union, I could come

out of the closet. I'm gay. People would ask me and I would say no, because in Latin America, they don't accept that. My family doesn't know yet, but I'm in the course of telling them now. That is why the union makes me be a leader, saying "not because you're black or you're brown or you're gay or you're this, we all come together and stand together and fight for it, for what is right."

I have the courage to tell people I'm gay and I see [more] respect from them than before. I learned [that] when I went to Indian gaming. I worked with this organizer and when he did my evaluation, I would say that I was gay to my friends, but not to the other organizers there. So he told me, "Why do you? It doesn't matter if you're black, white, brown, if you're short, big stomach, if you want to be respected you need to respect yourself first and be able to command respect." And he told me those words.

His lead organizer's message that the union wanted to support his self-respect as gay and Latino, and his pride in being gay was what made HERE a safe, home place.

Douglas also spelled out how being welcomed in HERE was key to his becoming a political activist, around sexuality as well as class justice. First, it freed him to act politically, to demand respect, as an out gay man: "I feel great. Now you know I'm out, and then whoever tells me something, if they just start to disrespect me I stop them because I said that's not right, I respect you and that's the way that I want to be respected."

It also expanded his social circles, and his sense of himself as able to be a resource for other gay people: "I go to the gay clubs. I go to all different places. And before I wouldn't go and now I do. In July I went to a party at Las Memorias/The Wall [a gay Latino organization that created a pioneering public art project commemorating those who died of HIV/AIDs]; and before I wouldn't. So I went there and I had fun and met a lot of people. The places that I go, sometimes they are not activists, political activists. And if I meet somebody, and I know they are have having trouble, I tell them I do this, and that's good."

The Women's Resource Center at California State University, Long Beach was a safe home for Norma Martinez because it resonated with the way women acted in her family. It was both Latina and gender friendly.

> When I went to Long Beach State, there was the identity club, which is La Raza, MEChA. I got involved with that, and I started working at the Women's Resource Center right when I went through summer bridge the summer before I started [college]. Growing up with a lot of women in my family—not only my immediate family. My mom has a lot of sisters. And it's pretty woman dominated, and a lot of them have had to do stuff on their own—which might not be very significant in American society, or it might. But in Mexico they tell you you have to be with a man and you have to do all this stuff. And they did everything on their own. So I was naturally strong to where women are at and wanting to work with women because that is who I felt most comfortable with.

Connecting with "Different Others"

Some narrators' consciously shopped and moved around, trying out a number of groups in search of kindred spirits and feelings of belonging. Other narrators' initial home places were multiethnic constellations of people of color, so that their sense of "we-ness" was variegated at the outset.

Liz Sunwoo is the only narrator who went to a multiracial high school that provided both a positive experience and one that supported her own emerging political identity, in her case as Korean.

> And when I went to high school, I just wanted to get involved with everything. I think that is something that still is part of me today. I love learning from people and interacting with as many people in different areas of life as I can. And that's really how I learn.
>
> I think in high school that was something that I was lacking. And because I was so introverted before, when I got to high school I started [in] a new playground, getting a chance to touch all these things that I have never touched before, and I just started talking to a lot of people. I went to a Catholic high school, and so there were no Koreans there—mostly white and heavily Latino and African-Americans, and then Vietnamese and Filipino. Me and my brother were the Koreans in the whole school.

I think I felt very comfortable. I mean of course it's always kind of awkward. By the end of my freshman year and the beginning of my sophomore, I just really felt very free to accomplish—very confident—more confident than before; I felt accepted. The thing about high school in Torrance—because it was so diverse, I felt like everybody was really open to each others' cultures, and like we never had a problem like many high school students today with race wars between different groups of students; it was never like that. I think all the minorities in the school all came together and we were always the ones leading the student government and always winning the homecoming queen, and you know, the white people they accepted us too—good environment for me.

TT: You knew that you were Korean-American?

LW: Yes, by my sophomore year, I was starting to write articles for the Korea Times, and after is when I decided I wanted to be a journalist. And so a year after the riots, I was spending the summer—because of the whole riot thing and there were a lot of college students and adults that were discussing a lot of ideas. And at that time I didn't know it was about power and about race, but you know they were discussing a lot of things that were going on in politics in the area, and I couldn't fully grasp them. But when I look back, after I came back after that summer, to high school, and the way I saw the world was just different.

When it came time for college, Liz decided, okay, I don't want to stay in L.A. anymore, so I went to Massachusetts to a very small school called Wheaton College in northeastern Massachusetts. I really started to get involved with the local cultural student alliance over there, and it really really pushed me intellectually, emotionally, and even physically to become active and also understand identity politics and power structures and all this kind of thing. I ended up majoring in African-American studies and political science—because I came in as an English major and they really really changed the way I thought. It was there where I really first started getting active in issues. At that time there were just a lot of campus issues. First I started with a lot of the student activism, like diversity among faculty, tenure for minority faculty, and there were a lot of cover-ups on campus. And then police brutality. I became one of the student leaders on campus. All of us had this multicultural alliance, and there was an independent faculty group that really supported us through it, because I think they really mentored me in the whole activism process.

Aquilina Soriano had a very difference experience at UCLA. Although she was active in environmental-justice issues, against the anti-immigrant Proposition 187, and worked with HERE on their campaign to unionize the New Otani Hotel while she was a student, she found it difficult initially to find an ethnic home place. Her search led her first to the Filipino club, "but I ended up jumping out of that because a lot of them were second generation students and they had different experiences." She then tried kindred student groups, MEChA, and through her boyfriend, the Native American student organization. Aquilina left school to spend a year in the Philippines working with activists there. When she returned, she began working full time at the PWC, where Tritia Toyota interviewed her, and became its executive director, as well as finishing UCLA with a major in Asian American Studies.

At the Claremont Colleges, Suyapa Portillo initially "wanted to study psychology because I thought that—at that time, in my narrow mind I thought that that would help me come back to my community to work with some of my compañeras that were having kids early." But she soon joined other students of color who organized to demand tenure for an African-American professor, and from there moved on to doing an internship with HERE Local 11, thereby shifting her framework for activism from personal service to members of one's ethnic community to organizing against racial and class barriers that held Latina/o as well as other people of color down.

As a teenager, well before he had any activist inklings, Javier Gonzalez was drawn to Mexico.

I always think that for some reason there's just a whole bunch of stuff that I had an interest in but never really explored it. For example, I have at home a book that actually—I was too embarrassed to check out books in high school. I didn't do well in high school at all. I was a big clown. So I do remember one time a group of friends and I went the public library and I was too embarrassed to check out a book so I took the little metal detector out of the book and I stole the book and I remember my friends all like tagged on the book. That was a big joke. It was a book on Mexican history.

Javier grew up in Santa Monica's one remaining Latino working-class neighborhood, but his family also spent time regularly with family in Mexico. Javier began to explore activism at Santa Monica College (a community college), and became much more involved after visiting the Zapatistas in Chiapas. However, when he transferred to UCLA, he focused his political energy off campus, helping to organize the Popular Arts Center, or Regeneración, a community-based arts and politics center in East Los Angeles that was part of a wide network of community-based progressive Chicana/o artists, musicians, and youth groups. When it dissolved, Javier worked for and received serious organizing training from Anthony Thigpen at AGENDA, a community group organizing in Latino/a and African-American neighborhoods (see chapter 1). After a brief stint organizing day laborers as part of a CHIRLA effort, Javier was recruited to Justice for Janitors, where his wife works. When I interviewed him, he was directing a project, collaboratively sponsored by union cleaning contractors and Justice for Janitors (SEIU Local 1877), that was investigating cleaning firms and practices. He began to think about activism while at Santa Monica College. He recalled deliberately shopping around and studying a wide variety of activist groups.

> I started listening to the activists on campus, started going to all the things. And then from there—I just always like to try to different things—student government. I was appointed vice chair in the interclub council so I had interaction with different clubs, and that's when I started hanging out with the Black Student Union, the Central American student groups, Mexican, the vegetarian club, which was the most radical club on campus—yeah they would do a lot of crazy stuff—environmental groups, gay and lesbian student union. That's how I started meeting them, and that opened up a whole bunch of different thoughts to me, and I started being able to pick and choose what I liked and I began to study different things.

Not all students of color gravitated immediately to ethnic identity groups. Michelle Mascarenhas and John Delloro felt marginal in high school because of ethnicity, but neither sought out ethnic studies homes, nor did they engage in antiracist activism on campus. Both came to acknowledge how their racial identities were personally and politically salient through connections with people of color who were like them, but who were also not like them. For Michelle, a radical change in identity came gradually, with actions leading reflection. For John, a moment of epiphany led him to radically reshape his actions.

Michelle Mascarenhas was an electrical engineering student at UCLA when the Gulf War broke out in 1991. She attributed her politicization to the war, even though she did not know at the time why this issue felt so resonant: "My third year [at UCLA] and the Gulf War arose . . . and [my boyfriend and I] just started reading a lot of stuff about what had gone on and questioning how the United States was involved, for oil basically. When it started, we went to meetings and forums to learn about how the issues were being framed by an alternative perspective. We heard Ramsey Clark and people like that. And then when the war broke out, we were demonstrating on the lines at the federal building every day."

Later, Michelle linked her family to the Middle East.

[My parents] met in the Middle East. My whole family migrated, over the last several generations, around the world from Goa. Although all my blood lines go back to Goa, I don't know when the last family member actually lived there. So my grandparents on both sides were born or as young children were in Uganda, and then went back to India, and then went to the Gulf, the Middle East. That is where my parents met. My mom went to boarding school in Jordan. And my parents met in Qatar. And they got married there. My parents stayed there [in Qatar] another ten years. My sisters were all born in Qatar. I'm the only one in my family that was born here.

KB: Wait a minute. Now the Middle East has a salience it didn't have earlier.

MM: With the Gulf War?

KB: Yeah.

MM: Well I think I might have had more of a connection to the place. I think Kuwait and Qatar are very similar; I learned that in the process of learning about Kuwait. I learned more about Qatar and became more interested in what that place was like

and what it was like for my parents, but I don't think that that
was so prominent in my thinking about it.

KB: . . . this is Karen's leading question: Did you feel that you had
a greater fund of hearing stuff so as not to be relying on the
media?

MM: Maybe, yeah. I mean not about Iraq, but I think I did have an
idea of Kuwait, if it was anything like Qatar, as being a very
undemocratic place. I didn't understand why we would be standing up for this place and the way that they were doing it pub-
licly. Because my parents told me stories of living in a house, and
a sheik driving by with a new wife and saying that she wanted
to live in that house and my parents were out the next week.

After the Gulf War I applied for and got an internship in the
Peace Corps and I went to southern Africa. I was there for—I
was supposed to be there for one quarter or three months. But
I was really having a good time and learning a lot about myself.
It was my first time out of country really, except for going to
Canada to visit my family, and I was on my own and just so dif-
ferent than engineering or anything else that I had thought of
before.

I was doing computer stuff actually, but working on a garden
program, a home-garden nutrition project, part of the thread
that brings to me to where I am today. I think just in developing relationships with other, mostly Americans, but even other
African students, and just hitchhiking around South Africa. I
really gained a sense of who I was in a different way. A lot of
my friends were African-American or Asian-American. We
were definitely the minority; the Peace Corps was mostly white.
And when we would hitchhike around together, Indians would
pick us up, or occasionally Coloreds. I think I learned a lot
about just who I was from that experience.

And it made me think about my experience in America in a
different way. I think also in becoming close to people in a way
I think I hadn't been able to do as much here. But I was open
to other ideas and ways of thinking.

I don't have a plan really, and it's partly because I think my
values have changed so much, or at least became what they are.

I couldn't really worry about my own livelihood in the same way anymore. It just didn't have the importance it did before.

Like Javier, John Delloro had already been thinking about social activism when he went to College of the Canyons, a community college. He, too, was active in student government, as he had been in high school, but John's politics were fairly conservative. His opposition to the Gulf War made him unpopular. "And it was a very trying moment because I remember being called things from—what was it? I was called a communist. I was called a new-age hippie, hippie with a haircut." Nevertheless, his safe space remained nonracial, social critique through music and poetry. Even as John's politics became less conservative, he did not develop an ethnic consciousness until some time after he transferred to UCLA around the time of the Los Angeles uprising, during a campus struggle against increases in student fees: "I ended up getting back into the whole fee-hike stuff. And I remember noticing how and at this time, I was still coming from the perspective of art, and that was how to protest the university. I wasn't thinking in terms of organizing. I was thinking more in terms of the arts and reaching people individually."

Contacts with "ethnic others," with politicized students of color, and with the struggle for Chicana/o Studies challenged his politics and his identity as non-racial.

The Chicano Studies hunger strike happened and I got into the whole thing of like how come we're worried about Chicano Studies when education is being cut. And at that time I was very anti-affirmative action, anti-ethnic studies. Anyone who said they were Asian-American, African-American, I thought was being very separatist and divisive. So when people asked me what my ethnic identity was, I would go—my racial consciousness was not there, period, and so I couldn't understand why people were willing to get arrested when they did the sit-ins and meetings.

Personal connections and personal testimonies were important for creating the space within which John felt able to hear different perspectives on race and political identities. Disrespect to the hunger strikers from white students heightened his interest in those with whom he disagreed.

One of the people who was working with me was one of those that got arrested, he was with the—what were they called again? Conscious Students of Color. Actually when he got arrested, I thought maybe I should look into why someone would do this. I remember the tent city [set up by hunger strikers and supporters of forming a Chicana/o Studies Department in the UCLA campus main quad], and I remember people sitting around [it], I don't want to be stereotypical, I was sitting there and they looked like they were from a frat, and they were laughing at the people in the tents. I remember feeling uncomfortable sitting there, even though I didn't support it.

And I decided to walk through the tent city, and that had a real impact on me because around the time there were some grade school kids who were visiting, and they were singing to the hunger strikers. I couldn't understand why people would go on a hunger strike for this. I remember saying you sang really well, and she said, thank you for supporting us. And she goes, you know it's important to learn my history and yours, and I'm like, you're supporting it and I never thought about it. And she started telling me what the murals, there were those big painted murals, is so-and-so. And I'm, God, I didn't know that. And then I thought, well maybe it's okay—it's important that you do that. But I didn't see it as important to me at that time.

And what happened was the USSA [U.S. Student Association] conference was happening right after the Chicano Studies hunger strike, in the summer '93, and a National People of Color caucus conference was happening right before the USSA conference. Because I was at the poverty carnival, I was trying to build a network with all the different community colleges and Cal States. So I went to the different campuses one by one, meeting with people and so I had all these contacts in community colleges. Because I tend to favor community colleges because I went to one and I learned a lot. Actually, I learned a lot more in the community college than I did in my undergrad years. And because I had all these contacts they said, can you advise some of those people to come to this conference, and I'm like, okay, and I start helping.

John's epiphany came when he realized that his refusal of an ethnic identity and opposition to racial politics rested on repressing the racism he'd experienced. It took personal connection and another student's personal testimony to facilitate it.

> I go pick up these two leaders at the airport, and I remember driving, it was a student of color and he started talking about issues of race and I would listen and I would joke around and they were really nice. There was this guy who was a student there, and he was very quiet and very involved with getting Tagalog taught on campus, and he was into poetry. He was writing poetry, and I said you write poetry and started to connect, and he started talking and then all of a sudden he starts telling me why he was involved in these issues and how for him it was important. I was opposed to Tagalog and all this poetry being taught in my English classes and he was talking how important it was to him.

At this point John's narrative became a testimonial for the effectiveness of personal narrative for connection and persuasiveness.

> And it struck me, because I was so used to people not hearing me or being called a banana or a coconut and being challenged like that, I get very defensive and I fight back. And he was just telling me what he was feeling; I even asked, and it got me thinking. The National People of Color conference caucus happened, and I went to the Asian Pacific Islander caucus meeting, and I started listening to people more, and then at one moment I suddenly realized how much self hatred I had without realizing it, and all of a sudden I started mouthing the racism that I dealt with growing up.
>
> But it was amazing I didn't even think. I didn't even blink an eye or wonder about the fact when I was in second grade in New Jersey, people calling me Chinese. I wasn't Chinese, but they would constantly say that about Chinese, Japanese, blah blah blah, whatever. It's funny how you kind of put that to the side and I started going back to remembering when I was in high school when someone actually put "nip" in shaving cream on our garage and I remember washing it off so that no one would see it, and I was amazed that didn't bother me as much.

Both John and Michelle became aware that their sense of being different did not come from something about them as individuals, but rather than from the racial way that society identified them. Absent awareness of being marked racially, they did not seek out co-ethnics or people of color in their quest for a socially safe space. Unlike Norma or Suyapa, whose sense of being racially othered, of ethnic identification, and quest for a home place preceded their political identity, John and Michelle developed their sensitivity to racism and their identification as people of color in the context of developing their present political identities.

For some narrators, the most salient connections with "different others" were transnational or with ethnic or national diasporas. In particular, their identification is with the heritage of political struggles that people of a diaspora have waged in whatever nation they have been. Immediately after his epiphany, John Delloro gravitated to the Asian American Studies Center, met Philip Veracruz, a founder of and the highest-ranking Filipino in the United Farm Workers union. He learned about the union's history and about friction over Cesar Chavez's visit with Marcos in the Philippines. "I started realizing that in identifying as Asian-American or Filipino, I'm in dialog with the struggles of my ancestors, which means I have the responsibility to continue those struggles."

At Wheaton College, Liz Sunwoo began to identify with Korea and to engage politically in issues around Korea, which ultimately led her to the Korean Immigrant Workers Alliance (KIWA): "I started getting involved in also international issues—a professor of ours got a group of us together to do a fast for North Korean famine relief. We did a long fast and at the end of the fast we all met in Boston with students from MIT and Harvard and everywhere, all over the Boston metropolitan area. We met at this one church, and there was a woman who did a documentary on the whole situation in North Korea. It was then that I actually met someone that worked for KIWA, who was working at the time during the summer for KIWA."

As with Liz and John, part of narrators constructing their ethnoracial identities as political involved constructing them across national boundaries, or transnationally, as based in a "home" country and in the United States. As part of constructing those identities, some narrators traveled to their home countries in search of meaningful activism and belonging. For Aquilina Soriano and Tori Kim, travel to their parents' home countries was especially important in leading them to think transnationally about their political identities.

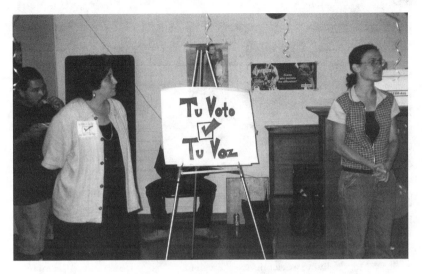

1. Stephanie Monroe (right) at living wage meeting. Photo courtesy LAANE

2. Living wage demonstration Los Angeles International Airport. Aisha Livingstone center. Photo courtesy LAANE

3. Santa Monica living wage initiative, Stephanie Monroe (right) and Aisha Livingstone (left). Photo courtesy LAANE

4. John Delloro (right) at UCLA teaching assistant union rally. Photo courtesy John Delloro

5. Joann Lo at Garment Worker Center rally against Forever 21. Photo courtesy Joann Lo

6. Michelle Mascarenhas (front left with baby) with Bay Area organizing committee before rally in Oakland, CA 2005. Photo courtesy Michelle Mascarenhas

7. Aquilina Soriano (left at mic) speaking at MIWON awards ceremony. Photo courtesy Aquilina Soriano

8. Liz Sunwoo (left). Photo courtesy Liz Sunwoo

9. Eileen Ma. Photo by Suyapa
Portillo, courtesy Eileen Ma

10. Suyapa Portillo Self portrait, courtesy Suyapa Portillo

11. Douglas Marmol. Photo courtesy LAANE

12. Milton Pascual (center). Photo courtesy LAANE

13. Quynh Nguyen (second from right) at Farmer John organizing drive, Vernon, CA. Photo courtesy of UFCW

14. Roxane Auer (right). Photo courtesy of Roxane Auer

Aquilina Soriano went to the Philippines to become involved in political work there before graduating from UCLA. Political work in the Philippines was a powerful formative organizing experience for her. In her narrative, the community of Filipinos takes shape as a borderless, trans-Pacific political community, as we will see in the next chapter. But she was also quite clear that going to the Philippines was a culture shock and a political education.

> I almost didn't speak a word of Tagalog. It was a pretty amazing life-changing event. I got exposed to how they are organizing there and how incredibly [powerful] the movement was. It was felt all over the nation and how united, not just on general progressive ideas but on specific things like how are we going to organize, what are we going to do.
>
> I came back and started working at the Pilipino Workers Center. It was sort of difficult, though. I had sort of a culture shock because it's, like, how do I maintain my commitment . . . I mean it's hard; we are in these nice cafes when people are suffering so much over there and sacrificing so much, but we negotiate because we are living here. You have to be able to navigate within the society here.

Tori Kim also traveled to her home country, Korea, but after college. When interviewed by Tritia Toyota, she was the staff attorney of KIWA in Los Angeles. Born in Korea, her family immigrated to Colorado when she was a young child. While at Harvard, she became politically interested in Korea through a class in Korean drum performance taught by a labor organizer from Korea. The music provided a means to address political issues—in particular, garment workers and labor issues in Korea—and whetted her desire to get involved in the labor movement in Korea. She deliberately sought out this experience as a way of negating what she saw as her privileged existence as a Harvard student. Grappling with the complexities of her own privilege and marginalization, and the differences between herself and her parents, were at the center of her experience: "It's very hard emotionally to deal with [being a privileged student], you have to buy into it and try your best to act like everybody else or you just become very marginalized."

Tori noted that the decision to give up one's class privilege was a political one that she shared with others, including Korean college students.

I think this is something that came out of the student movement in Korea, too. There was a point when there were a lot of college students who graduated and decided to go and work in factories because there was a sense that they wanted to give up their privilege as educated people and be part of the working class. I guess I kind of participate in the labor movement in that way. I was very intrigued by this when I was in Korea, to hear these stories. There were a lot of students—and factory workers—and they lived their life as workers and wanted to be a part of, I guess, not buying into that social division or class that society imposes on you—just wanting to be part of the people, I guess. I was very intrigued by that. And when I was in Korea, I chose to live in this very poor part of Korea.

I used to tell my parents about this and they thought I was completely [crazy]. They were like, "Well, actually, you were poor in this country." I mean not dirt poor, but from a perspective we are part of the working class in this country. So for me it was almost like internalizing the elitism of Harvard through thinking that I was so privileged, but I wasn't the one who was there working thirteen hours a day. I was young and never really had to fend for myself, I suppose it was easy for me to think that I had all this privilege or all these resources, which in fact, if you look at my family, it's not necessarily true. But in any case, I went through that stage.

Both Tori and Aquilina discovered that although they shared a great deal politically with activists in their parents' home countries, these were not places where they felt at home as political activists. However, they returned to the United States identifying simultaneously as members of a diaspora struggling against oppression globally and as part of a local constellation of oppressed groups.

In contrast, Javier Gonzalez's family is more involved in a transnational social circuit, with family members in Santa Monica regularly visiting those in Jalisco, Mexico: "All the kids would go to Mexico and my uncles would take us to the road to sell peaches on the side of the road and stuff like that. Our vacations were in Mexico. We spent all our summers in Mexico and we would be milking the cows and feeding the pigs."

Political activism in Mexico was integral to Javier's political identity from early on: "[Student organizing] wasn't what I wanted to do partly because I had been to Mexico a few times and I would see students organizing in Mexico City. And I would think student organizing in the U.S. was nothing compared to them. It's impressive stuff down there. So a group of friends and I started a study group, and then at least two of the friends ended up renting the loft and they wanted to have gigs in the loft and fund raisers. . . . So every show we ever did was for something. So we did shows for Mumia. We did shows for the Zapatistas. We did shows for a women's collective in Chiapas."

The center, Regeneración (Popular Arts Center) in Highland Park, organized several delegations to Chiapas. It also worked with a wide range of Chicana/o youth and community groups.

> Even back then I was always somebody that was really interested in the Latino immigrants so I had a lot of connections with Latino immigrant groups, solidarity groups with Mexico. You had Chicano groups in solidarity with Zapatistas, and Mexican immigrant groups and they didn't even talk, and that was pretty ridiculous so we had stuff with the National Commission on Democracy in Mexico. We had some contact with the Gardeners' Association, IDEPSCA's association with the project, with their domestica project; so we had a lot of contacts like that.
>
> [My wife and I] met in Mexico. We are from the same town. As it turned out, we were both from the west side of L.A. We saw each other again at SMC [Santa Monica College]. We were friends for about a year or two years and then we got—I always knew even when I was a kid I always liked going to Mexico and I always appreciated the fact that my dad took us and we knew about the ranch and where my grandfather lived and how he worked. So I always knew that I had to marry somebody that I could bring there and it was always really important to me.

Javier expressed clearly what Louisa Schein (1998) calls oppositional cosmopolitanism and Chela Sandoval calls differential consciousness. Both refer to a recognition that those to whom they are culturally connected in other nations are also struggling against oppression in their home countries, and the bond they share is a transnational struggle for justice, even as the specific strategies may differ. Several narrators who did not travel to home countries nevertheless shared in this oppositional diasporic identity.

Other narrators' senses of oppositional cosmopolitanism/differential consciousness came from the discovery, through travel, of political kinship with people who were not from their home countries or their ethnic group. Suyapa Portillo spent a year at the University of Chile after her first campus activism at Pitzer College. But others went places to which they had no obvious connection: Michelle Mascarenhas joined the Peace Corps and went to South Africa, where she connected to Americans of color and to South African "colored" and Asians; Joann Lo went to Australia, where she made links between Australian indigenous people and those of Taiwan; Stephanie Monroe went to Costa Rica to learn Spanish. In all cases, travel contributed to a transnational political sensibility, what Schein (1998) and others call transnationalism from below—that is, from the grassroots—especially through identification with a heritage of oppositional politics in those countries. However it was achieved, what all these oppositional perspectives share is a broader sense of political kinship that builds from a sensibility of racial and class oppression, but crosses ethnic and national borders.

PUTTING THE MARGINS AT THE CENTER OF POLITICAL THINKING AND CREATING A POLITICAL BORDERLAND

Race and ethnicity are central issues for activism in Los Angeles. The leadership and membership of organizations formed to deal with class-based issues, as well as those engaged in fighting racial and ethnic discrimination, were primarily people of color. Coalitions and collaboration among groups in Los Angeles were very multiracial and multiethnic, including whites. Each group had its own perspectives shaped by their particular experiences that informed their agendas for practice and their views of social justice. Those who worked in such coalitions found themselves moving from specific to wider understandings of the systemic nature of racial and class oppression. John Delloro's center of activism rapidly expanded from Filipinos and the UFW, to Asian-American garment workers, to workers of all races. Michelle Mascarenhas returned to UCLA from her Peace Corps travel to help found Voices, a feminist organization for women of color whose initial effort was to rethink myths about women and beauty from the perspective of women of color.

Quynh Nguyen's campus involvement with getting Vietnamese language classes led to a wider political vision of "us."

It just started out that I wanted to take Vietnamese, and some other students wanted to [take] Tagalog or Thai or their own language . . . We formed a coalition that became my life for five years.

Frankly as it started out, I just wanted to learn my language, I was self centered. Then it became for purely rhetorical reasons, about fighting Eurocentrism, about entitlement and coalition building and responding to community needs. And while I was spouting the rhetoric, I internalized it and realized it was true. And then the fight became much bigger. By the time I left, we won in our original goal, which was language classes. But by then our expectations and the hopes of the student movement had been raised so much, that as I sat on a faculty committee that formed because of our pressure, we suggested this whole Southeast Asian Studies program, which was formed years later and will eventually become a major.

At the Women's Resource Center at California State University, Long Beach, Norma Martinez developed a perspective that put the interlinked struggles against race, gender, and sexual oppression at the center of analysis. In Californians for Justice she found an organization that put the same complex set of margins at the center of their politics: "We are an organization that fights for gay rights, women's rights, or that are aware of the different issues. And so I thought this is the place to stay for me. But I have been here for three years. And also I think I have been lucky in finding really good spaces because, with organizing, not everyone addresses issues of homophobia and racism."

Joann Lo expanded her political center to include class when she went to Australia.

I began to look more at class and beyond just race and ethnicity. I spent a semester in Australia, and part of the program was learning about the aborigines there and what happened to them, how the government treated them as inferiors and lower class. And then, when I came back from that—that was my second semester

junior year. When I was on that semester abroad, I began getting letters from friends who were at Yale while I was in Australia and they
were telling me about the two unions at Yale who entered into a
huge contract fight with the university. And so I came back from
Australia wanting to do something beyond just the Asian-American
community, beyond race.

Because being perceived as working class in Los Angeles is so bound
up with being racially not white, white activists, especially if they have
no clear working-class history in their backgrounds, lack easy connection
points to why they worked as organizers around workers' issues. As we
saw in chapter 3, Stephanie Monroe valued a past family connection to
the working class as a kind of explanatory bridge for herself. And Roxane Auer looked to her Hungarian immigrant grandparents, less for any
"natural" connection to or identity with working-class people or people
of color, and more for a real history and an alternative to affluence and
whiteness, whose values were far from those she was coming to embrace.

Thus for Roxane, joining with "different others" to shift the margins to the center was a very different process than it was for narrators
of color. Although she was initially drawn to environmentalism for its
familiarity, as she came into contact with other activists,

Heal the Bay and conservation movements just didn't do it for me.
But there was a group on campus called the Environmental Coalition (EC), which was a combination of grad students and undergrad
who worked on issues of, I would say, more like globalization issues
than environmental issues. It was "Unocal and Pepsi out of Burma."
It was "free East Timor." It was any campaign against multinational
companies. They had an environmental twist to it because they were
polluting indigenous communities, but it was just definitely environmentalism with an edge that I could relate to more. It just
seemed they were getting more to the heart of the problem.

Through these groups Roxane made connections with kindred
"others": "Through the Environmental Coalition I got involved with
people from Communities for a Better Environment that were doing
environmental activism in southeast L.A., which is the part of L.A., having

grown up in L.A. and having spent my whole life in L.A., that I had never been to and never seen. So as soon as I drove down to southeast L.A. and saw the factories and saw the conditions that people were living in, I immediately was really inspired by that kind of work."

Figuring out how to fit, how to craft a political identity given her class position was not easy. Like Javier Gonzalez, she, too, shopped around, but less to educate herself on the spectrum of political possibilities than to find an explicitly political home: "I think when I started seeing people do something about [social injustice], I respected what they were doing and I didn't respect what I was doing, which was to just be kind of unhappy about it. And when I decided that, I was going through the process of what do I want to do with my life. I was getting closer to graduation; what job do I want? And every single job that I'd seen put in front of me through my parents and their friends, the idea of working in any of those jobs severely depressed me."

For Roxane, confronting her embrace of class privileges and then letting go of her expectations of continuing them allowed her to connect with "different others." Realizing that she could make that decision removed a barrier internal to herself to engaging in activism and with activists.

> I had this notion implanted in my brain from my dad, because I was raised with money, I would need to make money myself if I was ever going to be happy and if I was ever going to maintain the standard of living. And it weighed upon me very heavily.
>
> And I do remember having a day of epiphany where I realized—such a silly thought—but I realized how much money I make, that's ridiculous. It's not going to make me happy. I can do whatever I want to do. If I want to be an activist for a living, even though there's no money in that, I didn't even know there were jobs out there for that. If I want to take on this as a major part of my life, that's fine. I can go ahead and do that. I don't care how much money I make. I made that decision I don't care how much money, I'm going to go forward and drop that. I'm going to erase that thought. And that kind of sparked a whole freedom of investigation of what there was out there to do with your life.

There is nothing so heady, nothing that demonstrates political agency, being able to make a difference, as confronting power and winning. It is living testimony to the strength and efficacy of participation in a political community, of exercising political citizenship.

That discovery was Javier's equivalent to John's epiphany about race and Roxane's about privilege.

The big push that sort of changed my life direction most dramatically, I guess, when I was eighteen a group of friends and I went to a park, and we ended up getting beat up by the cops. And one of my friends, his grandfather was the president of the Santa Monica-Venice NAACP, but he got a lawyer and got the FBI and the LAPD to do an investigation and we sued. A bunch of stuff happened. There was a lot of press around it. So what ended up happening, one, I saw that people do do things. . . . The second thing was that the guys were pretty rowdy. We were a wild bunch of thirty young men, and we could be a handful. So for some reason, I wasn't a shot caller or leader of the group by any means, but for some reason I could get people to do stuff. So when they needed somebody to go to the press conferences, it was call me. When they needed someone to go to do interviews with the FBI or with the police or to do depositions with the police, they would call me, and I would somehow be able to show up with a group of guys. I wasn't a leader, though, because, when the thing came down, I didn't have any decision-making power. When we settled the case, I was just one of the many; so presumably I could get people there.

I don't think I was a leader of that group, I just think I could get people somewhere, and then let them make their own decisions. So those are the two things. After I got involved in that incident, that's what got my interest.

Roxane Auer linked her discovery that it is possible to make a difference in the world—and that she could be part of that process—directly to her psychological health.

A lack of hope about the world and life, a lot of that is still a struggle, and a lot of that was lifted when I first got involved in activism and more so when I got my first job doing it and felt like I was learning how to do it and was starting to become effective. The further I moved into feeling like I really was effective and, like, I was doing this and I could do it, the more I felt better. . . . And once I had that feeling of—that hopefulness and the height of some campaigns I feel just so good about the possibilities of life and about the possibilities of the human spirit, what people who come together can do.

Experiencing the power of his own ability to make a difference in the UPS strike changed Milton Pascual's life course immediately: "And I cried, 'Manuel, we won!' and I was crying for joy. We won the best contract in the U.S. And he was really happy for me. And I was like—I felt like I had accomplished something from taking those people with me and leading them into something that was tough for them. So the strike in general made me realize, what life is about. That's why I'm in here [as a union organizer for HERE]."

One's sense of agency is shaped by one's class in complicated ways. Javier and Milton grew up with the common sense that the "system" was hostile and that there wasn't much they could do about it. Stephanie, white and from an upper-middle-class family, was clear that she received a different message: "I did always grow up with the thought that I could—the possibility that I could do something about something bad that I saw. I was just too selfish to care. I was too busy in my junior high and high school activities."

Public acknowledgement is a kind of icing on the cake of agency. Having their opponents acknowledge activists' viewpoints or embrace their goals is a public recognition of activists' truth and effectiveness. Quynh Nguyen recalled the campus struggle a decade ago to establish a Southeast Asian Studies program and described the celebration of its opening as such a moment of recognition: "The great news is that two weekends ago I went to the opening [of the Southeast Asian Studies Center]. I was invited by a progressive professor who remembers the genesis in student struggle. Ironically, the event was now a touchy-feely celebration and everybody acting like UCLA wanted the program all along. But that is okay. We got it . . . ten years after we started; it was very moving. It adds to optimism and arrogance to do things no one thinks can win."

Javier recounted a similar acknowledgement from the police who beat them.

> We settled out of court. We had a strong case in terms of our testimony. We were all solid. It was all the same, we were all—it was a dramatic incident. It got a lot of press. The cops didn't want to settle. They internally disciplined some officers. Chief Gates over-turned it, as he did I think every single case. And then what happened was, this older white lady who was walking her poodle who saw the whole thing finally came out and said, "I saw the whole thing, they are not lying." That was one thing. The other thing was one of the police officers—actually the only black police officer that was there—ended up going to jail for rape and the D.A., the city attorney that was defending the police department, tried to get that suppressed. So they didn't want that to be admissible in court; and the day after the judge refused to suppress it, they called and offered [us] something like $200,000. And we had a meeting and they asked thirty poor kids from the neighborhood if they wanted to settle for $200,000, and everybody just raised their hands and said "where do I sign?"

Comparing these narratives of organizers who were college students with those of Douglas Marmol and Aisha Livingstone, both of whom came to organizing directly from the ranks of workers, illuminate the class variations in narratives as socially constructed political documents. The plot of college-origin organizers' narratives emphasizes the way that key experiences caused the narrator to radically change her or his viewpoint, sense of self, and life. The two rank-and-file organizers' narratives read differently; they are about discovery, but not transformation.

I realized that Douglas and Aisha were finding my questions about their early lives and politicization somewhere between less than useful and silencing for communicating what they wanted to say. They introduced a different repertoire of narrative personas than those of college-origin narrators. Neither responded to questions about how they became political with a life history. Instead, they described themselves as inherently and always class conscious, and hence as "natural" activists by virtue of their lived experiences and sense of fairness, a subjectivity (on this as a narrative expression of a working-class identity, see Passerini 1987).

Aisha Livingstone is an African-American woman, with grown children.[4] Although she remembers the civil rights movement from her youth, her work with the living-wage campaign for airport workers was her first foray into activism. She became involved in this campaign while she was a supervisor at one of the concessions at Los Angeles International Airport (LAX).

KB: The first question I want to ask is how you first became aware of social issues?

AL: Well, I first became aware of them at LAX [during the joint SEIU-HERE unionization drive for airport concession workers]. I was working for WH Smith [a newsstand chain that has airport concessions] and some people came around and started talking to us about the living wage and it was interesting to me, and that's how I really got involved.

KB: But when you were growing up as a kid.

AL: As a kid, I was always interested in people, their feelings, and how they were being treated, so I guess it was always in myself, it was always there but it just had to be brought out. And working at WH Smith brought it out.

Douglas Marmol also became involved in both union activism and the living wage campaign while working at the airport.

KB: So how did you first become aware of social issues.

DM: Like, in my country, I'm from El Salvador, and I come from a family that my uncle was a real activist in the revolution in El Salvador. His name is Miguel Marmol, and he helped build a lot of—you know Roque Dalton? He has some books that talk about my uncle, which is probably, that is why I got it in my veins. But first of all I used to—I work in Vons and that's how I got the view of what the union is about. But I knew that—I became a member, and then I used to pay union dues, by that I used to have free medical benefits, dental for me or my family.

Both Aisha and Douglas described themselves as self-evidently or always disposed to activism. For Aisha, it is rooted in her personality, the kind of person she is, "always interested in people, their feelings, and how they were being treated." Douglas, as a nephew of El Salvador's

most famous revolutionary, Miguel Marmol, who is the author and subject of that nation's master testimonio (Dalton 1987), attributes his willingness to become active in union struggles to his family heritage and
the self-evident benefits of a union. Neither described a disjuncture or
transformation of self; both emphasized continuity in perspective. Aisha
and Douglas also described becoming worker organizers as natural out-
comes of the conditions of their working lives.

> KB:　Tell me more about that [how working at WH Smith brought
> out her activism].
>
> AL:　Okay. When they started coming around and talking about the
> living-wage coalition, making more money was—and we were
> all interested in making more money. It was an increase in our
> salary so I thought that was good. I thought it was great because
> a raise at WH Smith was like a quarter—you got a quarter or
> twenty-three cents and, to me as a supervisor with the work
> that I was doing, it was just absolutely insanity to me, and for
> me to be able to get $1.25 more an hour, that would really make
> a difference.
>
> So I said to them, well how do we get this money. So they
> began to tell us that we had to file a petition and basically come
> to training and let our voices be heard. So I said, well I'm not
> ashamed or I'm not afraid to let my voice be heard as long as
> I'm in the right, so I'm all for that, so they started coming to
> my house and talking to me more about it. And I was all excited
> about it, and so I went to the meetings.

Douglas continued his answer to my query about how he first became
aware of social issues by describing his history of work and its attendant
insecurity, from unionized supermarket work to nonunion jobs at the airport in a variety of food service concessions where he met organizers from
HERE Local 814. And then his lead organizer "came and talked to us on
break. And, you know, right now we're fighting the company."

Neither Aisha nor Douglas were especially interested in explaining
why they became active because it was so obvious to them. Their passion, as we've seen, lies in the stuff of their activism, in the way participation in a union allows them to express, to act on the kinds of people
they are. Their taken-for-granted participation stands in sharp contrast to

most of the narrators who went to college, who emphasized events that caused a major transformation in the way they saw themselves and the world, which led to their becoming activists instead of striving for the personal or material success their college educations enabled.

Douglas's and Aisha's narratives, especially their silences on transformative experiences, make clear the central epiphany was less about how they saw the world than about the discovery of organizations that made it possible for them to do something about changing it, and in so doing to fully act on and express their true self. This was decidedly not the case in El Salvador when Douglas left during the civil war.

> In my country, it's a battle, things like that, because the government—you can ask, and if you get involved in the union or something like that, next day you're dead. And right here you have freedom of speech. You know, I can be with the general manager or the owner of company and I could tell him off, and I'm not, the next day I'm not dead. So when I go back to my country and things like that, they said, I cannot understand—I cannot believe how you are involved in the union, and nothing happens to you. My cousin works in the corporation and she said like five people got together and they were talking about the union, they got fired, and that makes me mad because if people cannot survive over there, then in this country we have to—we have to take advantage of this and that's how I think, it's why I got involved.

Where narratives of the college-origin narrators stress giving birth to new, more fulfilling selves, those of the two rank-and-file organizers emphasize the importance of organizations, and civil liberties that allow them to fulfill the self that has been there all along. For Douglas, this meant fulfilling a responsibility to those who do not have the freedom to organize on their own behalf.

The college-recruited and workplace-recruited organizers are not exactly the same social selves. The college-recruited organizers identify with ethnic cultural communities that are working class, while the two rank-and-file organizers identify as working class across ethnicity and race. The latter selves, I suspect, have been scaffolded and shaped by the foundational stories of the labor movement that stress class as transcendent, while the college-recruited selves have been shaped by the borderlands or intersectional perspectives and praxis discussed earlier in the chapter. As we will see in the next chapter, the foundational stories embedded in the organizational cultures of these two movements conflict as well as complement one another. The union foundational story is about class and economic justice. The intersectional foundational story emphasizes the complicated interrelations among people of color, of how racial and gender job-slotting can separate and divide workers as well as unite them, and about how to work across those divisions. Aisha and Douglas show that union discourses helped them to articulate and express politically their power and agency.

CONCLUSION

Narrators identified four structural moments through which they created political identities: a search for home; discovering kindred others; putting perspectives of the differently marginalized at the center of analysis; and discovering personal agency in collective action. Although I've presented them as if they were points in a sequence, this is not the case. They are moments that activists name as contributing to their political consciousness and agency.

Norma realized that acceptance in her white middle-class school was conditioned on rejecting her community. Suyapa saw herself in the eyes of the U.S. Border Patrol and realized that she was no longer normal or racially unmarked; Javier, Aisha, Milton, and Quynh discovered that they could undo injustice. For some like Javier, Milton, and Quynh, the epiphany lay in agency. For John it lay in recognizing his racial oppression. For Roxane it lay in realizing that she didn't have to reproduce her upper-middle-class standard of living. For Norma and Douglas, it centered on the discovery of a home, a social place that embraced them as the multifaceted people they are. For Tori and Aquilina, that home was a transnational political space. And for Joann, Michelle, and Suyapa the discovery that there were "other others" served a parallel energizing function.

What was an epiphany for some was learned early or taken for granted by others. For example, most narrators of color knew about racism from experiences early in life, and assume it is obvious how that knowledge shaped their politics. Even if John did not attribute his sense of difference to race, most others did. But because John gave a detailed analysis of how that discovery underlay his transformation, his narrative illuminates the structure of the moments in which racial identities give birth to part of political identities in other narrators as well. Likewise with agency. John, Michelle, Roxane, and Stephanie took their agency for granted, but because Javier and Quynh did not, their narratives analyze how its discovery underlay their creation of political subjectivity. These structural moments emerge from reading the interviews against one another, from putting them into conversation with one another. Reading what was a blinding flash in one narrative illuminates processes that were taken for granted in another.

Narrators described their personal transformations as moments of epiphany, moments that were emotionally intense experiences in which narrators saw their world, themselves, and everything else in new ways. The realizations they described in the previous two chapters let them see new possibilities in their personal lives, in their relations with others, and in their place in the world. And small steps in acting on their new knowledge set them upon a new and more meaningful life path. Narrators described these experiences as personal moments of giving birth to new political selves or identities.

For some, the epiphany came in naming the source of feeling marginalized, in discovering they were swans in a culture they treasured instead of ugly ducklings in a mainstream culture. For others, the key transformational moment came from collaborating with "other others," people of different ethnicities, classes, and gender, and putting the heterogeneous marginalized at the center of a transformed view, a critical angle of vision that linked multiple constituencies into an oppositional vision. For still others, the most powerful epiphany came from discovering they could change things by acting politically—and successfully—against discrimination from these vantage points.

The aggregation of personal moments of epiphany into a collective plot is the point at which personal stories become politicized. The plot is one of personally coming to consciousness through new knowledge and reorganization of the paradigm by which they understand themselves, now as sociopolitical actors in the world—a dialectical or reciprocal relationship between experience and its analysis. Each epiphany gains new and broader significance by being woven into this larger tapestry. This, too, is part of the structure of personal epiphany.

Narrators did not invent the collective plot that makes their personal realizations so powerful and personally liberating. The transformative effects of their personal epiphanies come in large part from a collective political narrative that is older than they are. Their narratives, singly and together, are part of a larger narrative of reinterpretation that, as I've indicated earlier, has been developed by scholars and activists in ethnic and women's studies that goes back as far as the 1970s (Cade 1970; hooks 1989). Grounded in the lives of women old enough to be these narrators' mothers, they continue to speak to the next generation. This confirmation also suggests that there are continuities across the generations in the political perspectives and the circumstances that gave rise to them, and that some of these theorists are themselves intergenerational bridges. Feminists of color especially have created a broad class of "intersectional," borderlands, and critical race theories that resonate with narrators' own experiences.

The narrative form has been central to creating these theories. By telling, sharing, and analyzing a multiplicity of life stories, testimonios, consciousness raisings, poetry, and fiction, feminists and ethnic-studies scholars have connected affect to intellect to create new and liberating theoretical perspectives. Both the collective narrative and the forms through which it developed were familiar to most narrators. That collective narrative and the narrative form offered models through which individuals can connect their personal experiences to the project of unthinking the world as it is, turning it upside down, and reconstituting it conceptually in radically different ways.

Activists' narratives describe the affective, emotional aspect of their liberation, and testify to the contagious power of narrative to stimulate it in others. John Delloro described the power of the testimonial form to break through his own defenses against recognizing racism, and incorporated it as the key turning point in his own rebirth as a political activist. His narrative and those of other organizers performs emotional as well as ideological work in creating counter-hegemonic political subjectivities for themselves and one another, as well as for a wider audience.

These narratives, at once deeply personal and broadly collective, share much with Morgen's foundational stories, the critical stories that social movements tell about themselves (2002). In the process of fashioning these narratives, social movements create a collective participant, a critique of the exiting state of affairs, and a vision of what could and should be. Political identities can be extremely liberating. For example, the women's movement, the black freedom movement, and gay and lesbian liberation created new social characters and scripts through public languages and discursive structures that gave millions of people the vocabulary and voice to become the narrators of their own lives, to create and share personal histories in which they analyze their current circumstances and create alternatives to it. Contemporary versions of collective, foundational stories enable this book's narrators to gain their voices.

Thus far then, I've suggested that there is a mutually reinforcing "virtuous circle" between personal realizations and a collective narrative that structures and gives narratives meaning as an alternative way to see oneself in relation to the wider society. The sense of personal liberation and new possibilities are the platform upon which narrators have created more specifically political subjectivities and political practices based upon them, to which we now turn.

CHAPTER 5

Democracy and Political Praxis

THIS CHAPTER EXAMINES THE connections between narrators' political experience and their visions of social justice and democracy. The first part revisits narrators' early political involvement and the networks they developed in a variety of campaigns and organizations during the early and mid 1990s. I argue that their early activism helped them to connect the dots between a multiplicity of issues, and to see the struggles for labor and immigrant workers' rights as part of a wider struggle for social justice.

The second and third parts of the chapter focus on the ways that narrators' participation in unions and immigrant workers' organizations built on these understandings and shaped their thinking about the kind of workers' movement they wished to build. Narrators gravitated to revitalized unions that were actively organizing workers of color and new immigrants, and to smaller immigrant workers' rights groups that were also beginning to form. These groups worked cooperatively with one another, and narrators moved among them. The second part examines the narrators' analysis of organizing as a form of democratic practice and a foundation for building democratic social movements. The third part deals with narrators' efforts to figure out the kinds of organizational structures, practices, and cultures that are needed to support a democratic social-justice movement.

ACTIVISM AND NETWORKS ACROSS ISSUES

Narrators' ideas about what's wrong with society, who has a stake in creating more democratic alternatives, and what those might look like come from two strands of their own paths to politicization. The first strand is experience with activism across issues and issue-based organizations locally. The second is activism across national borders. Together, they shape a politics that values knowledge and learning as foundations of activism and democracy.

A focus on the seven narrators who attended UCLA offers a window on the ways that the Los Angeles-based movements and networks in which they participated during their college years helped them to see connections among social issues. Workers' activism has been greatest in sectors of the labor force where Latina/o and Asian immigrants are concentrated, and organizers are mainly Latina/o and Asian-American. But working-class community-based activism has been sustained in African-American and Latina/o neighborhoods, where African-American organizers are concentrated. Narrators have retained ties with activists from their college years, both those who work on labor issues and those who now work in youth and community-based organizing efforts in Los Angeles. Their ties show that these predominantly Asian-American, Latina/o, and white narrators retain links to African-American activists, who are concentrated in organizing efforts in neighborhoods and on issues that are not workplace-focused.

The seven narrators were at UCLA in the early and mid 1990s, and graduated or left the campus between 1994 and 1996. All save one, who focused his organizing efforts in East Los Angeles community and cultural groups, moved in overlapping campus networks and knew at least one other narrator from campus activism. Five of the seven narrators were recruited directly into the union/immigrant worker part of the movement soon after they graduated or left college between 1994 and 1996.

To varying degrees, they've maintained connections with campus activists. Some of those ties now provide connections to two important community-based groups, AGENDA and the Community Coalition, which focus on neighborhood-based organizing in black and Latina/o communities, and youth organizing projects mainly in Latina/o communities. For example, John Delloro knows two AGENDA organizers from student days when they were all involved in Students First, the multiracial coalition of progressive students who captured student government and helped lead demonstrations against the University of

California's anti-affirmative action policies and Proposition 209. Kimi Lee, who heads the Garment Worker Center, was in student government at the University of California, San Diego in those years. But UCLA narrators know her from her role as statewide coordinator of the UC Student Association, where she spent three years coordinating student support for maintaining affirmative action. In turn, Lee met Marqueece Harris-Dawson, then youth organizer for the Community Coalition, when he brought high school students to protest at the UC Regents meeting.[1]

Lee subsequently went on to organize Southern California for Youth, a coalition of groups involved in education, leadership training, organizing among high school students, the criminalization of youth of color, and the racism of the criminal justice system. That coalition includes the Community Coalition's own youth group, led by another UCLA graduate and African-American activist of those years. In turn, six staff organizers at the Community Coalition are UCLA graduates.

To return to the narrators, John Delloro and Quynh Nguyen know the Community Coalition's current youth director, Albert Ratana, from UCLA activism. While at UCLA, narrator Roxane Auer met fellow student Yuki Kidokoro through environmental-justice activism. Yuki went on to become the lead organizer for Communities for a Better Environment, an environmental-justice group in south Los Angeles County that is also part of the Southern California for Youth coalition initiated by Kimi Lee.[2] They overlap with the Youth Justice Coalition, a partnership of several groups that focus on organizing youth within the criminal justice system, and also have some ties to Californians for Justice, narrator Norma Martinez's organization, which conducts political education and organizing among high school students.[3]

Youth organizing skyrocketed in response to the anti-immigrant and racist backlash between 1994 and 1998 that took the form of voter initiatives and anti-gang crackdowns that heavily impacted teenagers of color. Measures against bilingual education, for trying youth as adults, and denying services to undocumented immigrants politicized a generation of high school students, perhaps even more than college students. Noting that most of Community Coalition's staff first became active in campaigns against these voter initiatives, Marqueece Harris-Dawson described them as "great training grounds for creating organizers." They were the stimulus that led activists like Kimi Lee and other college students to begin organizing high school students. Many of these high school activists are now taking their places among the ranks of full-time community, youth, and labor organizers. Youth-organizing programs of a number of community, environmental justice, and criminal-justice organizations are linked together in formal coalitions, not unlike those of immigrant-worker organizations. They provide opportunities for activist high-school-age youth across the city to meet one another as well as to make decisions about political campaigns they wish to undertake (Brown 1999; Hamilton 1995; E. Kaplan 2003, 2005; Refuse and Resist 2001; Seif 2004). These organizations and networks emphasize political education for youth empowerment and leadership training by organizing ongoing academies, classes, and conferences.

Immediately or within a few years of leaving college, UCLA's Quynh Nguyen, John Delloro, and Roxane Auer joined Joann Lo, Suyapa Portillo, Eileen Ma, and Milton Pascual in being recruited or gravitating to HERE's hotel campaign and SEIU's hospital and nursing-home campaign. Tori Kim and Liz Sunwoo began working with KIWA, Aquilina Soriano with PWC, and Javier Gonzalez with SEIU's Justice for Janitors Local 1877. They have moved around, but largely within the constellation of groups engaged in immigrant-worker organizing and education. Javier moved from AGENDA and IDEPSCA to Justice for Janitors. Roxane and Stephanie Monroe gravitated toward the HERE-supported living-wage organizing at LAANE/SMART, and Roxane later joined the research department at HERE Local 11. Joann moved to the Garment Worker Center, and then to ENLACE, a training and education organization for organizations of low-wage workers. John remained with SEIU, but has changed locals; he still sits on the board of the PWC.

Although narrators developed their densest ties to other union and immigrant-worker organizers once they became involved full-time (chapter 2), they continued wider engagement to varying degrees. A number of narrators reported expanding their own political practice by participating in several forms of activism—besides their "day job." For example, Michelle Mascarenhas, the narrator most fully involved in activism outside workplaces, reflected:

One of the ways that I think I have grown most as an activist is working on projects outside of my work, like outside of my paid work, things like Common Threads, or with [a friend whose day job was with a union] on the board of the Venice co-op, and it wasn't so much the project in and of itself, but it was the processing of what we learned from that about organizations or about cooperation or about alternative businesses in a capitalist economy. The lessons that you learn and sharing that with someone else and working through those sorts of ideas brings you a common set of experiences that you can relate on and bring to your next challenge or your way of thinking about the alternatives.

Being able to rotate her angle of vision in the course of her political practice was important to Michelle's ability to develop politically. It also gave her a political network that has breadth as regards issues and activist communities.

Several other narrators and activists I interviewed referred to a quasi-organized social group of young organizers that cuts across issue domains. Formal and informal parties, friendships, and a variety of social and quasi-social events brought together people in labor, anti-globalization, immigrant rights, youth, criminal justice, and environmental justice activism. Narrators valued the network, but sometimes felt it was hard to keep up with all the meetings and sociopolitical events. But some degree of personal ties remained very important structures of narrators' political landscapes and understandings about the economic and ethnoracial interconnections among issues.

This rich fund of experience with intergroup cooperation, circulating though groups and organizations and building and maintaining political friendship networks, has generated narrators' own political knowledge and their recognition that this sort of knowledge is important for developing political agency and leadership in others.

Cross-Border Connections

Narrators attribute a great deal of their knowledge to political practice and personal experience going back to childhood that cross national and social borders. For several, their political identities and issues are transnational. Aquilina and Tori were among the narrators who traveled to their parents' home countries seeking cultural and political connections. They linked struggles in the Philippines and Korea, respectively, to those in the United States to shape their understanding of the big picture as a transnational or global one. Tori explained her organizing in the United States as part of a much broader activist social movement that for her exists beyond borders; and she sees the Korean labor movement as a model for her work in the United States: "[In Korea] there's a very strong labor movement . . . just hearing about these very intense fights and what happened was inspiring, and it kind of gave me a sense of rootedness, even though not necessarily to make a contribution there to Korean society. But feeling the connection to that kind of activism I think helped me here. I think back to that a lot when I do my work here."

Her work in Korea made it clear to Tori that she was culturally Korean-American, and not Korean. The connections to Korea that she returned with was of belonging to a transnational movement that joined her organizing in the United States to that of Korean workers in Korea, and connected her to political and cultural repertoires of resistance strategies (see also Park 1998).

Aquilina Soriano is directly influenced by the transnational nature of the Philippine community in Los Angeles, particularly as it applied to the Peoples' Movement at the end of the Marcos regime. During this period, thousands of Southern California Filipinos traveled to and from the Philippines, and created vast networks of opposition and fundraising, much of it underground. She now works with some of those same people who have transferred their transpacific organizing identity and experiences and sense of social justice to labor organizing. Contrary to the perception that most Filipinos are legal residents, many of them are undocumented. Their undocumented status underlies their poverty and the kinds of jobs to which they have access.

They have a wealth of knowledge about organizing, especially with Filipinos, so that is what gives us direction. We are starting with people who are not recognized in our community. Some of them come over on [student visas], some come through Mexico and then cross the border. Some come through Canada. Through Guatemala. [You'd be] surprised at how many undocumented Filipinos there are. Maybe ten people in a one-bedroom apartment; they divide up a living room with curtains, that's very common. If you talk to them individually, it's like almost all of them are undocumented.

Thus, her "locality" is also transnational because the people with whom she works have formed migrant circuits that now constitute much of the Filipino community in Los Angeles and Southern California, fostering a diasporic identity and strategies among them.

Norma Martinez stressed that crossing social borders is as important as crossing national ones for creating the political practices and visions needed to build a social movement in today's world. Her organization, Californians for Justice, is not transnational, but its work crosses social borders within the United States. It has contributed to her understandings of how different axes of one's social being are connected and mutually defining within one country.

> [Our organization] has a clear mission—we are an organization that fights for gay rights, women's rights, or that are aware of the different issues. And so I thought this is the place to stay for me. I think I have been lucky in finding really good spaces because, with organizing, not everyone addresses issues of homophobia and racism. Recently I have been finding out, "Well doesn't that organization talk about it?" And it doesn't. So again I feel like I have been really lucky in finding a place where all of that gets talked about and that we don't—if a member is homophobic, we don't just say forget it, we are not going to. For example, somebody might support affirmative action but they might not support us working for an issue that fights for gays, lesbians, and bisexuals and so they have to want it all or none. I have been lucky in finding a place like that because that's what I believe in.

By virtue of direct and indirect connections to sectors of transnational migration circuits, narrators have developed understandings of the ways in which workers' struggles in the United States are deeply connected to those around the globe. While not all narrators have participated directly in political activism in other countries, all of them have been involved in activism across issues in the United States, at least while they were in school. Although Norma's organization, which focuses on political education and activism among high school youth, may well practice the broadest range of interconnections on a daily basis, most narrators stay at least somewhat connected to issues beyond labor through friendships with other activists or inter-organizational mutual support. Their activism gives them a big-picture understanding that the myriad issue movements, local and national, are all part of a bigger struggle. Narrators find that this can be empowering, understanding oneself as part of a global movement, with an extraordinary fund of experience and diversity of cultures.

As Roxane Auer said,

> I want some education on the global economy. I have done local work and I think that is a key piece to me figuring out what it is we need to do to change the world—it's funny to say that, to change the world, but it's just to figure out the global economy. I had so much fun figuring out where corporations get power from their local government, donating to build and things like that, that I think figuring it out on a national level and a global level would also give me a greater feeling of empowerment.

Political knowledge has also led her to identify capitalism as the thread that links issues and groups. But knowing that also makes for frustration with a social justice landscape organized around particular issues and constituencies. Narrators also recognize that knowing all this can be overwhelming, and that this can lead, paradoxically, to feeling disempowered. They often talked about feeling overwhelmed, as though whatever they are engaged in, they should also be fighting a million other injustices, that knowing so much led them to feeling disempowered. Roxane Auer talked about these feelings as well:

> My passion is campaigns to win, the campaigns that are anticapitalist, anti-corporate. Not just anticapitalist, anti-corporate, but actually fighting for something that is going to fundamentally change the balance of power, and I think that is why I have been attracted to the unions so much. It doesn't fill everything. That is something that I think every activist comes to have to face. You are never going to find a job that makes you feel like you're working on all of it at

once, that you're doing "the thing" that needs to be done. And maybe that's what we are missing right now . . . even if it's something outside of their work that they are involved in—political party, an organization, an anticapitalist organization.

In part, narrators felt that their political education gave them a solid foundation for understanding the connections among social movements in today's world. But the fragmented organizational nature of the movement also constrained their ability to build their political practice in ways that would enrich the connections that strengthened specific struggles for justice and fostered their visions of more fundamental social change.

WHAT DOES DEMOCRACY LOOK LIKE INTERPERSONALLY?

Like most people today, narrators do not have direct answers to this question, but they do have answers that that are implicit in their accounts and evaluations of their own political activism and the practices and organizational cultures of the groups with which they work. I will first examine their views of what democratic organizing should look like at an interpersonal level, and then look at their views—positive and negative—of organizational culture and structure. Implicit in their reflections is the belief that building interpersonal and organizational democracy are projects for now. In this respect, narrators agree that modeling the changes they wish to see is important. That is, they believe that democratic social movements should create democratic practices, cultures, and organizational forms that prefigure, or create in the present, elements of the society they envision and advocate for the future.

Organizing as Building Democratic Leaders

The double-edged nature—empowering and disempowering—of political knowledge notwithstanding, narrators were united in a very strong belief that organizing is about empowering workers, and that knowledge is an important part of that process. An APALA report of Asian-Pacific American organizers' and union officials' views explained, "Organizers organize because they want to empower workers to build a movement to change society" (Yasuda 1998).

This statement seems to be self-evident, and by the time I became immersed in interviews with narrators, it seemed obvious to me as well. However, it is worth focusing on its emphasis: that *empowered workers* will build a movement to change society. It casts organizers more as teachers and mentors than as institutional movement builders. It is a specific, though not unique, view of democratic practice and ideology.

Contrasting narrators' views with other views of democratic organizing helps to appreciate its specificity. First, it differs greatly from progressive movements that focused on mobilizing and leading masses of people in big demonstrations, what the Student Nonviolent Coordinating Committee's (SNCC) Bob Moses referred to as the mobilizing tradition along the lines of Martin Luther King's organizing, as discussed in the introduction. Those movements presumed already-knowing actors, or at least they de-emphasized building leadership on an interpersonal level in their organizational practices. Instead, the nature of these organizations' democratic mission was to bring together enough people to demonstrate the popularity and "rightness" of ideas to participants and adversaries alike, to show that a particular demand or claim was the democratic will. Many social movements, including much of union culture, especially that which constructs the job of organizers as galvanizing masses of workers, embeds ideas of democracy as a mobilization and demonstration effort. A focus on empowerment emphasizes building interpersonal relationships between activists and potential constituents.

Second, narrators' focus on outreach to potential constituents sets them apart from other social-movement versions of democracy that also emphasize democratic practice, knowledge, and leadership development at the interpersonal levels. For example both SDS chapters and early feminist consciousness-raising groups in the student and women's movements of the sixties and seventies placed great emphasis on practicing democracy and building leadership in their interpersonal relations and group processes. Francesca Polletta (2002, 1120–1148) has described SDS's implicit model of democracy as that of a group of friends, all peers. That model, and the organizational practices that stemmed from it, she argues, were created in the organization's youth, when members were homogeneous in background and experience, and were engaged in creating a new political perspective. Likewise, consciousness raising and its vision of democracy and empowerment through group process and interpersonal relations among relatively homogeneous small groups of friends (Ibid., 149–175). These models of democracy were particularly effective models for collective development of the already-converted, or at least for those consciously dissatisfied with the status quo. Narrators share elements of SDS and consciousness-raising processes, but differ in that their focus is outward, to reach new people and communities, to develop new political participants, and to create democratic practices that work in heterogeneous groups. In this respect, their closest model is SNCC in the early and mid 1960s. SNCC also saw organizers as mentors and teachers (Polletta 2002; Payne 1995). They aspire to SNCC's Bob Moses' description of Ella Baker, "What she did for us, we did for the people of Mississippi," and to Barbara Ransby's tribute to Baker, "A Freirian teacher, a Gramscian intellectual and a radical humanist" (Ransby 2003, 330, 357).

Like SNCC organizers, narrators see themselves building democratic leadership in chains of teaching and learning. Their ideas about organizing are also rooted in their own political development. They sought to provide workers with the knowledge and confidence to analyze the world from their social locations, and to create opportunities for them to experience themselves as effective actors in making things change, in much the ways they had experienced their own coming to voice and agency.

However, narrators' emphasis on personal agency, or capacity to take effective political initiatives, is also in part a consequence of their structural position in unions. Organizers and local workplace leaders bridge institutional goals and perspectives and those of potential constituents, so that their focus is necessarily on dialog, discovery, and personal change (Brodkin Sacks 1988; Robnett 1996). Their emphasis on education for political agency is also part of a much broader politics that has come to characterize independent workers' centers and working-class organizing in communities of color nationally. I will return to this point at the end of the chapter.

Narrators found the goal of building democratic leadership through teaching to be the most important and perhaps the most emotionally rewarding part of their organizing practices. Several described their organizing practices as consciously modeled on Paolo Freire's *Pedagogy of the Oppressed* (1972). They distinguish teaching, or the interpersonal aspect of organizing, from other aspects of their organizing work. "We call it solid organizing," said Aquilina Soriano, to distinguish it from other kinds of organizing: "There is also organizing, which is getting out a general message and getting out flyers and stuff like that, which is also important. But [with] the solid organizing we get people actively involved in the organization with an understanding of what is going on and becoming politically conscious."

Aquilina's "solid organizing" for Milton Pascual rests on building friendship: "That's what organizing is, having relationships with the workers, having really close relationships. There's this lady who works at CA-1, a nonunion place, and [she and] I became so close. She has three girls. She's from the same country that I'm from, El Salvador, and she asked me, my daughter's Quinceañera is coming and I would like you to be like the godfather of the cake. I feel honored by it because nobody [ever says that] unless they really appreciate you and really trust you, and when you have that, that is because you have built a great relationship with them."

Narrators likened the reciprocal aspect of friendship to that of organizing. They embraced "solid" interpersonal organizing, willingly working long hours for long periods of time because it is intrinsically rewarding and often exhilarating.

Narrators have an implicit but detailed model of this aspect of their organizing practice as democratic. In their practice, teaching brings together three processes. The first stresses knowledge building, or helping those they teach to analyze and expand their experiences, and hence knowledge base. The second, glossed as empowerment, is about helping them to apply that knowledge to political practice. The third is mentoring, where organizers build reciprocal relationships that model the kind of political leadership they seek to build in those they organize.

In addition to resonating with Freire, narrators' descriptions of political organizing resonate with their descriptions of what they learned from parents and mentors, which they in turn are passing on to those they organize. Their views of organizing as interpersonal teaching thus draw upon their parents, whose journeys across borders opened up new ways of being women and men and new possibilities for forging lives, and upon narrators' own learning from crossing social borders and political activism. In these ways teaching becomes a practice of making democratic political citizens, regardless of one's legal status.

KNOWLEDGE BUILDING. The main way narrators help those they organize build their political knowledge is by helping them reexamine and reinterpret their experience, singly and as part of a group, in much the same way they themselves became politicized. Describing how she began to organize a living-wage group, Roxane Auer emphasized her need to begin with people's understandings and experiences. Referring to organizing the Valley Jobs Coalition for LAANE (see "Union-Initiated Community Organizations" later in chapter) around a living wage, a project she shared with Quynh Nguyen, who worked with the United Food and Commercial Workers union (UFCW), she met with those she was organizing regularly just to talk about their lives, issues, and problems: "You can't bring people to do the task that you set them to. You need to discover what it is that makes their life difficult, whether or not they are single parents or going through a divorce. I want to get to know people so I can understand their talents and decide how this can be better for them, how they can grow. And that's the only way you can really get people to step forward as leaders, take them from where they are at."

Aisha Livingstone was a supervisor at a WH Smith concession at Los Angeles International Airport. When HERE and SEIU organizers for a living wage and mandatory employer contributions to health benefits for airport concession workers told her about the drive, it made obvious sense to her. In her case, as we saw in the previous chapter, the new knowledge was that an organized effort to make it happen existed.

Expanding workers' knowledge base by showing them the economic context within which they worked is another part of this process. Javier Gonzalez described this approach to knowledge building while working with the CHIRLA/IDEPSCA day-laborer organization.

Pico and Main [a casual labor market], it's like three hundred guys standing for work so that's what I would also do. I have a big picture. And so I would try to implement that in my work. And I got a lot from Anthony [Thigpen, director of AGENDA]. So I would get the day laborer and say, what kind of job do you do? and they would say, I load containers, rolls of clothing or material, and I would say, you know where the containers come from? and they would say no. And I would say let's go have lunch. So I would take them down to Long Beach, to the Port of L.A. and say, this shit, all of comes from who knows where—from China, from Mexico. It comes in these containers in these boats. Look how big those boats are, something like 10,000 containers on each boat and there's money here. And they are going to build this big Alameda corridor, they are going to build a big super train so it can get down to downtown L.A. in five minutes and then in downtown L.A. all these teamsters come in these trucks and put the stuff in these trucks and drive it down to the garment manufacturers or retail or wholesalers and sell it and then they are coming to pay you $4 an hour to unload it. And don't you think there's money there? This is a strong economy in terms of this industry here and yet this industry pays crap. So don't you think we could charge more? Don't you think instead of charging $4 an hour, we should be charging minimum $7? The only way we can charge the minimum $7 is if we all get together and do it together. Because if somebody charges $5, it ruins the whole thing.

EMPOWERMENT. Empowerment is about what people do with new understandings. Javier described one outcome of putting the knowledge gained into practice: "So then we start having all these meetings and we rented this big ugly vacant lot with all these trees and bushes and everything, We got like sixty guys to get off the corner on a Saturday and clean the whole thing up in one day. We thought it would take us two weeks to clean up that lot, and we did it in one day."

The ideal outcome of empowerment is that workers can organize themselves. Describing the bittersweet outcome of an organizing drive that did not emphasize empowering workers, Joann Lo welcomed the leadership that workers developed that helped her leave an unsatisfactory situation: "I eventually quit, which was a hard decision, because I loved the workers there and they were great. On the one hand, I didn't want to leave them and leave them with the union people who were going to stay. But on the other hand, I began to feel that they were much stronger. They were already beginning to learn to organize themselves and speaking up more. They were having their own meetings, and so in a way I felt like my job was done and I needed to move on."

When I interviewed them, both Douglas Marmol and Aisha Livingstone were workers who had recently become organizers themselves. Their perspectives highlight the kinds of empowerment narrators seek to facilitate. Douglas is a member of HERE and has taken several leaves from his job to work as an organizer for his union as a result of an innovative clause negotiated into the contract. The joint SEIU-HERE-LAANE effort to gain a living wage for airport workers was Aisha Livingstone's first contact with political activism, for which her employer, WH Smith, soon fired her. She then became an organizer with the campaign.

Douglas describes his political practice as replicating his own path to politicization: "I can organize them right now by visiting them; it's more effective because we are organizing and they see me and they follow me, and all that, but I need to prepare them for that one day I'm not going to be there. And they need to stand up for themselves when I'm not there, so that's my plan."

Aisha focused on unpacking the explosion of energy and sense of possibility that the word "empowerment" contains when she described the center of her organizing passion.

> It was rewarding because I was able to go house to house and sit down and talk to those people and get them to see, get them to really see what was being done to them, that their rights had just been stripped away from them. . . . Reward came when I was able to totally get someone to say, okay you're absolutely right. And I'm all for it, I will go—you tell me what I should do and I will follow. And that was a great reward. When I'm around people, that gets my adrenaline going, so my mind says, what can I do next to help you because, if I'm helping you, I'm helping myself.

Aisha and Douglas became worker-organizers because the changes in people they helped to bring about also gave them an exhilarating sense of their own agency. This was the part of organizing that moved them most strongly.

MENTORING. Aisha's and Douglas's analyses get at two key elements of mentoring—reciprocity and modeling democratic political practice—that are important to narrators' understandings. Eileen Ma described the element of reciprocity in a mentoring relationship as regards knowledge and practice. Organizers may have knowledge and interpretations that those they organize do not, but mentoring demands their openness to that of others: "Several years ago I read Paolo Freire, and I really believe that you need to come with some humility to whatever organizing work that you do. You can't feel like you have all the answers. So you have to come to it knowing that you're no better than anyone else; you're going to help try to figure stuff out, and at some point if someone has a better idea or a better way of doing things, you have to be ready to relinquish your position."

Mentoring also embeds the idea of modeling democracy, and training others that this is what organizing practice looks like, passing it on as chains of teaching and learning where leaders are links in the chain. As Stephanie Monroe put it, "A leader to me is someone who helps grow the movement and so it is someone who knows how to mentor people. It's someone who knows how to have other people reach their full potential, how to bring people together." Mentoring relationships represent a way of creating a model of democratic practice for the future by enacting them in the present.

Eileen Ma was perhaps the most experienced union organizer I interviewed. She became a field trainer for the AFL-CIO's Organizing Institute and a leader in APALA after graduating from Columbia University in 1993, spending four years organizing, training, and speaking one-on-one with workers and organizers across the country.

Most inspiring in this work was being in the field in so many communities and experiencing firsthand the diversity of the U.S.—from white auto and grocery workers in the Midwest, to migrant Latino and Asian farm and factory workers in the Northwest, to black poultry and meat processing-plant workers and laborers in the Southeast, to healthcare workers of all races and ethnicities in

California, Florida, and New York. This work taught me to appreciate both the differences and commonalities among these workers and communities, and confirmed that all communities have their own leaders and visions for change.

For Eileen, "the process is really important and not the end result. It's the battle, doing the work humanely and respectfully." Here, the "end result" referred to specific goals of a campaign. Like other narrators, she sees a union election, a good contract, and getting payment of back-wages as part of a very long battle for social justice. Specific victories are part of changing people as well as their circumstances. And over the long haul, there can be no social justice movement without large-scale democratic consciousness. In this respect, democratic mentoring is a simultaneously means and end to creating democratic consciousness and citizenship.

I think that it is fair to say that narrators place a great deal of emphasis on creating democratic practices and on training those they organize to exercise democratic leadership. Organizers, leaders, and activists should be mentors in the sense of modeling this kind of practice. It should build the knowledge and experience in others that allows them to become mentors and leaders in their own right.

But a number of narrators, especially women of color, were also deeply critical of union practices that de-emphasized worker ownership and leadership development in favor of short-term mobilizations for specific goals. Reflecting back in 2006 on the Catholic Healthcare West organizing drive in which she served as a lead organizer, and on her union experience more generally, Eileen wrote that while she is "proud of the organizing work accomplished among healthcare workers in south L.A., this experience was a painful reminder that the internal conflicts that had marked many of the other campaigns I had already experienced in the AFL-CIO and many unions— including questions of worker ownership, leadership development and transfer, democratic practice, racism and sexism—were not an aberration."

Like Joann and others, Eileen's experience led her to believe that worker ownership and leadership were possible, and what organizing should be about building. She was frustrated by organizational priorities on winning that made these goals take a back seat.

However, narrators recognize the limitations inherent in thinking of organizing as being only about interpersonal practices and goals. First, in the sense of offering a vision for the future, the only vision in this way of thinking is that it is a means to more democratic praxis, which is also the end or vision driving the whole endeavor. It is also a non-vision of what democracy might look as socially institutionalized, and begs the question of how to think about decision-making as a process undertaken by groups and organizations. That is, it begs the question of organizing what? And toward what end?

When I interviewed her, Eileen Ma was working at UCLA's Labor Center as a reflective break from labor organizing. She credited the critical angle of vision that her experience gave her, but also confronted the limitations built into labor union goals.

> I think there's some interest in organizing immigrant workers, there really is, about getting as many people as possible to attain this middle-class dream. And I think that's fine; people should be comfortable, and most of the workers want that. But there's something that is more deeply corrupt about the system than just the fact that people aren't paid enough or aren't able to buy the things that they want. In a lot of ways—I mean as a whole reordering of priorities on how we live our lives and what we think we need and what we think sort of a decent life is. And at this point for most people it is making as much money as possible, saving as much as possible for their kids, and having a comfortable lifestyle. And I think that there should be some value placed there, or some equality because it just doesn't make sense to me that the world was meant to be great for 30 percent of the people or less, and cruddy for the rest of it.

Narrators are aware of these limitations, and equally aware of the importance of ongoing institutions to social movements. In particular, they stressed the institutional contributions to social movement culture, structures, and repertoires of political practice, and their continuity.

WHAT DOES DEMOCRACY LOOK LIKE IN ORGANIZATIONAL PRACTICE AND CULTURE?

Narrators are engaged in building democratic citizenship in the different kinds of organizations—labor unions and smaller immigrant-worker centers—that make up the field of labor and immigrant-worker organizing. Unions are relatively large and hierarchical. Despite new leadership, they are part of a labor heritage with its own culture and repertoire of strategies and tactics. The new immigrant-worker organizations and centers are small, with young staff, minimally hierarchical, and in the process of inventing repertoires and cultures. These groups built informal and formal coalitions among themselves and with unions. Union locals tended to be independent of one another, and worked more often in parallel than collaboratively.

Among these organizations, intergroup relations were a mix of coalition, complementarity, and conflict. Union recruiting brought activists of color from across the country to Los Angeles; union jobs sustained them and supported directly and indirectly networks among activists of color. Young immigrant-worker organizations attracted new activists, politicized new constituencies, and expanded repertoires of worker activism. Likewise, unions supported new takes on old issues, most notably city- and county-based living-wage legislation, that brought a variety of immigrant worker and community groups together in coalitions.

The arena of labor and immigrant workers' rights organizing in Los Angeles during the 1990s involved a great deal of formal and informal coalition work. It also involved a great deal of inter-organizational mobility. As they moved among immigrant worker organizations and unions, narrators created new strategic and tactical organizing repertoires, and also a consistent set of critiques of union practice.

Narrators' critiques of union practices and their efforts to build new and more democratic practices address in different ways an important and perennial social-movement problem: how to transform democratic interpersonal and organizing practice into organizational culture, structure, and practice. Narrators' critiques stem from their political belief that, to paraphrase Kathleen Yasuda (1998), it takes empowered workers to build a movement to change society, and that organizing is about helping to develop such workers. Narrators' organizing practice seeks to embody the interpersonal democracy it preaches. Narrators also addressed the organizational aspects of institutionalizing interpersonal democratic practice by building new workers' groups with minimal divisions of work and authority, and struggling to find appropriate ways to democratize practices, structures, and cultures in unions, which necessarily have much greater divisions of labor and authority.

Institutionalizing Democracy in Immigrant Worker Organizations

Immigrant worker organizations are responses to society-wide racializing practices that constrict the lives and priorities of new immigrant workers, and call for new kinds of outreach and ethnically based organizing and coalition. Thus when narrators discussed the organizational landscape of worker organizing, immigrant workers' groups took on a special significance that stemmed from their innovative strategies and democratic practices more than from their present size or power.

Unlike unions, newer immigrant worker and working-class community organizations like CHIRLA, KIWA, PWC, and the Food Security Project do not have a traditional repertoire of organizational forms that they can draw upon for building collective political agency. Rather, they have been engaged in inventing new traditions. For the most part, these mix organizing around issues and helping people solve concrete problems, legal or otherwise. We can think of them as embracing a range of strategies from social-service delivery to building autonomous political organizations. At the social-service pole, these organizations invent new forms of outreach, information and service provision like legal clinics, English classes, and women's groups. At the pole of forming new organizations, recognizing that unions are not always the most appropriate way for workers in every situation to organize, these groups invent new forms of worker and working-class organizations. For example, CHIRLA has organized a day-laborers association, as Javier Gonzalez described earlier, and a domestic workers' cooperative. (On CHIRLA's Domesticas cooperative, see Hondagneu-Sotelo 2001, Hondagneu-Sotelo 1994, and Hondagneu-Sotelo and Riegos 1997.) And the Garment Worker Center organizes women's groups for the development of leadership among women (Louie 2001).

Tori Kim, KIWA staff attorney, emphasized that the key was to develop an organizational form with some flexibility: "I think it's important that the immigrant-based worker organizations that are now beginning to blossom in a lot of different cities are outside the union structure, very community based. [It's important to] come from an organization that can really reach out to these immigrant communities in an appropriate fashion, and to organize and empower workers to improve their conditions and their economic status."

KIWA has focused simultaneously on helping and organizing Latino and Korean restaurant workers in Korean-owned restaurants in Koreatown. Liz Sunwoo, KIWA community organizer, talked about involving Korean immigrants trying to get back-wages from a restaurant owner.

> We have been negotiating with the owner for such a long time. We had a lawsuit with the owner, had a claim with the Department of Labor, but all of a sudden he filed bankruptcy. It's sad because this happens all the time. None of them [the workers] were activists. It's hard because we're trying to show Koreans [they can be] empowered, it's okay to come forward and it's okay to fight for your rights. A lot of them were so bitter. They hate America and that feeling that they came to America [to have better lives]. It's such a sense of fear for them to come forward.

However, when KIWA won a legal settlement against another restaurant owner, Tori Kim stressed further steps that KIWA planned to make the victory an educational springboard for what could be possible.

> I mean we were doing [the legal case] together, so that was good because it became a multicultural legal team to make sure that it did not turn into a racial conflict, which it often does in L.A. So I think KIWA, being involved in that way, was good to say we are part of the Korean community and we are supportive because this is a worker issue, it's a labor issue in our community even though these are Latino workers with a Korean employer, but we still see it as the question is the justice for the workers. [The workers] are happy with [the settlement]. What is good about this case, in addition to money, is that they also agreed to a variety of future reforms, so we are going to be monitoring the restaurants by reviewing time cards and interviewing workers for the next three years, and we are going to do a labor seminar for the workers, for the current employees. They are going to put together a personnel policy to set out clear guidelines.

Tori described the willingness to be flexible that allowed KIWA to move from offering assistance to helping members build a restaurant workers' organization.

> We started this campaign about three years ago. When we first started, we had a walk-in clinic for the workers who came in with a variety of problems going on in their workplace. Through that there was definitely a trend—most of our cases were coming in through the restaurants in the area. So we decided we wanted to do more than just helping individuals getting back-wages. So we have done a lot of public education, we have picked fights with some employers, and through that we also generated a lot of publicity, and then recently we just launched our Restaurant Workers Association; and that is going to be a separate group run by restaurant workers. They're recruiting members for that.

In organizing a restaurant-worker association, which is in the process of becoming self-governing, KIWA seems to be moving in a direction similar to CHIRLA.

PWC, a newer organization, is still seeking a form and base. They are working with Filipinos in specific apartment buildings around amnesty and immigration issues. Aquilina Soriano describes the process of simultaneously listening to people's priorities and seeking to facilitate their move to being able and willing to act on their own behalf. Her description captures the making-it-up-as-we-go-along quality expressed by others.

> So now what we have done is started a food distribution at different apartment buildings. It is hard for us to start organizing an industry, so we have gone to the apartment buildings, where we are now working ten, fifteen different apartment buildings. We do food distribution there and that is how we build our relationship. We talk to the managers and then we talk to a couple of the people, they said that they are able to get other people to come out. We have done it for over a year now, so we have established a relationship and we are consistently there. Then through them we find different people have different [problems], so we handle individual cases and help out

however we can help out. One person who is working as a security guard at Armand Hammer [Museum], was denied his pension; we were able to get him his pension.

Aquilina's vision for an organizational structure of PWC is as a membership-based organization, which at once funds and creates an invested constituency, along the lines of a mutual assistance organization.[4] "In the future as we go, we'll build basic membership to be based on, like a thousand people giving $20, better than just getting one grant. That's a long-term plan." In this respect, the PWC would depart from the other immigrant-worker organizations, which are made up of a small paid staff who work to organize constituents into several of their own membership associations, where they determine their own programs.

However, what all these organizations share is a mission of developing workers' sense of their own rights and abilities to get them, and facilitating collective forms of political agency by fostering appropriate organizational forms, autonomy, and networking with parent organizations and other organizations.

ONGOING COALITIONS. Narrators and other organizers in immigrant-worker organizations have taken the lead in creating new, specific-issue coalitions across ethnicities that include their own organizations and create links to a much wider range of groups. Thus, the Coalition of Immigrant Worker Advocates joins KIWA, CHIRLA, Sweatshop Watch, and the Maintenance Cooperation Trust Fund (MCTF), which comes out of SEIU's Justice for Janitors, around issues of fair treatment for immigrant workers. The Multi-ethnic Immigrant Worker Organizing Network (MIWON) includes KIWA, PWC, GWC, CHIRLA, and immigrant workers in the groups they've organized—Filipino workers, garment workers, restaurant workers, and the day laborers and domestic workers associations. MIWON's focus is legalization for undocumented workers and developing leadership and power in Los Angeles's immigrant communities.

Michelle Mascarenhas emphasized another dimension to building collective political initiative through organization building. She works to create groups and institutions in working-class communities where people can experience practices and ideals that are positive alternatives to the ways things are usually done. Acknowledging that fighting injustice is worthy political work, she nevertheless finds that building organizations that enact democratic alternatives to the status quo are personally more satisfying for her.

> Part of what we are trying to do is build models or have programs in place. I was thinking about what are we going do when the revolution comes? So we go up against capitalism or we go up against the corporations and we fight them and we win. What do we do with that? So many of my friends that work for labor unions or work on economic-development issues or economic-justice issues in the city can't talk about environmental issues at their workplace or with their coworkers or can't talk about community development. I think what we are trying to do is be more holistic in what we talk about and what we do.
>
> So in a program like the salad bar [in school cafeterias] we talk about creating work in cafeterias near where people live, that are unionized jobs. It's not the greatest thing in the world, but it's people engaging in their communities. In Santa Monica we encourage them to hire parents, so there are moms back in the cafeteria or dads even, observing what their kids are eating, having an influence on that. It's trying to think how you get people to engage at all different levels and work on all these different issues at the same time.

Michelle's statement unpacks several strands of narrators' ideas about building democratic political and cultural citizenship. They include experiencing collective effectiveness against opposition, but also include building a sense of entitlement to and responsibility for setting a collective agenda of issues, and for inventing better alternatives to the status quo, things that other narrators also wish for.

In sum, immigrant workers' groups represent one set of solutions to the problem of how to institutionalize democratic organizing practices. Their solutions focus on organizing within and across immigrant working-class communities, developing innovative strategic repertoires, and building new forms of organization. The latter emphasize creating relatively small, non-hierarchical organizations that can practice collective decision-making, minimal division of labor, and hence experience with developing multiple skills and the perspectives that come from varied experience. That solution solves the problem of size by supporting the birth of new organizations, also with relatively flat organizational structures that are tied together by a larger structure of coalition and mutual institutional support among these groups.

DEMOCRATIZING UNION PRACTICE AND CULTURE. One size does not fit all. Unions, with their complex hierarchies, relative financial stability, and funds of historical experience are crucial to this landscape of worker organizing. None are more important than unions and locals that are struggling to revitalize organizing and retool unions to be institutions that reflect the needs, priorities, and hopes of the working class. That is why narrators gravitated to them in the first place. Their critiques come from recognition that hierarchy and division of labor have their place and are necessary correlates of unions' contributions to a workers' movement. The challenge is to find ways to create democratic, empowering practices and cultures within union organizational structures.

Reflecting across their experiences in hierarchical organizations and small groups—from campus days and from organizing practice—narrators construct an argument that organizations should contain democratic social spaces, that is, specific social contexts governed by cultural practices that nurture personal capacities for agency and leadership development among those they organize and their own staff. Narrators' critiques also come from rotating their angle of vision from the way they experience their own work as organizers to the way they see their organizations' treatment of the workers they seek to organize.

Their criticisms focused on unions' practices that undercut narrators' understandings of organizing as about teaching workers to become democratic activists and leaders, and their goal of a labor movement that would be led by women and men of color, and shaped by their priorities and perspectives. This argument took the form of two intertwined critiques. The first was about the ways that unions' organizing practices did and did not embody a view of workers as potentially empowered leaders. The other was about practices that conveyed a view of leadership and empowerment (to workers and union staff) as some mix of white and male. Narrators' criticisms are important not only for pointing to problem areas, but also for insights they contain about what more democratic practices and worker empowerment could look like. Because the most sustained critiques came from women of color among the narrators, they also illuminate ideas and insights their experiences contribute to the wider workers' movement.

Democratic Spaces. From the immigrant worker groups, where it seemed to emerge naturally from a fairly nonhierarchical organizational structure, narrators brought a sense of what democratic organizational space could look like. A collegial model of equality that combined collaborative decision-making, a minimally hierarchical organization of work, and personal autonomy loomed large (Fujino and Leung 2000). Aquilina Soriano emphasized the commitment to shared mission at the base of a collegial (or here, family) model in speaking of her coworkers at the Pilipino Workers' Center: "A lot of people that I work with closely I feel like they are my family too. Because we do so much and we go through so much struggle together. Although I don't think you have to feel like family to be able to work together. You know, but it's even more than just friends. You know it's more because you also have a vision of how you want to create change and make a difference and experience the struggling together and trying to figure things out and staying and working for something that is very strong."

Speaking of KIWA's executive director, Liz Sunwoo highlighted the relatively egalitarian flavor of work distribution and personal autonomy that such an atmosphere sustains.

It's only a title, and there's no distinction; he answers the phones sometimes even a lot, and he gets involved on the front lines. And we never have that supervisor kind of feeling. And basically anyone they hire they trust that you're working—like I said we are working for something greater. I think because it's hard to find a lot of progressives, and within Korean-Americans, it's very difficult. And so they value that general appreciation of each other for being there. And you know, it's weird, when I started working here, it's more welcoming, and they really treat you with respect even though I think Koreans, like you're supposed to treat older people with more respect, but I feel people [treat me respectfully] even though

I'm the youngest. Even with our interns [we let them know] we love you so much and we try to always talk to them about what is going on and making them feel comfortable.

Because we don't have any form of supervisor kind of structure, it's basically everyone works on their own projects and makes sure it gets accomplished. At KIWA they are really open to new ideas and that's what they want.

Narrators did not expect unions to abolish their division of labor and organizational complexity. The challenge was to figure out how to create a more collegial organizational culture that attached decision-making components to work responsibilities.

For example, in explaining what he would need to sustain himself as an activist over the long haul, Javier Gonzalez emphasized that he needed personal autonomy and flexibility in his work, but he also says that he can't do only what he likes.

I think I will do this for a long time. I don't think I will get burned out. If I get burned out, I can take three days off and rejuvenate myself. I know how to relax when I need to. People get mad at me at staff meetings [for] cracking jokes and it upsets me. Don't tell me not to joke around because that's my personality, that's how it's going to keep me active in stuff all my life. So if I'm working sixty hours a week, trying to figure that out, that's fun to me. But if I'm working sixty hours a week trying to fax the payroll—I hate that stuff—so you can pick and choose what you want to do and take your days off when you want them, not when your organization wants you to take them.

In a seeming about-face, Javier also offered a view that organizational structures and missions should be scaffolds for personal growth, rather than part of a zero-sum game. "To me activism, it means always growing as a person and always being more fruitful in your organization and doing what is necessary, and not just what you like. If you're in activism, you don't do what you like."

Narrators' wrestled with what a union organizational culture and practice should look like that supported, rather than squashed, growth and leadership development among staff and the workers they sought to organize. Their answers shared much with historically persistent critiques of the ways unions tended to treat their organizers and workers (Yasuda 1998; Mantsios 1998).

On the one hand, Quynh looked back on her first union campaign as an organizer for HERE, parachuted into a Texas decertification campaign for six months. Quynh felt the euphoria and intense community with the workers that marked a total work and life fusion: "I was in the middle of Texas, no family, no support group. The workers and organizers became my best friends and support group and there was a lot of bonding and bingo going on." But the flip side of total immersion and complete independence was a disconnect from her own life and needs beyond the campaign.

> Though I was married when I started organizing, I only eventually recognized the work that it takes to maintain my family. I wouldn't say by any means that I have learned to balance. It is a constant struggle. When I first started shifting from organizing is everything to organizing is not everything, the justification was that I needed family so I could be happy so I could continue organizing. Now it's I need all of it for a full life and to function either at work or in my family. Work and family are really the only two realms because, if you're going to work on both that hard, then things like friendships and other interests, even if they are political activities, really fall by the wayside . . . especially now that I have kids of my own. On the other hand, having children of my own really makes my work come full circle. I understand so much more what is at stake for workers like my parents, why they fight and the tremendous risks they're taking.

In "organizing is everything" models, organizers are instruments rather than among those whole people the movement serves. Such practices implicitly accept mainstream notions that to be part of a collective project necessarily requires sacrifice of individuality, wholeness, and autonomy as the only way to further collective or organizational goals.

Roxane Auer argued that there are ways for political organizations to treat organizers as whole people, agents with complex lives, without diminishing their commitment to the organizational mission. The collegial model she experienced at LAANE allowed her flexibility in controlling her work time, and autonomy in this arena represented delegating responsibility and concomitant authority, which in turn showed the trust that was a foundation of an organizational culture built on respectful relationships: " 'I trust that you will get the work done.' This is the kind of employer I want to work for. She said, you can have any time off you want. I know that you're going to win and do the best job you can on this campaign, and I know you wouldn't take the time when you need to be at work. If somebody gives me that much respect and freedom, there's no way I'm going to damage that relationship by taking time off when I'm supposed to be at a hearing speaking."

At the base of collegial reciprocity is recognition that workers (including staff) are more than instruments of organizations—or employers. Social-justice organizations need organizational practices and cultures that reflect their mission, that practice the social justice they seek. By finding ways to treat staff and those they organize in ways that scaffold their well-being *and* organizational goals, narrators are pushing for prefigurative visions of democracy and social justice at the organizational level. Here, Roxane makes that argument by unpacking organizational practices and cultures that treat staff as instruments instead of people who serve and are simultaneously served by the social-justice struggle.

> There is some education that needs to go on within the progressive community. I don't think education is necessarily the right word, but a shift in attitude. We have a problem with people keeping their lives healthy, exercise, mental health, relationship health, health in a lot of ways. I don't think it's healthy to obsess over your job. People are working long hours for low pay and need mental-health time if you're going to keep a staff for a long term and institute a little bit more of a policy of relaxing on those issues and actually speaking about them, like having a staff meeting and devoting a half hour to people talking about, okay, is anyone having a hard time in their lives because of the work hours and can we talk about it, have it out there. People talk about it among themselves in hushed whispers

sometimes, and any time you have that, it's a problem. I have seen a number of good organizers leave.

Her thoughts are in line with historically persistent critiques of the ways unions have treated their staff, and thus reflect ideas deeply embedded in union culture (Yasuda 1998; Mantsios 1998).

In line with this history, narrators were clear that treatment of staff and treatment of those they organize are deeply connected. For unions to be able to get employers to respect their workers, they need a culture that models respectful organizational relations, and this should begin at home. They pointed to the contradiction of unions fighting for decent hours, vacations, and respect for workers but not according them to their own staff. Quynh Nguyen summarized a widespread perception: "We had an entire APALA conference about this—how to retain organizers conference—dozens and dozens of organizers talking about that for three days. It was suggested by a few disgruntled organizers, young activists like myself. Some of the highlights that I remember were democracy and voice. That is the most common complaint of people who leave at this age, feeling like they have no control over their lives and their work, while ironically we are theoretically organizing for workers to have more control over their life and work."

Eileen Ma pushed this analysis a step forward when she asked, ought not organizers and unions demand the same treatment for those they organize as they wish for themselves? Ought not unions also to be about challenging the inhumane organization of work and jobs more broadly? "Whether it's an injection-molding plant or a poultry plant or a hog plant or whatever, people are just really sort of used as machines there and have very little opportunity to move out of that. Because, even if the idea of getting a union is basically to get more wages, it's never to say, wait, I shouldn't have to do this job at all." She sees the labor movement as needing to question more deeply the organization of work in, and values of, capitalist America as a part of its political education.

In a similar way Tori Kim argued for the importance of questioning another aspect of labor force structure, specifically ethnic job slotting and an economy with ethnic enclaves as a big part of such a structure: "When you look at Korean workers and why they continue in the substandard conditions, I think part of it is the immigrants have a hard time finding jobs outside like Koreatown for example. And these ethnic enclaves have to do with lack of opportunity for immigrants, non-English speaking communities, or people of color. And that whole issue has been very sidestepped in the whole affirmative-action debate."

Thus far, narrators are building a model of staff and workers who both serve their organization and have a legitimate claim on that organization to serve them in their multifaceted lives. By emphasizing the need to rethink staff jobs, and constructing work as part of life within activist organizations, they are taking an important step to envisioning what work and jobs should look like more generally in a democratic society. But as Tori Kim points out, the experiences of workers are powerfully structured by their race and ethnicity, and gender.

Gender, Race, and Democracy. Racism and racialization were what propelled most narrators to become political activists, so it is no accident that fighting racism is central to their social-justice practice. They want to organize in low-wage workforces and in communities of color because people in those places are conscious of xenophobia and racism and struggle with it on a daily basis. As Quynh Nguyen noted,

> There's also a lot of Asian-American organizers who are young people who are recruited out of ethnicity or race-specific movements, recognize that this is a large part of our political identity and a large part of our political motivation. So also what keeps us motivated and going is some connection to those communities and those workers. One of the reasons I'm at UFCW is because the industry and the union affords me the opportunity to work with Latino and Asian workers and communities at various times. I think all of us have thought the union could do more, whether it's more community service or more socially involved with or more democracy.

Just as women of color predominate in low-wage, closely supervised, and intensely driven jobs in the industries in which unions are seeking to organize, so, too, are they a large portion, often the majority, of union organizers. But women of color are underrepresented in higher positions with more authority to shape union practice.

A number of narrators argued that unexamined union cultures and practices marginalized women of color and the democratic perspectives on organizing they advocated. Roxane Auer and John Delloro both specified the sexist baggage carried by cultures of workaholism in union organizing. When organizations construct organizing as heroic immersion, and hence demanding a great deal of self and family sacrifice, they affect women and men unequally. Although organizing may encourage gender-blind workaholism, given the sexism in the wider culture, it also supports heterosexual men exploiting their women partners to do the lion's share of family work and take a back seat to their male partner's heroic career. A number of women also argued that for unions to exalt heroic self-sacrifice in organizers encourages general devaluing of serious intimate relations and the time they need. This devaluing of intimate relations may affect men less than women, so men may embrace heroic self-sacrifice more readily and be rewarded and taken more seriously within the culture of organizing.

Other narrators argued as well that having a race- and gender-conscious organizational discourse was crucial to changing practice. Reflecting critically on unions' public and internal blindness about race and gender, several narrators saw this as an inability or unwillingness to confront biases and practices that worked especially against women of color as union staff and as workers that unions sought to organize. Although Joann Lo saw some changes among organizers of her generation, she did not see them in larger institutional practices.

> In my generation [of union organizers] there are a lot more women. At 399 there are definitely more women. I think it's beginning to change, at least with the organizers—not so much above, in management positions in the union. When the new international director came in, management favored the men, and promoted this one international organizer who had about much experience as me and some other organizers. I think that is what happens. But for me, working with a lot of other women has been good and it is very nurturing, and we support each other a lot and we help each other.

Eileen Ma pointed out that such institutional blindness allows practices that carry important messages about unequal political agency by race as well, especially among women of color who predominate among organizers and in many of the workforces that activist unions seek to organize.

> It happens on two levels. One is what I have experienced personally as an organizer, where if I say something, it could be the same thing that a white male is saying but the white male is given a lot more credibility. And I feel like I have experienced the same thing with white women where they're in relative positions of power and yet they are of the status quo, or they don't really have a clear understanding of how a woman of color may see things a little differently because, either consciously or not, they don't create that space for people to either express it or challenge it. That happens on a staff level. It's frustrating for me as a young Asian woman organizer of color. Ultimately that can be limiting because my opinions are inevitably not taken as seriously. You feel it, and I definitely feel it in the labor movement. I have noticed, for some reason, men of color have an easier time tolerating it and staying in the movement. Or just as men of color, I don't know if they see less of a compromise.

Dan Clawson (2003, 55) points out that women are a quarter of all lead organizers, and in bargaining units that are heavily female, they are 42 percent of lead organizers, and that jobs that are low paid and mainly women's are the fastest growing. And the women in these jobs are predominantly women of color. Eileen Ma connected the treatment of women organizers of color to treatment of the women workers of color who predominate in tourism and health care.

> I think that people don't necessarily think seriously about what the workers think or say, or that it's important. So many of the workers are women of color; it's shameful that all these women are supposed to jump because we say jump, or that they don't have more of an opportunity to develop themselves as leaders. I think that we talk too much about leadership development and don't do anything about it; it's contradictory because the reality is that the chances of

a woman worker of color organizing into a union and then rising to the decision-making positions in the union are slim or nonexistent. White-led, dominated, I think that can't guide us in a movement. Whatever campaigns that I work on have to be really about inclusion in a real way in respecting people's differences, and especially allowing space for women of color, who I think don't really have the space for their ideas and their visions, in the organizing I see.

Narrators' critiques are not unique. They are similar to those of the largely college-recruited young organizers in Daisy Rooks's study (2004) and to many of the activists in the new workers' organizations studied by Vanessa Tait (2005), as well as those in Kathleen Yasuda's analysis (1998) of the recommendations of Asian-American organizers in APALA. Pretty much across the board, narrators who worked in unions wanted them to recruit more organizers from the workplace and to connect much more closely with immigrant working-class communities. APALA's recommendations also gave a great deal of attention to ways unions should engage systematically in building cultural citizenship among members and within working-class communities of color. These ranged from membership education and training programs, building ownership and leadership among workers in a campaign, avoiding the abrupt pulling of organizers after a campaign, and structuring organizers' work to allow them community involvement and engaging more generally in work with communities of color (Yasuda 1998).

Narrators' criticism of sexism and racism is part of a larger view that organizational leadership structures are visual representations of how far unions that seek to represent low-wage workers of color are from that goal, and from modeling the range of practices that narrators see as crucial for building an inclusive and democratic workers movement. These include: creating collegial models of work in which responsibility and authority were delegated together; a work culture that respected the work but devalued workaholism and supported multifaceted social relationships as part of constructing organizing as a long-term career that would sustain family life and friendship over the long haul; and an explicit institutional discourse and consciousness about race and gender practice.

Unions were not the only organizations whose practices narrators challenged. Suyapa Portillo detailed the struggles over sexism she and other women waged in the early years of KIWA's existence.

The women organizers at KIWA were also struggling within the organization for respect for women organizers, a safe workspace, and decision-making power. Organizational narrowness at the time and an unclear sexual harassment policy, which did not offer protection to women and interns working in the organization, led us to quit en masse in 1997. We women, who did most of the work with the bases, were not part of decision-making. KIWA suffered greatly. The resistance to organizational change led us to this action, which affected our work with the community. I am confident that the decisive moment created openness and change within the organization, which now has women organizers in decision-making positions, something that in our time did not exist. KIWA is now a more inclusive and dynamic organization, even though the history is hidden and names forgotten. My satisfaction is knowing that we struggled and respected and protected the organization at our own expense by not filing a sexual harassment suit in order to not destroy it. Growing pains within this and other organizations around Los Angeles challenged me to see the problems and discrimination women and queer organizers face in Los Angeles.

Suyapa, Eileen, Joann, and others laid out the complexity of the struggle over how shared ideals confronted real-life organizational practices. They developed their ideas about, and deep appreciation of, democracy and inclusiveness from their organizing work as women of color and queer women in less-than-perfect organizations, but organizations that were nevertheless committed at some level to much of their vision of social justice. The challenge was, and remains, how to remain connected to particular social-justice organizations and to simultaneously struggle within them for full inclusiveness and democracy.

Union-Initiated Community Organizations. Union-initiated community organizations have formed a kind of more open space within union structures that narrators have welcomed because these organizations are more amenable to creating the kinds of inclusive and democratic institutional practices they seek. Such structures also form bridges between workplace and community-based organizing. Narrators have participated in two major union-initiated coalitions, and one smaller one, initiated by Quynh and Roxane. I met Milton, Douglas, and Joann while they worked with a joint effort by HERE, LAANE, and SEIU to apply the Los Angeles County Living Wage Ordinance to workers at concessions at the Los Angeles International Airport, as well as to initiate unionization efforts. And Stephanie, Roxane, and Aisha worked together on a collaboration between HERE and LAANE/SMART to address the same combination of issues in Santa Monica. LAANE/SMART organizers also closely worked with the airport union organizers.

Finally, Roxane, working with LAANE, and Quynh, working with the United Food and Commercial Workers union, initiated a similar living wage and unionization effort by creating the Valley Jobs Coalition in Los Angeles's San Fernando Valley. Quynh elaborated on prodding her union to support this new kind of community-based organizing, a somewhat more autonomous form than mobilizing known supporters for a union demonstration.

I asked to be put on community organizing in a union that I think has traditionally done it very differently. A few weeks ago, before the big supermarket opened in the Valley, a sign of where community organizing was going, which has been going on for about two, two and a half months, was that we had a community rally in front of the store which had not opened yet. There wasn't a major push of any kind for a union turnout; we wanted [this] very much to be a community event. It was primarily some fifteen community organizations, mostly from the Valley, ranging from social-service groups to religious groups to citizens groups, senior citizens groups to neighborhood-watch type parent groups. Very early in some shallow way—not shallow because shallow would be a "you scratch my back I scratch your back" kind of mobilization, and it wasn't. It wasn't like that at all. It felt really good because it also showed the potential for me to see and for the union to see the possibilities, both in terms of political movement and in terms of the practicality of serving this particular campaign. So there is now a Valley Jobs Coalition, and it had two meetings, but it's yet to be seen how permanent and how deep it will go. But if it succeeds, it's definitely filling a much-needed niche.

In this particular case, the resulting organization drew people and organizations from a geographical area into an issue-based coalition around living-wage jobs. It was not drawn from a preexisting community so much as its goal was to create issue-based constituencies in a particular region of the city by building a group that was diverse racially and by class, and provide an organizational venue for their collective action on the issue of jobs. Ideally, Quynh and Roxane hoped to link it but not tie it to the union.

Like recruiting union staff from the ranks, community-based unionism is also part of the organizing repertoire of left-leaning unions (D. Frank 1985; Lichtenstein 2002). Roxane expressed a view widely held among narrators in advocating this kind of union involvement in communities, and openness to issues beyond their traditional concerns.

> [Good unions] are working with the community. I think they care about other issues and they are actually giving money and time and effort to campaigns that are not directly related to the union because they care. We have turned out for rent-control issues in Santa Monica because a lot of the people involved in SMART are also involved in Santa Monicans for Renters Rights. We have gotten involved with community groups in Santa Monica that work with people who need low-income housing and gotten some of our members into renting units in Santa Monica who then turned around and became members of the Santa Monicans for Renters Rights.

Just as narrators have generated their visions about what the interpersonal aspects of democratic organizing look like from their experiences in unions and new immigrant-worker organizations, so, too, have they generated their visions of institutional practice. By working comparatively across the two kinds of organizations, narrators have developed new visions of how democracy can become integral parts of very different kinds of organizational structures. Democracy is practiced as a relatively egalitarian process with minimal division of work in the small, face-to-face immigrant-worker organizations. As new constituents and constituencies are incorporated, they spin off their own ideally autonomous groups that practice democracy in similar ways. In larger, already-existing union locals with established hierarchies and complex divisions of labor, and varying degrees of hierarchical relations to their main international union, narrators urge commitment to organizing as leadership building. They wish to create democratic work spaces small enough within the organization to allow for delegation of a sphere of authority and decision-making commensurate with responsibilities. And not least, they agree that the white and male biases built into union culture work especially against women of color, but as well against men of color and white women.

CONCLUSION

I would argue that the organizing practices and structures of unions and new immigrant-worker organizations embody two different, implicit visions—and discourses—about the nature of the working class. I read the combination of narrators' critiques of unions and their descriptions of how immigrant-worker organizations function together as calling into question prevailing notions about the working class as an already existing entity. The practices and structures of immigrant-worker organizations seem to treat in practice the working class as a *potential* but not yet existing coalition of groups with overlapping, but far from identical interests. Their practices of organizing as building individuals' capacity for direct democracy and leadership are part of the longer heritage of radical democracy in American history indicated at the beginning of the chapter. But here that view of democracy is deployed toward negotiating conflict and cooperation across differences—in both interests and identities—with, ideally, negotiating more inclusive visions of working-class issues and priorities. Union structure and discourse presumes an already-existing working class with a uniform class basis for that identity and a "natural" basis for unity that rests in (even if it extends beyond) the labor "contract."

To narrators, visions of class as preexisting seems to erase the very real race, ethnic, and gender differences in the ways low-wage workers experience their lives, and consequently shape their priorities. Such erasure is counter to narrators' own experiences of the centrality of racialization—whether along lines of color or immigration status—in shaping their political identities and the way they see the world. Far from least, racialization shapes their understandings of capitalism as resting as much on race and racialized constructions of gender as it does on exploitation of wage laborers. Presuming class as a unity then forecloses the organizational spaces and practices that would allow negotiating differences; and it also pauperizes the discourse through which people can formulate them.

In the organizational forms that narrators have helped to create, and in their participating in a landscape composed of progressive unions seeking to change the practices, priorities, and cultures of organized labor, narrators are part of a wider social movement led by people of color and new immigrants. Vanessa Tait (2005) has argued persuasively that this new wave of what she calls poor workers' unions has been developing since the late 1970s. She traces the beginnings of independent immigrant-worker organizations back to the Chinese Staff and Workers' Association (CSWA), organized by waiters in New York's Chinatown in 1978 after restaurant unions refused assistance (Kwong 1987; Tait 2005, 165–176).

By the 1990s, when narrators were becoming part of the Los Angeles activist landscape, independent workers' centers had developed across the spectrum of immigrant, Latina/o, and African-American communities. Some are organizations of women workers, especially among garment workers (Louie 2001), and they are in the forefront of what feminist movements look like today. According to Tait (2005, 166), there are more than a hundred worker centers in cities and among agricultural workers in addition to CSWA.

> The Latino Workers Center, Awaaz and Sakhi for South Asian Women, and the New York Taxi Workers Alliance, all in New York City; La Mujer Obrera in El Paso, Texas; Asian Immigrant Women's Advocates in Oakland; Korean Immigrant Workers Alliance in Los Angeles; and the Miami Workers' Center in Florida. Others, such as the Worker Organizing Committee in Portland, join immigrant and native workers under one umbrella. A few serve mostly nonimmigrant workers, such as North Carolina's Black Workers for Justice and Virginia's Appalachian Women Empowered.

Although they have roots in antiracist movements as far back as the 1940s and 1960s, these organizations represent something qualitatively new and politically very significant. Independent worker centers, which include Los Angeles's KIWA, PWC, and the Garment Worker Center, are an important part of this new national wave of grassroots politics within the working class. These organizations have sustained relationships of cooperation and struggle with labor unions. On their own and joining with progressive forces in unions, they have put some movement back into the union movement. But they have also struggled against entrenched legacies of conservative union oligarchies, sexism, and racism to build more democracy and bottom-up organizing into unions, as well as to expand labor's repertoire of issues and strategies. Together these new worker organizations and more activist and community-based unions form an arena of organizing that came into its own during the 1990s. In this arena, a much-needed discussion is beginning about the nature of working low-income America in today's global political economy—whether it is a pre-existing unity or a potential coalition. That discussion is also about the scope and priorities of a social movement that seeks to represent its needs.

Conclusion

I'VE ARGUED IN THIS BOOK that it is the birth of individual and collective political identities that give social movements their palpable energy, excitement, and sense of possibility, and that these identities shape the politics of the movement and its particular vision of democracy. I sought to make explicit three aspects of that process. First was the emotional structure of personal transformation and the epiphanies that changed narrators' lives. Second, I suggested that those epiphanies have the meanings they do because they fit into and help build a larger, collective narrative that creates a specific kind of working-class social actor or political identity for which this movement speaks. Third, this collective social actor has its own kind of democratic political ideals and practices that flow from the ethnic, racial, gendered, and class conditions of its life.

By way of conclusion I want to take up two questions, about identities and democracy, that these narratives raise. I believe these questions are relevant to today's political climate. The first question is about the ideological work that the narratives perform in shaping a social movement. What kinds of counter-hegemonic social selves do they create, and how do they help us to think about building a movement that deals with multiple forms of marginalization? Second, where do narrators fit into the heritage of democratic social movements? And what can we learn from them about the historical fragility and difficulties of sustaining such movements?

IDEOLOGICAL WORK OF
POLITICAL IDENTITIES

To ask how political identities perform ideological work is to ask how a particular portrayal of a social self offers models, values, and discourses that differ from the prevailing, or hegemonic, portrayals of those social selves. The idea of ideological work comes from Antonio Gramsci's theories about ideological struggle (Sassoon 1980; Gramsci 1997 [1971]). Gramsci, like Machiavelli, noted that rulers cannot stay in power by force alone; they must also rule ideologically, shape the ways the majority of people think, or, as Stuart Hall famously put it, their ideology must be everyday common sense (Hall 1988, 1996). The identities that social movements present to the public are strategically chosen and tend to be homogeneous. As Laura Pulido (1998) and Lynn Stephen (1997, 2005), among others, have argued, these identities are designed to show why the movement's demands are moral and natural, the right thing to do for those the movement represents. Activists hope that the public identity and its embedded analyses will resonate with and come to be owned by masses of people, specifically those who are the potential constituents in whose name a social movement acts. Rulers and revolutionaries struggle to convince masses of people to see themselves and their place in the world as these leaders do because these views embed very different commonsense views of the people's allegiances, rights, and interests.

Counter-Hegemonies

I have argued that these narratives have done this ideological work. That is, they created a public, counter-hegemonic political identity of a (variously) racialized immigrant working-class culture (chapter 3). Thirteen of sixteen narrators are children of immigrants, and nine are women. Their narratives create a collective and public working-class political subjectivity from these vantage points. Thus, what workers and working-class issues look like to the narrators are shaped by the experiences of working-class people who are of color, immigrants, and women. The content and interpretations in those identities challenge and offer alternatives to mainstream ideology about the nature of immigrant cultures, aspirations for assimilation, and visions of success. The identities' embedded politics affirm the value of one's own culture and reinterpret its content to emphasize hard work as a basis of cultural entitlement, and cooperation as a mode for a culturally worthwhile life.

Narrators' construction of an immigrant working-class constituent goes beyond challenging mainstream ideology and also takes on union ideology about working classness. These narratives put race and ethnicity in the center of their political identities. Narrators emphasized the ethnic and racial division of work, and differences in social rights and entitlements based on race and ethnicity. They showed how these differences shaped the perspectives and priorities of working-class immigrants in particular ways. By doing that, they also challenged union politics based on class as a natural identity derived from shared work interests, transcending other aspects of one's social being. They did not see class solidarity as a spontaneous identity for political activism. Their narratives offer an alternative view of those who work for wages, as less a preexisting class and more as a potential coalition of people with diverse and potentially conflicting, but also overlapping and shared, interests and experiences.

Multiple Marginalities

Coalition is at the heart of narrators' political project in other ways as well. Theories of intersectionality or multiple marginalities underlie the task narrators set for themselves in building social-justice campaigns and organizations. These theories rest on the idea that social personhood has many dimensions, among which race, ethnicity, class, gender, and sexuality are particularly salient. That is because these dimensions are socially structured bases for according very different degrees of social entitlements and privileges. Thus, any individual's social personhood is made up of a mix of socially entitled and socially subordinated statuses. Social movements and politics created by what I have been calling the nineties cohort deal with, or try to, all forms of socially structured marginalization and subordination.

This cohort differs from earlier social-movement generations in insisting that people cannot unite or form coalitions against one form of subordination, like class, without also combating other forms of inequality. The particularly difficult challenge is to figure out how to create a movement or organization made up of people who themselves embody this necessarily complex mix of entitled and marginalized statuses. How does an organization handle the inevitable mix of perspectives that come from class, race, gender, and sexuality privileges—and marginalizations along those same axes of social being?

And most important, what insights do the perspectives of different marginalities and privileges contribute to thinking more inclusively? The public, strategic, and counter-hegemonic political identity of the labor movement in Los Angeles is of immigrant men and women workers. In this book, it has a kind of hegemonic counter-hegemony. But it has been created and supported by political activists who depart in multiple ways from it. To get at the insights that come from perspectives that depart from the main story line, I want to examine the differences in the narratives of organizers recruited from the workplace against those recruited from college, the narratives of white women against those of organizers of color, narratives of women of color against narratives of men of color, and those of gay and lesbian narrators against heterosexual ones. Doing this helps clarify the very real challenges involved in dealing with multiple marginalities, or multiple kinds of subordination, in practice.

The narratives of Aisha Livingstone and Douglas Marmol, both recruited to organizing from low-wage jobs, depart in significant ways from the dominant narrative thread. We have seen that they did not explain their involvement as the result of a journey to awareness of exploitation and racialization. That consciousness was self-evident. The other striking departure was Douglas's discourse of a working class as naturally united or uniteable across race and ethnicity, and the silence about race and ethnicity in Aisha's narrative. In contrast to college-recruited narrators, they articulate the traditional union discourse of class unity, and take as common sense that their corporate employers treat them unfairly.

Nevertheless, these two narratives contain their own energizing epiphanies, but they are more about finding a place that allows them to make a difference in the world by developing and expressing their true selves. The narratives share epiphanies with those of immigrant women garment workers in Miriam Ching Yoon Louie's Sweatshop Warriors (2001). Louie describes their transformation in identities from sweatshop workers to sweatshop warriors. The issue was never about justice (they knew the system was unjust), but about their own power to change it. And Louie argues that their presentation of this identity is now part of a collectively owned identity that embodies its own social movement repertoire about how, for what, and why immigrant workers should become involved in and own this struggle: "The women who weather the transformation from sweatshop industry workers to sweatshop warriors could be designated the Living Cultural Treasures of our communities, and their campaigns and creations, Intangible Cultural Assets. In fighting to maintain their sense of dignity and self worth, they are learning and teaching the fine art of how the people can win justice and release their pent-up human suffering and potential" (Louie 2001, 247).

Aisha's and Douglas's narratives illuminate another aspect of ideological work that the narratives of college-recruited narrators who are children of immigrants perform, namely that they are explanations of a road not taken. By attention to the multiple forms of racial, ethnic, and economic barriers they encounter in mainstream environments, these narrators explain why they have chosen to identify with and work for working-class co-ethnics rather than to become upwardly mobile in the mainstream. These narratives speak about potential privileges and explain why they rejected them.

It is important to emphasize that I am not saying that workers see class while college-recruited activists emphasize ethnic and racial oppression. There is a great deal of evidence that the immigrant workers who are in the forefront of labor organizing are quite aware of the interaction of both. The large numbers of immigrant-worker organizations that have sprung into being since the late 1980s, and their anti-xenophobic activism as well as economic-justice efforts, attest to that consciousness (Tait 2005; Louie 2001).

Narratives of Stephanie Monroe and Roxane Auer, both middle-class white women, grapple with the question of why they are in a movement for immigrant working-class people, but they do so in different ways. Stephanie offered two explanations, first of early childhood experiences with poverty and having the experience of being a racial "other," but more proximally of discomfort with middle-class models of womanhood and attraction to those she found among her working-class friends of color. Not unlike the narrators who went to college who are children of immigrants, Stephanie explained her participation around forms of mainstream oppression, in this case gender, that she experienced. Roxane's narrative focuses directly on her privilege—class and race. Although she identifies herself as feminist, she does not explain her activism as about gender. A central thread in Roxane's narrative is frustration that she has no coherent story in the sense of an explanation to herself of how she came to know that immigrant-worker activism is the path for her.

Her narrative and Stephanie's illuminate some unfinished business of understanding not only multiple marginalities, but also their counter-point, multiple privileges. The main explanatory road is to explain participation in social-movement activism as a response to experiences with marginalization or subordination. Indeed, that is at the heart of theories of intersectionality. But Roxane's narrative reminds us that socially-structured privileges are under-theorized or under-understood in a particular way. Writings on intersectionality say a great deal about ways that privilege refuses to recognize itself, to take preferential treatment as one's entitlement, and so on. But there is not a collective, socially shared narrative of why or how activists come to deal with their entitlements within social movements and explain that process to themselves and others.

Narratives of women of color argue explicitly that a combination of unexamined male and white privilege within the movement has all too often led to their being treated as second-class activists who are taken less seriously and held back from organizational leadership. In addition, these unexamined privileges have also retarded organizational commitment to the concerns and priorities of women of color.

Their narratives also raised the issue of movement constructions of womanhood. One of the ideological contributions of their narratives was to offer culturally-rooted models of womanhood that emphasized strength, a strong sense of social connection to others, social justice, and standing up against sexism at work and in personal relations. Their critiques suggest that those visions of womanhood are not universally shared, or even recognized in the movement. They highlight the unfinished business about the racialization of sexism and male privilege.

Finally, there is the relative silence on queer sexualities. Neither Eileen Ma nor Suyapa Portillo, who are out and identify as queer, nor me, who is also out as a lesbian, addressed it. In a recent exchange, Eileen Ma reflected that heterocentrism, the presumption of heterosexuality, discourages talking about one's relationships or sexuality by subtly setting a context where "it seems peripheral or like a whole other issue." Our collective silence may well be the effect of heterocentrism, but why does sexuality seem like such a separate issue?

I think that part of the answer comes from Douglas Marmol's narrative, when he constructs gay sexual identity as at once a personal and a political identity. He first became involved with the union because of the obvious importance of its economic goals. But he attributed his commitment, his ability and willingness to become a leader to his lead organizer's explicit acceptance. From the explicit message of organizational respect and support for his entitlement to respect from others, Douglas created a political practice for himself that combined union activism with a certain amount of gay activism. This suggests that part of the process of integrating multiple forms of marginality into a movement involves conceptualizing those identities in public and political ways.

Narratives highlight strands of shared identity that are ongoing and constitutive of a particular movement. Those strands do analytic work inside a movement. Each embodies or "speaks for" analytic parts of the larger political project—which is to articulate which goals speak to different constituents and why. The narratives that form the core of this book come from organizers who were college students and who are children of immigrants. They bear a doubly borderlands perspective. As organizers, they are situated between their group or institution and potential constituencies, and as children from working-class immigrant communities who went to college, they stand between the cultures of their communities and that of the mainstream. They put in the foreground the racializing assaults on their families, communities, and culture by the dominant culture. They redefine working class issues as racial, gendered, and about immigration as well as about economics. Their strand is the public face of a progressive working-class movement. Their construction of a working-class political actor does a great deal of ideological work in defining what social justice means and how to practice it. But it is also a work in progress.

These narratives are reflective analyses of a quest to find a place where the activists can exercise agency in ways that are moral and personally meaningful, and to show how the exercise of political agency constitutes a social self through meaningful life activity. Some parts of this quest and one's connection to others are clear; others are more intuited. Paying attention to the narratives that differ on particular points from the book's main narrative and paying attention to the differences and silences across the narratives let us see the gaps and the very real challenges involved in putting multiple marginalities, or multiple kinds of subordination, at the center of politics.

THE FOUNDATIONS OF DEMOCRATIC SOCIAL MOVEMENTS

Narrators' insistence on bottom-up organizing, democratic organizational practice, deep organizing, community-labor coalitions, and much greater attentiveness to issues of race, ethnicity, and gender are in accord with what scholars and activists seeking to revitalize the labor movement advocate as necessary and effective (Bronfenbrenner and Juravich 1998; Bronfenbrenner et al. 1998a, 1998b; Bronfenbrenner and Hickey 2003; Clawson 2003; Milkman and Voss 2004; Mantsios 1998; Yasuda 1998).

But narrators also share ideas about democracy with a longer and broader historical tradition of democratically based political activism that has been a current in a variety of social movements in the United States. This tradition hasn't gotten the attention it deserves in part because we tend to study movements by issue, rather than to compare the ideas and practices of democracy across social movements. I would like first to show that narrators' ideas about democracy have much in common with parts of the civil rights, New Left, and women's movements of preceding decades. Then, within this larger context, I will ask why democratic forms and practices seem so fragile and short lived, and have to be invented seemingly from scratch, over and over again.

Narrators seek to build a labor movement by community-based organizing in immigrant communities that is both rooted in those cultures and that politicizes already existing democratic values and practices. They see a reciprocal relationship between the constituency of a movement and its organizational culture. The fact that working-class Los Angeles is heavily female, largely immigrants and U.S.-born people of color, shapes the scope of working-class issues and the political culture of their movement. Like other advocates for revitalizing the labor movement, they insist that naming and dealing with race and racism among workers as well as by employers be at the center of political practice, that working-class issues should be those that women and men of color face beyond, as well as on, the job, and that unions' internal practices be based upon gender and racial respect. This includes challenging a culture of heroic organizers who mobilize workers rather than build their capacity to lead themselves for being undemocratic, sexist, and paternalistic.

There is a great deal of evidence that successful democratic social movements are built upon the foundations of local cultures and social relations, especially the values and ties that structure people's relationships of everyday interdependence. A central, but often implicit, corollary to this point is that the very fact of constituents' familiarity and mastery of those everyday values and practices is empowering. Sarah Evans and Harry Boyte (1986) underscore this point in arguing that non-political voluntary organizations and kindred "free [social and cultural] spaces" serve as repositories of democratic practice and skill development.

Mobilizing interpersonal networks, voluntary organizations, and the everyday ties of trust and reciprocity upon which they depend has an impressive track record in the annals of grassroots political activism. Focusing on women's ways of organizing in a variety of grassroots and democratic movements offers another way to see the connection of movement cultures to constituents' local cultures and practices. Carol Stack (2000) has shown in an ethnographically detailed way just how African-American women in the rural South organized from scratch a social movement that was built from daily ties of kinship, friendship, and local values of caring and mutual assistance. Elsewhere I have shown that the movement to unionize workers at Duke Medical Center rested upon politicizing already existing workplace networks and patterns of informal leadership among African-American women hospital workers (Brodkin Sacks 1988). Mary Pardo's (1998) study of working-class Mexican-American women's mobilization against toxic pollution in East Los Angeles shows how women's informal leadership came from church- and neighborhood-based networks to become the local activist culture of a powerful grassroots environmental-justice struggle. Temma Kaplan (1997), Cynthia Hamilton (1995), and Harriet Rosenberg (1995) have all shown how culturally specific democratic values and preexisting local networks in African-American, African, and white communities structured the environmental-justice movement from Africa to Love Canal to Los Angeles. Jael Silliman and her collaborators, as well as Sandra Morgen, Cynthia Hamilton, and Temma Kaplan, have argued more generally that women's network-based activism in environmental justice and the health movements of white women and women of color embody culturally specifically women's and feminist ideals of democratic process (Bookman and Morgen 1988; Hamilton 1995; Kaplan 1997; Morgen 2002; Silliman et al. 2004). Perhaps the most detailed demonstration of how social movements created democratic structures based on models of social relations familiar to their constituents in their everyday lives is Francesca Polletta's study (2002) comparing a variety of twentieth-century pacifist social movements.

The organizational landscape that narrators have helped to build also shares a great deal with the organizational landscape of other democratic social movements. As we have seen, for narrators, building organizations that practice democratic agency is an equally central part of their mission because they help to create informed political actors. One part of this job is to help constituents figure out their shared priorities and the appropriate organizational forms for achieving them. The other part is to remain connected to those they organize, to serve not only as a personal resource but also as a scaffold for nascent organizational forms and a bridge to other organizations and networks. Thus, political connections are maintained through both personal networks and organizational coalitions. They envision democracy as a combination of organizational autonomy among groups and democracy within groups. In short, narrators' social-change landscape looks like a network of democratic organizations tied together by overlapping and changing coalitions and by personal networks of activists. In this mesh, progressive union locals serve as important organizational nodes, of both support and contention.

Resource mobilization theorists of social movements see such an organizationally rich mix of institutions and actors as facilitating the growth and success of social movements (Morris 1999; Edelman 2001; see also Schneider and Schneider 2003 for parallels with anti-Mafia movements in Palermo). Vanessa Tait (2005) and Dan Clawson (2003), among others, have argued that a landscape of organizational forms similar to that in which narrators are engaged has worked synergistically to generate the recent revitalization of the labor movement nationally. Recent willingness of progressive unionists to innovate and to organize is a case in point. It has been stimulated by the vitality and success of grassroots organizing by independent workers centers; unions in turn have supported these groups, especially financially. Some of that synergy, positive and negative, operates in the organizational field of the Los Angeles labor and immigrant workers' movement. Narrators with activist backgrounds became union organizers and pushed against institutional practices for more democracy. Unions offered a home and an income for activists, bringing greater numbers of potential organizers to the city's labor activism community.[1]

Grassroots movements made up of small democratic groups have also built larger and more permanent forms of organization that embed aspects of direct democracy. The women's health movement of the 1970s and 1980s, as well as women's leadership in the environmental-justice movements in the United States and in antiapartheid struggles in South Africa, changed over time. Starting as localized struggles, they have developed into formal national and international networks of activists, and into national institutions coordinating ongoing national activism. Such movements come to constitute themselves as wider national or global movements less by a single unifying organization than by a mix of interpersonal networks of people and local organizations, specific events like conferences or demonstrations, or coordinated local events (Bullard, Taylor, and Johnson 1998; Hamilton 1995; Kaplan 1997; Morgen 2002; Silliman et al. 2004).

Although reliance on networked small organizations may seem like a fragile organizational field, Polletta found that when democratic groups had close ties to other such groups, they were more likely to survive because they found in one another mutually reinforcing support for democratic ideals and practice (2002, 217). In their organizational emphasis on autonomy, decentralization, and situational concerted action, narrators connect to earlier democratic movements with small, horizontal organizations like the antinuclear and peace movements, the New Left, and with much of second-wave white feminist organizing (Darnovsky, Epstein, and Flacks 1995; Epstein 1991; Morgen 2002; Silliman et al. 2004). Small, autonomous, local-issue-based groups loosely linked through networks and ideals seem also to characterize the recent anti-globalization landscape as well.

The Fragility of Movements

Yet successful social movements and the energies that fuel them are fragile and relatively fleeting. Polletta and Clawson have argued that success or failure of a social movement is in part determined by "windows of opportunity," and by internal divisions or weaknesses of their opponents that are beyond movement control (Polletta 2002; Clawson 2003). When movements ebb, strong national organizations can become institutional shells with no social or political mission, as was the AFL-CIO for many decades. And small democratic organizations and the networks that sustain them may disintegrate and their participants disperse. By the late 1960s, organizations that formed only a few years earlier on commitment to building democracy and a "beloved community" began to fall apart. Dissention and division (greatly aided by police provocateurs) tore apart the black freedom movement, the New Left, and the women's health movement (Payne 1995; Morgen 2002).

Even if social movements are short-lived, one could argue that the explosive energy they generate comes from the process by which they create new political identities with new perspectives and social visions. Those identities, perspectives, and visions affect more than a movement's participants and live on long beyond the movement. They are kept alive in the transformed selves of their participants who become keepers of a repertoire of political experience and knowledge that is part of a long tradition of democracy.

Generations of Cohorts

I want to conclude by returning to what these narrators have shown us about the importance of cohort-based networks to their identities and the shape of their movement's organizational field because I believe it may help to explain why democratic social movements seem to reinvent similar ideas about democracy again and again from scratch.

The book's focus on narrative highlights the importance of cohort-based activism in Los Angeles, what I've called a nineties cohort. Most of the narrators came of political age in their college years. They formed political networks among their peers on campus and at other campuses. They were recruited to unions from their campuses. Narrators make it clear that they remade themselves by talking back to the value-laden demographic categories of mainstream imagination in a peer-structured context. Their new political identities came from a mix with "other others" in a range of campus-linked struggles. Colleges and high schools are age-specific institutions, and have long been hothouses for generating local peer cultures, popular and political.

In this respect, narrators share a great deal with the high school- and college-age men and women of SNCC's Mississippi Freedom Summer, of Students for a Democratic Society and other sixties campus-origin groups, and of the early women's liberation movement. The ideas of those movements about making democracy and the political identities those movements represented were, as Francesca Polletta (2002) argued, fashioned from the class, race, and peer cultures from which their participants came. Many college and high school students in those years became activists, many briefly, a few lifelong, some part time and others full time. But the repertoire of political identities they developed in their years of activism continue to explain what social justice looks like and for whom. The practices and structures of democracy of their era's activism tend also to be what democracy looked like for cohorts who learned politics in that generation.

However, many movements, for example labor and environmental justice, develop from communities and workplaces with people of all ages. Nevertheless, the networks of organizers who sustain such movements across space are drawn largely from a young-age cohort that seems to create a set of signature identities, discourses, and practices that characterizes a movement. If social movements in general and democratic ones in particular are fragile and ephemeral for reasons not of their own making, we still have to ask why they seem to be reinvented anew, often by those with no or little knowledge of what went before. Even if we recognize that there are also traditions of intergenerational political mentoring, some personal like Ella Baker, some of it institutionalized in organizations like the Highlander School, the occasional ethnic and women's studies courses, and union educational programs, we also need to recognize that there are forces that also structure generational discontinuity. Some of that discontinuity has to do with the different structural places of older and younger activists. For example, while the narrators name a number of 1960s and 1970s activists as important political mentors, they also encounter that older generation of activists as officers of progressive unions and other kindred institutions with which they work. And, as suggested earlier, the responsibilities of officers give them priorities and perspectives that are very different from those of organizers, so that they often see the same things quite differently. Also, union officers' structural positions shape their relationships to organizers toward hierarchy more than reciprocity. At the same time, peer groups or teams in unions and immigrant-worker organizations, and, I suspect, social-justice religious movements, can be quite age-diverse and still support creating new political identities and practices.

In sum, I am suggesting that generational cohorts are a kind of incubator and home place for the radical transformations in worldview and self that provide the contagious social energy and optimism of grassroots social movements. High school and college, and youth organizations and political-education programs for high school students, combined with the assignment of organizing to young people, offer a local and more recently a national and even transnational networked structure for building cohort-based activist political cultures. In groups that emphasize organizing new constituencies, organizers are the points of contact between the internal culture and assumptions of their organizations and the local cultures and practices of their constituents. As such, they are the most likely to be in the forefront of creating new and locally situated forms of democracy. Still, social movements are episodic by nature and have an uphill climb to transmit one generational cohort's knowledge and repertoire of democratic practices to the next. The silver lining is that democracy continues to be rediscovered and reinvented by new generations.

APPENDIX A   STUDY DESIGN AND USE OF NARRATIVE

THIS STUDY REALLY HAS TWO ORIGINS, the accidental and purposeful. It did not begin as a book, but rather as a number of interviews to help me design a larger participatory study of labor and immigrant-worker organizing in Los Angeles. As a faculty member, I had been active in a number of the campaigns on the UCLA campus, speaking out in support of affirmative action and opposition to UC measures and ballot measures outlawing affirmative action; organizing faculty opposition to the first Iraq war; supporting creation of a Chicana/o Studies department; speaking out against racist and sexist practices by fraternities; and supporting graduate teaching assistants' right to unionization. In the course of these campaigns I met a large number of student activists and came to admire their commitment. I was also intrigued with the ways they went about organizing, and with their political ideas. Together with a few of those activists and a colleague at UC Riverside, we formed Common Threads, a community and educational group of women in support of garment workers' efforts to unionize. That activism brought me into closer contact with immigrant workers, many of whom were young, articulate, and political.

A few years later, I volunteered in living-wage efforts and in a community group supporting HERE's hotel-worker organizing, where I encountered unions that were creative and activist in new, exciting ways. In the course of all this work, I again met those I first knew as students as full-time social-justice organizers. By the summer of 1999, when I had a sabbatical, I decided to design a project that could figure out what was new and different about this wave of activism that was clearly energizing a wide spectrum of the city. By way of figuring out the landscape, I began to interview relatively young organizers in activist unions and community groups about how they came to be full-time social-justice activists, and what social justice and democracy looked like to them.

I selected organizers to interview on the basis of convenience and referrals by interviewees, a combination of snowball and opportunistic methods. I had two streams of snowball—those I already knew and those who were involved in a joint organizing effort by SEIU and HERE to unionize workers at Los Angeles International Airport concessions. However, the two streams of interviewees overlapped quite a bit in that organizers tended to know one another across groups. I also followed a number of referrals to people who worked in community-based organizing around educational and employment equity. Tritia Toyota interviewed three organizers whom she knew in two immigrant workers groups, the Korean Immigrant Workers Association and the Pilipino Workers' Center. I conducted interviews between the summer of 1999 and the spring of 2000; Tritia conducted her interviews in the fall of 2001.

We interviewed organizers about three things: their personal journeys to political activism, their experiences as activists and organizers, and their work histories and social networks. We asked them to analyze specific political events and events in their lives, and to reflect on them as well as to reflect on how they came to be where they are and the social visions they have. I developed a list of questions (see appendix B), which Tritia and I shared with interviewees at the beginning of the interview. We used it mainly as a guide, to prompt these activist narrators' memories and encourage me to pursue their analyses. For the most part, however, the interviews did not follow the questions but usually took the form of open-ended conversations. As we seemed to be winding down, I often showed the questions to the narrators again, and asked if there was anything we had not covered that they wanted to talk about—or what we had missed that wasn't on my agenda of questions. Interviews ranged from an hour and a half to over six hours—the latter were conducted in two or three sessions. The taped interviews were transcribed as they were completed, beginning in fall 1999. I reviewed and corrected the transcripts against the original tape, and sent those transcripts to the interviewees as I went along.

As I worked with the transcripts, it became clear that they were loaded with important insights, and that they told a collective, analytic story about the nature of an emerging political cohort and the politics it was creating. This story needed its own book.

I am using narrators' real names. This goes against prevailing practices in most social science disciplines. Because this book is about their intellectual and political ideas, using pseudonyms would appropriate their passions, analyses, and histories. I want to recognize the authorship of the ideas and their contributions to social-movement history in proper scholarly form. At the same time, there are very good arguments for not identifying people. We may inadvertently expose events or statements that could prove embarrassing or damaging to them in ways we could not anticipate. My decision to make the narrators' review and release of their transcripts critical to my working with them stems in part from these considerations.

That decision is also rooted in notions of participatory research in several streams of progressive anthropological, feminist, and ethnic studies, all of which emphasize research with people as collaboration between peers (Gluck and Patai 1991; D. Smith 1999; L. Smith 1999).

I began working with the transcripts slowly, as interviewees reviewed them, made such corrections and deletions they wished, and approved their use. However, the realities of my relationship with narrators were that our priorities differed. Their priority was the business of political organizing, and mine was writing about them. Thus, time and circumstances shaped how much attention each narrator was able to give to editing his or her transcript and, later, to feedback on early drafts of the book manuscript. Some gave a great deal of time to editing their transcript; others simply said it's okay to use the transcript as is. All save one narrator approved use of their transcript; one interviewee, despite good intentions, has still not reviewed it. Consequently, I've included in the book only the narratives of the sixteen interviewees who completed the process.

Appendix B   Organizer Survey

Organizing directors at HERE Local 11/814 and SEIU Local 399, and LAANE/SMART's community outreach director allowed me to make an informal presentation and discuss my research during their regular organizers meeting and to distribute a short written questionnaire about organizers' backgrounds, where their families live, whether they immigrated to the United States, the class and ethnic composition of their schools, how they became political, social descriptions of their closest friends, and where they hope to be in five years (see below).

It was conducted informally—how could it not be among organizers? While people were writing their answers, many asked questions for clarification—especially how old could you be and still be a young organizer—and talked with each other about the questions. I asked people to include their age, but if they were older than thirty and felt young, to include themselves in the survey. Some people spent a great deal of time and many gave thoughtful and insightful answers. I stayed through the meetings and people gave me their questionnaires as they finished them, sometimes long after the meeting had moved on to other business. I also had a number of longer, informal conversations with organizers who were interested in the project. I surveyed a total of sixty-five HERE, LAANE/SMART, and SEIU organizers. Tables 1, 2, and 3 focus on the forty-two organizers who were thirty and under, and compare them to narrators. However, the backgrounds and networks of those under thirty did not differ much from those over thirty.

Questionnaire for SEIU, HERE and LAANE/ SMART Organizers

My goal is to get some sense of demographics of young organizers in L.A. and see ways that experiences of those I interviewed map onto this wider picture.

1. Describe yourself re: age, gender, race/ethnicity, politics, etc. anything else that's important.
2. Did you or your parents immigrate to U.S.? From where? Do you have family in more than one country?
3. If you crossed the border, what kind of experience was it?
4. What kind of K-12 schools did you go to? (i.e., one with students like you? Bused to school where students were different ethnicity, race, class?)
5. In school, college, neighborhood did you experience racism, marginalization? Did/how did that influence your politics?
6. What was the first time you did anything political, or had a political "aha!"
7. Can you make a (short) list of your history of activism that led you to where you are now?
8. Who are your closest political friends (by where they work/job; not their names).
9. Which other organizations should I go to that young activists gravitate toward?
10. Where would you like to see yourself in 5 years?
11. Anything else I should have asked about?

TABLE I

Gender and ethnic backgrounds of union organizers thirty years old and younger and narrators

	Union organizers 30 and under	Narrators
Total	42	16
Women	28 (70%)	12 (75%)
Men	12 (30%)	4 (25%)
Gender unspecified	2	–
Asian-American	7 (4F, 3M) (18%)	8 (7F, 1M) (50%)
African-American	3 (3F) (8%)	1 (F) (6%)
Chicana(o)/Mexican/Latina(o)	14 (11F, 3M) (36%)	5 (2F, 3M) (31%)
Not white	24 (62%)	14 (88%)
White	15 (8F, 5M) (38%)	2 (2F) (13%)
Women of color	18 (46%)	10 (63%)
Men of color	6 (15%)	4 (25%)
Race, ethnicity unspecified	3 (2F, 1M)	–

TABLE 2

College attendance of union organizers thirty years old and under, and over thirty years old

	Total ≤ 30 yrs.	College ≤ 30 yrs.	Total > 30 yrs.	College > 30 yrs.
SEIU 399	29	20	11	8
LAANE	3	3	4	3
HERE	10	6	8	6
Total	42	29	23	17
Percent	–	69%	–	74%

NOTE: The percentage of college attendees may be higher than what is shown in the table because I did not specifically ask about college attendance, but rather counted only those questionnaires that explicitly mentioned college experiences.

TABLE 3

Organizers' political friendships categorized by friends' type of organization

Type of organization	HERE	LAANE/SMART	SEIU
Own & affiliated organizations	28	8	2
Other unions and labor organizations	19	7	6
Campus ethnic clubs	12	1	2
Community/human rights organizing	13	3	1
Other (prison, antiglobalization, antiwar, independent media, environment)	6	2	3

NOTE: Not all organizers who were surveyed answered these questions; some who did gave several answers to each, so the numbers of organizations don't add up to the number of organizers.

Notes

Introduction

1. For a review of resource mobilization theories see, among others, Edelman 2001 and Morris 1999. On the effectiveness of grassroots organizing in union organizing, see Bronfenbrenner et al. 1998, and Bronfenbrenner and Hickey 2003.
2. I don't want to minimize the importance of creative strategies, images, organizational forms, and coalition building that underpin social movements. Those have been amply described in the resource mobilization literature referenced above as well as in the works of Kate Bronfenbrenner and her colleagues, and will be part of this discussion as well.
3. Many union organizers also come from the ranks of workers, but, as progressive unionists argue, not enough. Indeed, there is a long-recognized and often-critiqued tradition within labor unions of recruiting organizers from among college students (Ganz et al. 2004). This tradition was revived with the initiation in 1996 of the AFL-CIO's Union Summer program of intense recruitment of organizers on college campuses across the country (Lichtenstein 2002, 262; Mantsios 1998).

Chapter 1   The Context of Labor and Immigrant Workers' Rights Activism in Los Angeles

1. Los Angeles in the 1990s seemed to buttress resource mobilization theories that show social movements flourishing best in an environment where there are many different social movement organizations actively pursuing change in competition and cooperation with one another, and where there is innovation and creativity in their tactics. This kind of social field encourages people's hopes of being able to effect real changes (Morris 1999; Edelman 2001).
2. "Chicana/o" refers to a Mexican-American. "Latina/o" refers more generally to people of Latin-American ancestry.
3. Mandla Kayise, interview 4/30/03.
4. David Kamper, personal communication on the Student Association of Graduate Employees (SAGE).
5. The other two, the Domestic Workers Association, a cooperative business run by domestic workers, and the Sidewalk Vending Coalition, to protect the rights of sidewalk vendors (Hondagneu-Sotelo 1994; Hondagneu-Sotelo, P. Riegos, and C. Riegos 1997; Valenzuela 2001; Hondagneu-Sotelo 2001), do not employ any narrators, nor do they loom large in the networks of other labor and immigrant workers' organizations.

6. This measure was passed by Governor Gray Davis and subsequently repealed by incoming Governor Arnold Schwarzenegger. On a related issue, see Seif 2004 on the struggle to pass AB 540, which gained in-state tuition for undocumented students in 2001.

CHAPTER 2   NARRATORS AND NARRATIVE

1. Government determination of whether people are immigrants or refugees shapes the legal framework that governs their lives in the United States; both statuses are limiting, but in different ways. For the most part, refugee status is applied to those fleeing communist governments. Refugees often do not get to choose when or to what countries they will be sent, and are not under the same set of restrictions in the United States that immigrants face. See Sucheng Chan (1991), *Asian Americans: An Interpretive History* for the nature and consequences of refugee status for Asians.
2. The percentage in the larger sample may be higher because I did not specifically ask about college attendance, but rather counted only those questionnaires that explicitly mentioned college experiences.
3. Passerini (1998) argues that what oral histories do and do not say about the past can illuminate the nature of ideological contestation on the left at the time, and help to better understand underlying political activism or apathy in the past, as well as the nature of political subjectivity formation more generally; also see Passerini 1987.
4. Stephen (1994) and Mitchell (2002) have been highly critical of efforts to delegitimate Rigoberta Menchú's work because of errors of fact, and because it is political. They argue that the entire *testimonio* genre is indeed political, but that this hardly disqualifies its truth. Rather, testimonios are much more complex linkages between individual memories of shared events and the contexts of their tellings. Truth, they emphasize, lies in the shared underlying meanings as part of a collective tapestry of memory and embedded understandings of its meanings.
5. Narrative, whether an individual's life history, daily conversational analysis, or oral history of the times, is a superb way of learning about the meaning of events and relationships for participants. On this there is solid agreement across disciplines from feminist and ethnic studies to anthropology, linguistics, social psychology, and oral history. See Moraga and Anzaldua 1983; Asian Women United of California 1989; Kim et al. 1997; Kennedy and Davis 1993; Weston 1991; Personal Narratives Group 1989; Saldivar-Hull 2000; Agar 1980; Bruner 1986; Peacock and Holland 1993; Grele 1998; Perks and Thompson 1998; Frank 2000; Garro and Mattingly 2000; Ochs and Capps 2001.
6. Sonia Saldivar-Hull (2000) makes a similar argument with respect to feminism of color more generally, showing how writers, scholars, and artists have used the testimonio form to create border-crossing political and cultural perspectives.

CHAPTER 3   POLITICAL IDENTITY STARTS AT HOME

1. Not her real name. I've used pseudonyms for all childhood friends.
2. It is striking that activists of the nineties as well as a wide swath of activists of the sixties see their parents as positive influences on their activism, not least as

role models. This stands in contrast to the popular notion that white activists of the sixties generation were in rebellion against their parents. According to McAdam (1988), the white volunteers of SNCC's Mississippi Freedom Summer shared other activists' admiration of their parents. The idea of the sixties embodying a youth rebellion against its parents may need some modification, even regarding the white New Left.

CHAPTER 4 MAKING IDENTITIES POLITICAL

1. I thank Eileen Ma for comments that helped clarify my thinking about borderlands theories. These theories have been most fully developed by the Chicana lesbian feminists Cherríe Moraga and Gloria Anzaldúa, children of the Southwest borderlands. Along with Sandra Cisneros, they are perhaps the most widely read and have created theories of borderlands through poetry, novels, and personal testimonies.
2. Nelson Lichtenstein has noted the importance of participating in a successful struggle for inspiring young activists to take up social change activism over the long haul (comments delivered at Rebuilding Labor Conference, UCLA Institute for Labor and Employment, May 17, 2002).
3. Environmentalism seems to be coded as white and middle class by a number of activists. Joann Lo also identified her high school interest in environmental issues as middle class. "I think that came out probably because it was a middle-class high school, sort of maybe up to upper-middle class. People didn't talk much about class in that setting, but environmentalism was a good thing, something to work on, and like recycling was important and that kind of stuff." And Aquilina Soriano noted that in her Orange County high school, the environmental club was as political as it got.
4. Aisha Livingstone is significantly older than other narrators, but those who directed me to her included her as part of their cohort.

CHAPTER 5 DEMOCRACY AND POLITICAL PRAXIS

1. Marqueece Harris-Dawson interview, February 28, 2003.
2. Kimi Lee interview, March 14, 2003.
3. Kim McGillicuddy interview, February 24, 2003.
4. La Hermandad was a very successful mutual aid organization among working-class Mexican immigrants throughout Southern California in the 1950s and 1960s (Garcia 1994).

CONCLUSION

1. All is not rosy. The organizing team responsible for the Justice for Janitors success in Los Angeles ran a slate of officers and won leadership of that local, only to be ousted and the local put into receivership by the SEIU. See Tait 2005, 251–252.

References

Acuña, Rodolfo. 2000. *Occupied America: A history of Chicanos*. New York: Longman.

Acuña, Rodolfo and others. 2003 (no longer available). Open letter to our African-American sisters and brothers. http://www.bellyofthebeast.org/illvoces/openletter.html.

Agar, Michael. 1980. Stories, background knowledge and themes: Problems in the analysis of life history narratives. *American Ethnologist* 7: 223–239.

Allen, James Paul. 1997. *The ethnic quilt: Population diversity in Southern California*. Northridge, CA: Center for Geographical Studies, California State University at Northridge.

Allen, Paula Gunn. 1992. *The sacred hoop: Recovering the feminine in American Indian traditions*. With a new preface. Boston: Beacon Press.

Anzaldúa, Gloria. 1999. *Borderlands = La Frontera*. San Francisco: Aunt Lute.

———. 2002. Preface. In *This bridge we call home: Radical visions for transformations*, ed. Gloria Anzaldúa and AnaLouise Keating, 1–5. New York: Routledge.

Anzaldúa, Gloria, and AnaLouise Keating, eds. 2002. *This bridge we call home: Radical visions for transformation*. New York: Routledge.

Asian Women United of California, ed. 1989. *Making waves: An anthology of writings by and about Asian American women*. Boston: Beacon Press.

Bailey, Eric. 2004. Causes of labor, gays join at event. *Los Angeles Times*, May 6.

Bernal, Dolores Delgado. 1998. Grassroots leadership reconceptualized: Chicana oral histories and the 1968 East Los Angeles school blowouts. *Frontiers: A Journal of Women Studies* 19 (2): 113–142.

Bernstein, Mary. 2002. The contradictions of gay ethnicity: Forging identities in Vermont. In *Social movements: Identity, culture, and the state*, ed. D. S. Meyer, Nancy Whittier, and Belinda Robnett, 85–104. New York: Oxford University Press.

Bookman, Ann, and Sandra Morgen, eds. 1988. *Women and the politics of empowerment*. Philadelphia: Temple University Press.

Breines, Wini. 1992. *Young, white, and miserable: Growing up female in the fifties*. Boston: Beacon.

Brodkin, Karen. 2003. On the politics of being Jewish in a multiracial state. *Anthropologica* 45: 57–66.

Brodkin Sacks, Karen. 1988. *Caring by the hour*. Urbana: University of Illinois Press.

Bronfenbrenner, Kate, Sheldon Friedman, Richard W. Hurd, Rudolph A. Oswald, and Ronald L. Seeber. 1998a. Introduction. In *Organizing to win: New research on union strategies*, ed. Kate Bronfenbrenner, Sheldon Friedman, Richard W. Hurd, Rudolph A. Oswald, and Ronald L. Seeber, 1–16. Ithaca, NY: Cornell University Press.

_____. eds. 1998b. *Organizing to win: New research on union strategies*. Ithaca, NY: Cornell University Press.

Bronfenbrenner, Kate, and Robert Hickey. 2003. *Blueprint for change: A national assessment of winning union organizing strategies*. Ithaca, NY: Cornell University Press.

Bronfenbrenner, Kate, and Tom Juravich. 1998. It takes more than house calls: Organizing to win with a comprehensive union-building strategy. In *Organizing to win: New research on union strategies*, ed. Kate Bronfenbrenner, Sheldon Friedman, Richard W. Hurd, Rudolph A. Oswald, and Ronald L. Seeber, 19–36. Ithaca, NY: Cornell University Press.

Brown, Deborah Elder. 1999. Don't mess around with the toxic crusaders: Nevada Dove, Fabiola Tostado, Maria Perez. *Time*, April 26.

Bruner, Jerome. 1986. *Actual minds, possible worlds*. Cambridge, MA: Harvard University Press.

Bullard, Robert. D., Dorceta E. Taylor, and Glenn S. Johnson, eds. 1998. Environmentalism and race, gender and class issues, part II. Special issue of *Race, Gender and Class* 6 (1).

Cade, Toni, ed. 1970. *The black woman: An anthology*. New York: New American Library.

California Budget Project. 2003. *Working, but poor: California's working families that fail to make ends meet*. http://www.cbp.org/2003/030519WorkingButPoor.pdf.

Chan, Sucheng. 1991. *Asian Americans: An interpretive history*. Boston: Twayne.

Christian, Barbara. 1988. The race for theory. *Feminist Studies* 14 (Spring): 67–80.

Clawson, Dan. 2003. *The next upsurge: Labor and the new social movements*. Ithaca, NY: Cornell University Press.

Common Threads Artists. 1998. Hidden Labor, Los Angeles. http://www.publicartinla.com/Downtown/HiddenLabor.

Dalton, Roque. 1987. *Miguel Marmol*. Willimantic, CT: Curbstone Press.

Darnovsky, Marcy, Barbara Epstein, and Richard Flacks, eds. 1995. *Cultural politics and social movements*. Philadelphia: Temple University Press.

Davalos, KarenMary. 1998. Anthropology and Chicana/o studies: The conversation that never was. *Aztlan* 23 (2): 13–45.

Davis, Mike. 2000. *Magical Urbanism*. London: Verso.

Delloro, John. 2000. "Personal is still political": Reflections on student power. In *Legacy to liberation: Politics and culture of revolutionary Asian Pacific America*, ed. F. Ho, 227–234. San Francisco: Big Red Media and AK Press.

_____. n.d. *"Personal is still political": Reflections on student power*. Unpublished manuscript.

Downs, Sarah Don. 2005. *Ties that bind: New methods of worker empowerment in the Los Angeles garment industry*. Los Angeles: UCLA Department of Anthropology.

Edelman, Marc. 2001. Social movements: Changing paradigms and forms of politics. *Annual Reviews in Anthropology* 30: 285–317.

Epstein, Barbara. 1991. *Political protest and cultural revolution: Nonviolent direct action in the 1970s and 1980s*. Berkeley: University of California Press.

Evans, Sara M., and Harry C. Boyte. 1986. *Free spaces: The sources of democratic change in America*. New York: Harper and Row.

Fantasia, Rick. 1995. From class consciousness to culture, action, and social organization. *Annual Review of Sociology* 21: 269–287.

Fisk, Catherine L., Daniel J. Mitchell, and Christopher L. Erickson. 2000. Union representation of immigrant janitors in Southern California: Economic and legal challenges. In *Organizing immigrants: The challenge for unions in contemporary California*, ed. Ruth Milkman, 199–224. Ithaca, NY: Cornell University Press.

Flacks, Richard. 1971. *Youth and social change*. Chicago: Markham.

Flores, William V. 1997. Epilogue: Citizens vs. citizenry: Undocumented immigrants and Latino cultural citizenship. In *Latino cultural citizenship: Claiming identity, space, and rights*, ed. William V. Flores and Rina Benmayor, 255–278. Boston: Beacon Press.

Flores, William V., and Rina Benmayor, ed. 1997. *Latino cultural citizenship: Claiming identity, space, and rights*. Boston: Beacon Press.

Frank, Dana. 1985. Housewives, socialists, and the politics of food: The 1917 cost of living protests. *Feminist Studies* 11 (summer): 255–285.

Frank, Gelya. 2000. *Venus on wheels: Two decades of dialog on disability, biography, and being female in America*. Berkeley and Los Angeles: University of California Press.

Freire, Paolo. 1972. *Pedagogy of the oppressed*. Trans. M. B. Ramos. New York: Herder and Herder.

Fujino, Diane, and Kye Leung. 2000. Radical resistance in conservative times: New Asian American organizations in the 1990s. In *Legacy to liberation: Politics and culture of revolutionary Asian Pacific America*, ed. F. Ho, 141–158. San Francisco: Big Red Media and AK Press.

Ganz, Marshall, Kim Voss, Teresa Sharpe, Carl Somers, and George Strauss. 2004. Against the tide: Projects and pathways of the new generation of union leaders, 1984–2001. In *Rebuilding labor: Organizing and organizers in the new union movement*, ed. Ruth Milkman. Ithaca, NY: Cornell University Press.

Garcia, Mario. 1994. *Memories of Chicano history: The life and narrative of Bert Corona*. Berkeley and Los Angeles: University of California Press.

Garro, Linda C., and Cheryl Mattingly. 2000. Narrative as construct and construction. In *Narrative and the cultural construction of illness and healing*, ed. Cheryl Mattingly and Linda Garro, 1–49. Berkeley: University of California Press.

Giddings, Paula. 1984. *When and where I enter*. New York: Bantam.

Glenn, Evelyn Nakano. 1994. Social constructions of mothering: A thematic introduction. In *Mothering: ideology, experience and agency*, ed. E. N. Glenn, Grace Chang, and Linda Rennie Forcey, 1–29. New York: Routledge.

Gluck, Sherna Berger, and Daphne Patai, ed. 1991. *Women's words: The feminist practice of oral history*. New York: Routledge.

Gottlieb, Robert, Mark Vallianatos, Regina M. Freer, and Peter Dreier. 2005. *The next Los Angeles: The struggle for a livable city*. Berkeley and Los Angeles: University of California Press.

Gramsci, Antonio. 1997 [1971]. *Selections from the prison notebooks of Antonio Gramsci*. Trans. and ed. Quintin Hoare and Geoffrey Nowell Smith. New York: International Publishers.

Grele, Ronald J. 1998. Movement without aim: Methodological and theoretical problems. In *The oral history reader*, ed. Robert Perks and Alistair Thomson, 38–52. London and New York: Routledge.

Hall, Stuart. 1988. The toad in the garden: Thatcherism among the theorists. In *Marxism and the interpretation of culture*, ed. Nelson Cary and Lawrence Grossberg, 35–58. Urbana: University of Illinois Press.

―――. 1996. The problem of ideology: Marxism without guarantees. In *Critical dialogues in cultural studies*, ed. David Morley and Juan-Hsing Chan, 25–46. New York and London: Routledge.

Hamilton, Cynthia. 1994. Concerned citizens of South Central. In *Unequal protection: Environmental justice and communities of color*, ed. R. D. Bullard, 207–219. San Francisco: Sierra Club Books.

―――. 1995. Industrial racism, the environmental crisis, and the denial of social justice. In *Cultural politics and social movements*, ed. M. Darnovsky, B. Epstein, and R. Flacks, 189–196. Philadelphia: Temple University Press.

Ho, Fred, ed. 2000. *Legacy to liberation: politics and culture of revolutionary Asian Pacific America*. San Francisco: Big Red Media and AK Press.

Holland, Dorothy, and Jean Lave, ed. 2001. *History in person: Enduring struggles, contentious practice, intimate identities*. Santa Fe, New Mexico: School of American Research Press.

Hondagneu-Sotelo, Pierrette. 1994. *Gendered transitions: Mexican experiences of immigration*. Berkeley: University of California Press.

―――. 2001. Latina immigrant domestic workers: Pathways for upgrading cleaning and caring jobs. *Aztlan* 26 (2): 173–182.

Hondagneu-Sotelo, Pierrette, and Cristina Riegos. 1997. Sin organization, no hay solucion: Latina domestic workers and non-traditional labor organizing. *Latino Studies* 8 (3):54–71.

hooks, bell. 1989. *Talking back*. Boston: South End Press.

Horne, Gerald. 1995. *Fire this time: The Watts Uprising and the 1960s*. Charlottesville: University of Virginia Press.

―――. 1996. Black, white, and red: Jews and African Americans in the Communist Party. In *The narrow bridge*, ed. M. Brettschneider, 123–135. New Brunswick, NJ: Rutgers University Press.

Hurtado, Aida. 2003. Voicing Chicana feminisms: Young women speak out on sexuality and identity. New York: New York University Press.

Ito, Leslie, director. 2005. Grassroots rising: Asian-American workers in Los Angeles. In *California documentary project*, documentary film. Distributed by Visual Communications Los Angeles, lito_arts@yahoo.com.

Joseph, Miranda. 2002. *Against the romance of community*. Minneapolis: University of Minnesota Press.

Kaplan, Erin Aubrey. 2003. Maria Brenes, student teacher. *LA (Los Angeles) Weekly*, November 7–13.

―――. 2005. Reviving education: Grassroots advocates for public schools are raising their voices—and getting heard. *LA (Los Angeles) Weekly*, May 13–19.

Kaplan, Temma. 1997. *Crazy for democracy: Women in grassroots movements*. New York and London: Routledge.

Kennedy, Elizabeth Lapovsky. 1998. Telling tales: Oral history and the construction of pre-Stonewall lesbian history. In *The oral history reader*, ed. Robert Perks and Alistair Thomson, 344–356. London and New York: Routledge.

Kennedy, Elizabeth Lapovsky, and Madeline D. Davis. 1993. *Boots of leather, slippers of gold: The history of a lesbian community*. London and New York: Routledge.

Kim, Elaine H., Lilia V. Villanueva, and Asian Women United of California, ed. 1997. *Making more waves: New writing by Asian American women*. Boston: Beacon Press.

Kroskrity, Paul V., ed. 2000. *Regimes of language: Ideologies, politics and identities.* Santa Fe, New Mexico: School of American Research Press.

Kwong, Peter. 1987. *The new Chinatown.* New York: Hill and Wang.

_____. 1997. Manufacturing ethnicity. *Critique of Anthropology* 17 (4): 365–389.

Lichtenstein, Nelson. 2002. *State of the union: A century of American labor.* Princeton, NJ: Princeton University Press.

Lipsitz, George. 1998. *The possessive investment in whiteness: How white people profit from identity politics.* Philadelphia: Temple University Press.

Lopez-Garza, Marta, and David R. Diaz, ed. 2001. *Asian and Latino immigrants in a restructuring economy: The metamorphosis of Southern California.* Stanford: Stanford University Press.

Lorde, Audre. 1982. *Zami: A new spelling of my name.* New York: Persephone.

Louie, Miriam Ching Yoon. 2001. *Sweatshop warriors: Immigrant women workers take on the global factory.* Boston: South End Press.

Louie, Steve, and Glenn Omatsu, ed. 2001. *Asian Americans: The movement and the moment.* Los Angeles: UCLA Asian American Studies Center Press.

Lynd, Staughton. 1999. The local union: A rediscovered frontier. In *The transformation of U.S. unions: Voices, visions, and strategies from the grassroots,* ed. Michael Cummings and Ray M. Tillman, 191–203. Boulder and London: Lynne Riener Publishers.

Mantsios, Gregory, ed. 1998. *A new labor movement for the new century.* New York: Monthly Review Press.

Mascarenhas, Michelle, and Robert Gottlieb. 2000. *Report of Farmer's Market Salad Bar Program in Santa Monica-Malibu Unified School District.* Los Angeles: Community Food Security Project, Urban and Environmental Policy Institute, Occidental College.

McAdam, Doug. 1988. *Freedom summer.* New York and London: Oxford University Press.

Milkman, Ruth, ed. 2000. *Organizing immigrants: The challenge for unions in contemporary California.* Ithaca, NY: Cornell University Press.

Milkman, Ruth, and Kim Voss, ed. 2004. *Rebuilding labor: Organizing and organizers in the new union movement.* Ithaca, NY: Cornell University Press.

Milkman, Ruth, and Kent Wong. 2000. *Voices from the front lines: Organizing immigrant workers in Los Angeles.* (English and Spanish). Trans. L. E. Rabadan. Los Angeles: UCLA Center for Labor Research and Education.

Mitchell, William P. 2002. Stolen glory: David Stoll and Rigoberta Menchu: A view from Peru. *Anthropology News,* May.

Moraga, Cherríe, and Gloria Anzaldúa, ed. 1983. *This bridge called my back: Radical writings by women of color.* New York: Kitchen Table Press.

Morgan, Robin, ed. 1970. *Sisterhood is powerful: An anthology of writings from the Women's Liberation Movement.* New York: Random House.

Morgen, Sandra. 2002. *Into our own hands: The women's health movement in the United States, 1969–1990.* New Brunswick, NJ: Rutgers University Press.

Morris, Aldon. 1999. A retrospective of the civil rights movement: Political and intellectual landmarks. *Annual Review of Sociology* 25: 517–539.

Naples, Nancy A., ed. 1998. *Community activism and feminist politics: Organizing across race, class, and gender.* New York and London: Routledge.

Ochs, Elinor, and Lisa Capps. 2001. *Living narrative: Creating lives in everyday story-telling*. Cambridge, MA: Harvard University Press.

Omatsu, Glenn. 1994. The "Four Prisons" and the movements of liberation: Asian American activism from the 1960s to the 1990s. In *The state of Asian America*, ed. Karen Aguilar San Juan, 19–69. Boston: South End Press.

Ong, Paul, Edna Bonacich, and Lucie Cheng, ed. 1994. *The new Asian immigration in Los Angeles and global restructuring*. Philadelphia: Temple University Press.

Pardo, Mary. 1998. *Mexican American women activists: Identity and resistance in two Los Angeles communities*. Philadelphia: Temple University Press.

Park, Edward J. W. 1998. Competing visions: Political formation of Korean Americans in Los Angeles, 1992–1997. *Amerasia Journal* 24 (1): 381–387.

Passerini, Luisa. 1987. *Fascism in popular memory: The cultural experience of the Turin working class*. Cambridge, UK: Cambridge University Press.

————. 1998. Work ideology and consensus under Italian fascism. In *The oral history reader*, ed. Robert Perks and Alistair Thomson, 53–62. London and New York: Routledge.

Paul, Jacquie. 2004. Serving up healthier. *The Press-Enterprise* (Riverside, CA), May 11.

Payne, Charles. 1995. *I've got the light of freedom: The organizing tradition and the Mississippi freedom struggle*. Berkeley and Los Angeles: University of California Press.

Peacock, James, and Dorothy Holland. 1993. The narrative self: Life stories in process. *Ethos* 21: 367–383.

Penezic, Vida. 2005. Women in Yugoslavia. In *Dialogue and difference: Feminisms challenge globalization*, ed. Marguerite Waller and Sylvia Marcos, 57–77. New York: Palgrave MacMillan.

Perks, Robert, and Alistair Thomson, ed. 1998. *The oral history reader*. London and New York: Routledge.

Personal Narratives Group, ed. 1989. *Interpreting women's lives: Feminist theory and personal narratives*. Bloomington: Indiana University Press.

Polletta, Francesca. 2002. *Freedom is an endless meeting*. Chicago: University of Chicago Press.

Popular Memory Group. 1998. Popular memory: Theory, politics, method. In *The oral history reader*, ed. Robert Perks and Alistair Thomson, 75–86. London and New York: Routledge.

Pulido, Laura. 1998. Development of the "people of color" identity in the environmental justice movement of the southwestern United States. *Socialist Review* 96 (4): 145–180.

————. 1999. Rethinking environmental racism: White privilege and urban development in Southern California. *Annals of the Association of American Geographers* 90 (1): 12–40.

Ransby, Barbara. 2003. *Ella Baker and the black freedom movement: A radical democratic vision*. Chapel Hill: University of North Carolina Press.

Reagon, Bernice Johnson. 1986. African diaspora women: The making of cultural workers. *Feminist Studies* 12 (1): 77–90.

Refuse & Resist. 2003. Los Angeles city council votes immigrant rights resolution. http://www.refuseandresist.org/imm/122001lacouncil.html.

Robnett, Belinda. 1996. African-American women in the civil rights movement, 1954–65. *American Journal of Sociology* 101 (6): 1661–1693.

Rooks, Daisy. 2004. Sticking it out or packing it in? Organizer retention in the new labor movement. In *Rebuilding labor: Organizing and organizers in the new union movement*, ed. Ruth Milkman and Kim Voss, 195–224. Ithaca, NY: Cornell University Press.

Rosenberg, Harriet G. 1995. From trash to treasure: Housewife activists and the environmental justice movement. In *Articulating hidden histories: Essays in honor of Eric R. Wolf*, ed. Jane Schneider and Rayna Rapp, 190–206. Berkeley: University of California Press.

Rothman, Jack. 1999. *Coalescing the Los Angeles progressive community: Views of activists and organizational leaders*. Los Angeles: Center for Labor Research and Education, School of Public Policy and Social Research, UCLA.

Rundle, James. 1998. Winning hearts and minds in the era of employee involvement programs. In *Organizing to win : New research on union strategies*, ed. Kate Bronfenbrenner, Sheldon Friedman, Richard W. Hurd, Rudolph A. Oswald, and Ronald L. Seeber, 213–231. Ithaca, NY: Cornell University Press.

Russel y Rodriguez, Monica. 1994. Protests, resistance, and the fight for Chicana and Chicano studies at UCLA. Paper presented at the meetings of the American Ethnological Society Annual Meeting, Los Angeles.

Saldivar-Hull, Sonia. 2000. *Feminism on the border*. Durham, NC: Duke University Press.

Sassoon, Anne Showstack. 1980. *Gramsci's politics*. London: Croom Helm.

Schein, Louisa. 1998. Forged transnationality and oppositional cosmopolitanism. In *Transnationalism from below*, ed. Michael Peter Smith and Luis Eduardo Guarnizo, 291–313. New Brunswick, NJ: Transaction Books.

Schneider, Jane, and Peter T. Schneider. 2003. *Reversible destiny: Mafia, antimafia, and the struggle for Palermo*. Berkeley and Los Angeles: University of California Press.

Scott, Allen J. 1996. The manufacturing economy: Ethnic and gender divisions of labor. In *Ethnic Los Angeles*, ed. Roger Waldinger and Mehdi Bozorgmehr, 215–246. New York: Russell Sage.

Seif, Hinda. 2004. "Wise up!" Undocumented Latino youth, Mexican-American legislators, and the struggle for higher education access. *Latino Studies* 2: 210–230.

Silliman, Jael, Marlene Gerber Fried, Loretta Ross, and Elena R. Gutierrez, ed. 2004. *Undivided rights: Women of color organize for reproductive justice*. Cambridge, MA: South End Press.

Sklair, Leslie. 1998. Social movements and global capitalism. In *The cultures of globalization*, ed. Fredrik Jamison and Masao Miyoshi, 291–311. Durham, NC: Duke University Press.

Smith, Dorothy E. 1999. *Writing the social: Critique, theory, and investigations*. Toronto and Buffalo: University of Toronto Press.

Smith, Linda Tuhiwai. 1999. *Decolonizing methodologies: research and indigenous peoples*. London and New York: Zed Books.

Solinger, Rickie. 2001. *Beggars and choosers: How the politics of choice shapes adoption, abortion, and welfare in the United States*. New York: Hill and Wang.

Southern California Association of Governments. 2001. The state of the region 2001. http://www.scag.ca.gov/publications/sotr01/sortofc.html

Stack, Carol. 1996. *Call to home: African Americans reclaim the rural South*. New York: Basic Books.

Stephen, Lynn. 1994. The politics and practice of testimonial literature. In *Hear my testimony*, Maria Teresa Tula and Lynn Stephen, 223–234. Boston: South End Press.

_____. 1997. *Women and social movements in Latin America*. Austin: University of Texas Press.

_____. 2005. Gender, citizenship, and the politics of identity. In *Social movements: An anthropological reader*, ed. June Nash, 66–77. Malden, MA: Blackwell Publishing.

Stiglitz, Joseph E. 2002. *Globalization and its discontents*. New York: W.W. Norton.

Su, Julie A., and Chanchanit Martorell. 2001. Exploitation and abuse in the garment industry: The case of the Thai slave-labor compound in El Monte. In *Asian and Latino immigrants in a restructuring economy: The metamorphosis of Southern California*, ed. Marta Lopez-Garza and David R. Diaz, 21–45. Stanford: Stanford University Press.

Sweatshop Watch. 2005. Advocates discuss future of California's garment industry. *Sweatshop Watch* 11 (1): 1, 6.

Tabb, William. 2001. *The amoral elephant: Globalization and the struggle for social justice in the twenty-first century*. New York: Monthly Review Press.

Tait, Vanessa. 2005. *Poor workers' unions: Rebuilding labor from below*. Cambridge, MA: South End Press.

Tillman, Ray M., and Michael S. Cummings, ed. 1999. *The transformation of U.S. unions: Voices, visions, and strategies from the grassroots*. Boulder and London: Lynne Rienner Publishers.

Toyota, Tritia. 2004. Reconstructing a collective Asian American political identity: Political projects among new Chinese American activists. PhD diss., UCLA Department of Anthropology.

Valenzuela, Abel, Jr. 2001. Day laborers as entrepreneurs? *Journal of Ethnic and Migration Studies* 27 (2): 335–352.

Waldinger, Roger, and Mehdi Bozorgmehr, ed. 1996. *Ethnic Los Angeles*. New York: Russell Sage Foundation.

Waldinger, Roger, and Claudia Der-Martirosian. 2000. Immigrant workers and American labor: Challenge or disaster? In *Organizing Immigrants: The challenge for unions in contemporary California*, ed. Ruth Milkman, 49–81. Ithaca, NY: Cornell University Press.

Waldinger, Roger, Chris Erickson, Ruth Milkman, Daniel J. B. Mitchell, Abel Valenzuela, Kent Wong, and Maurice Zeitlin. 1997. Justice for janitors: Organizing in difficult times. *Dissent* (Winter): 37–44.

Waldinger, Roger, and Michael I. Lichter. 2003. *How the other half works: Immigration and the social organization of labor*. Berkeley and Los Angeles: University of California Press.

Welton, Neva, and Linda Wolf, ed. 2001. *Global uprising, confronting the tyrannies of the 21st century: Stories from a new generation of activists*. Gabriola Island, British Columbia, Canada: New Society Publishers.

Westerman, William. 1998. Central American refugee testimonies and performed life histories in the sanctuary movement. In *The oral history reader*, ed. Robert Perks and Alistair Thomson, 224–234. London and New York: Routledge.

Weston, Kath. 1991. *Families we choose: lesbians, gays, kinship*. New York: Columbia University Press.

Williams, Raymond. 1973. *The country and the city*. London: Chatto and Windus.

Wong, Kent, ed. 2001. *Voices for justice.* Los Angeles: UCLA Center for Labor Research.

Yasuda, Kathleen. 1998. Why Asian Pacific organizers leave: What are they looking for? The unfulfilled promise of organizing. Working paper, Asian Pacific American Labor Association.

Youth Power Change. http://www.sscnet.ucla.edu/YPC/1960_chronology.html.

UCLA ARCHIVAL SOURCES

UCLA Yearbooks
UCLA Archives: Box 15 Students of UCLA, Student Activism Collection.

Daily Bruin electronic archives

Students First sweeps runoff offices. May 12, 1995. http://www.dailybruin.ucla.edu/news/articles.asp?ID=5515.

Young issues Prop 187 statement. November 30, 1994. http://www.dailybruin.ucla.edu/news/articles.asp?ID=4460.

Index

activism: antiracist, 4, 107; antiwar, 25, 26, 29; Chicana, 95; collective, 98, 99, 120–126; community-based, 22, 131; democracy and, 160–164; early, 130–138; economic, 25; ethnic, 18, 116–119; feminist, 25; full-time, 14; gay, 176; gender and, 160–164; goals of, 15; grassroots, 178; for immigrant workers' rights, 17–42, 31–40; for job access, 18; for labor rights, 4, 31–40, 99; learning as foundation for, 131; across national borders, 131; and networks across issues, 130–138; personal meaning in, 10, 156; political, 13, 30, 114; progressive, 32; racial, 116–119, 160–164; shared, 95; social, 109; social justice, 1, 3; student, 13, 25, 27–30, 104; by students of color, 18; successful, 120–126; synergistic growth of, 17; union, 31. *See also* movements
activists: analysis of politicization process by, 10; gaining personal meaning from social movements, 10; organizing, 12; reinterpretation of local culture by, 10; student, 11
Acuña, Rodolfo, 58
affirmative action, 24, 27, 30, 132, 160
AFL-CIO. *See* American Federation of Labor–Congress of Industrial Organizations

African-Americans: in low-wage employment, 160; as union organizers, 160
African Student Union, 27
AGENDA, 46, 106, 131, 143; training in, 22
Allen, James, 20, 22
Allen, P. G., 49
American Federation of Labor–Congress of Industrial Organizations, 39; Asian Pacific American Labor Alliance and, 39, 40; immigration policy and, 3; organizing by, 1; Organizing Institute, 30, 31, 39, 145; Union Summer Program, 39
Anzaldúa, Gloria, 15, 49, 195*n1*
APALA. *See* Asian Pacific American Labor Alliance
Appalachian Women Empowered, 168
Asian-American Students Association, 99
Asian American Studies Center, 112
Asian Immigrant Women's Advocates, 38, 168
Asian Pacific American Labor Alliance (APALA), 31, 33, 39, 40, 138, 145, 159, 163; narrator membership in, 46, 47; Organizing Institute, 99
Asian Pacific American Legal Center, 38, 39

About the Author

KAREN BRODKIN is a professor of anthropology and women's studies at the University of California, Los Angeles. Her current research is about social activism in Los Angeles. Her previous book is *How Jews Became White Folks and What That Says About Race in America.*